EROTIC HUSTLE

REDEFINING SIN THROUGH SACRED SEXUALITY & PSYCHEDELICS

LANA SHAY

an imprint of Sunbury Press, Inc.
Mechanicsburg, PA USA

an imprint of Sunbury Press, Inc.
Mechanicsburg, PA USA

For information about special discounts for bulk purchases, please contact Sunbury Press Orders Dept. at (855) 338-8359 or orders@sunburypress.com.

To request one of our authors for speaking engagements or book signings, please contact Sunbury Press Publicity Dept. at publicity@sunburypress.com.

FIRST VERBOTEN BOOKS EDITION: August 2022

Set in Adobe Garamond | Interior design by Crystal Devine | Cover by Tobi Afran. Cover image photographer: David Miller. Image on back of book (with Rose): Elise Gee. | Edited by Sarah Peachey.

Publisher's Cataloging-in-Publication Data
Names: Shay, Lana, author.
Title: Erotic hustle : redefining sin through sacred sexuality & psychedelics / Lana Shay.
Description: First trade paperback edition. | Mechanicsburg, PA : Verboten Books, 2022.
Summary: Lana Shay is on an altruistic mission to bring light to the dark underworld of the sex industry. Fast cash lures Lana into a decade of stripping, webcamming, sensual massage, and moonlighting as a dominatrix. Erotic Hustle invites readers into a world of the therapeutic uses of psychedelics and the tantric approach to conscious sexual exchange.
Identifiers: ISBN 978-1-62006-912-7 (softcover).
Subjects: SOCIAL SCIENCE / Human Trafficking | SOCIAL SCIENCE / Sexual Abuse & Harassment | SOCIAL SCIENCE / Women's Studies.

Product of the United States of America
0 1 1 2 3 5 8 13 21 34 55

Continue the Enlightenment!

Dedicated to my younger sisters, Leah & Cali.
May you know your worth and
stand in your power.

CONTENTS

"There is no greater agony than bearing an
untold story inside you."

—Maya Angelou

INTRODUCTION

The intention of this book is to unite the pieces of myself that I've separated by adopting not only one alias but five and allowing them to hide in the shadows. In writing this book, I fully claim myself as one integrated being. The many names of Lana Shea Baumgartner are that of one infinite, eternal, whole human being (thank you to my teacher Devarshi Steven Hartman for this powerful combination of words). In publishing this memoir, the intent is to serve as an example. For anyone with the deep desire to just simply be, may you live without fear of full expression. From this point on, I will not hide any part of myself from anyone. I will not rob myself of my wholeness.

This book is not only my integration and healing journey—it's a call to action. Women who choose to claim their power can shift the world's consciousness. If we don't claim our power, it can and will be used by others. Working in strip clubs opened up a world of opportunity for me and offered priceless lessons. However, I am living someone else's dream inside those walls. I wasn't giving those countless hours in the VIP to myself. I was ultimately giving it to the club owner. I played by someone else's rules. No longer. In some ways, we must conform to play this game of life together, but we can create any reality we want. We all get a shot at this game. I'm stepping up to bat. For more than a decade of my lifetime, strip clubs across the United States have been my classroom. This book is what I've learned and continue to learn. I'll point out the "gifts" I've received from my experiences.

Thank you for allowing me to share my experience with you through this book. I do believe that you will enjoy the ride.

1

WATERING THE SEED

How far that little candle throws its beams! So shines a good deed in a naughty world. —Shakespeare

Light travels at a constant speed. Traveling in all directions at 186,000 miles per second, the light from a single candle illuminates the confines of any space. My father often reminded me of the speed of light when I've called him on long drives. He vents about the current news and children ripped away from their "immigrant" parents; parents placed in holding cells for days, weeks, or years. Without fail, we always arrive at the abuse he experienced as a child. And once in a blue moon, we'll dig into the federal prison system and his years of being incarcerated. My eyes well up with tears, and I feel my chest tighten. His words invoke imagery that ripples through my body, knotting my stomach. His voice is hoarse and rough from years of smoking cigarettes, and every few sentences are interrupted by a bout of deep coughing and spitting up mucus.

"When I got on the plane, I had no idea where they were taking me. No one told me or anyone else, just like the children separated from their parents seeking asylum. I remember they had us on hard plastic seats with no cushions so we couldn't stash anything. There were a bunch of Cubans on the plane who didn't speak any English, and it was hot as hell, and they could only say 'water.' They started to scream and yell after a few hours and didn't understand that the enforcement officers on the flight were telling them to shut up or they wouldn't serve them water. The rest of us were quiet—the ones of us who spoke English—because we were all thirsty and sweating our asses off. They kept us waiting almost eighteen hours before they gave us water. We were starved and parched until we reached our stop. I remember my mouth felt like it was glued shut, and my tongue was stuck to the roof of my mouth. We had shackles on our feet, and they were so tight when we went to deplane, the metal on our ankles would cut into our Achilles, and it was hard to walk. Some of the guys that were smarting off got locked in cuffs with a black box in the middle. It would make it hard to eat or drink or do anything because their hands were so far apart."

My mind felt frantic, and my heart sank as the questions swirled. How could any human being do this to another? Who deserves to endure these conditions? How is this fair? How can this be justified? Why did I choose to live on such a cruel planet? He continues without pause, describing the dark rooms he was locked in, cockroaches and rats running on the floor, and low-quality food. "I remember the guard coming up to the cell with a metal pitcher, and I thought it would be iced tea like it was every day, but when it came out, it plopped in my metal cup. I asked what it was, and the guard said, 'It's milk.' I said, 'This isn't milk! There are chunks in it; this is cottage cheese. This milk went bad a long time ago.' They put some sort of strawberry flavoring in it to color it red to disguise it." I imagine my father, emaciated, being served a glass of spoiled milk and rotten garbage on a piece of metal.

His story has weighed heavily on me for as long as I can remember. I feel my face flush, and the tears come again. For me, this pain runs deep. Generations deep. It's pre-verbal. He tells his stories with so much emotion and enthusiasm, and there's always a punchline. Despite the humor, the depth of pain feels infinite. He tells the story about the spoiled milk as if it were a joke, but it doesn't feel like comedy to me. Ever since I can remember, I have been sensitive to the pain of others. That pain cuts straight to the heart when the connection is blood.

* * *

At six years old, I can still recall the intense emotion that consumed my entire being when my mother and I were leaving a grocery store, and

I noticed a man by the entrance in soiled clothes, his features weathered by the elements. His appearance and the dirty paper coffee cup in his hand were off-putting to me. I asked my mother, "Is he okay? What's wrong?"

She replied, "He's fine, honey. He's homeless."

The concept baffled me. "Why is he homeless? Can't he live with us?"

My mother modulated her voice in the way she does when she feels deep empathy, "Ohhh honeyyy . . ." She tried to explain why this wasn't an option.

"But doesn't he have a family?" I asked.

Something about that man and that situation has stuck with me. It's one of my earliest memories of human injustice. This was not only an injustice, but also an obvious indication that the system was broken. My upbringing was filled with inquiries about such things. Much of my perspective came from my mother, as it does for many of us. My mother, damaged from her own challenging experiences, brought many vital lessons into my life. She was in touch with her spirituality. There was no dogma in the faith I learned at home. She was open to Eastern religions and would reference past lives and reincarnation matter-of-factly. After my grandmother died, we'd see this same white rabbit at a local park, time and time again. My mother said it was my grandmother greeting us. The fact that she even noticed the rabbit was telling. The homeless man's predicament baffled me, this empathy and compassion my mother expressed; wasn't this how all humans navigate life?

One night, on our way home through a stretch of farmland in Fitchburg, she hit a cat. She immediately stopped the car and burst into tears. She pulled a blanket out of the trunk and wrapped the cat in it, placing it on the floor at my feet and telling me to look after it while we raced to the nearest veterinarian. She paid $500 out of her pocket for the care of this cat, even though we were struggling financially. The cat was put to sleep in the end, as it couldn't function normally with the severe injuries. We returned to the farm close to where we'd hit the cat a few days later, and she confessed to the owner. The owner said tons of cats lived on the farm, and he wasn't concerned about one missing cat. My mother was relieved yet saddened even more, knowing that no one missed the cat. "Poor little mahw mahw," she said as she looked at me with tears in her eyes. We had endearing names for all animals. I'll never forget this memory as one of my mother's many ways of moving through the world with ultimate compassion and empathy.

My father's childhood home was void of love with two alcoholic parents and one living brother. He believes his first brother, whom he never met, was shaken to death. Instead of receiving hugs and affection, my father was beaten with wire hangers and belts. The physical abuse was believed to be warranted for things like sneaking a glass of milk out of the fridge after they'd forgotten to feed him for a day or making too much noise opening a door. Fortunately, I didn't exist in physical form to witness any of this. But I am witness to how it has affected his life. It's etched in his cells. I believe this pain and trauma travel through time, and I carry it with me today. Every day my father relives the trauma in his head. He lives in despair. He's never been married and has never experienced a stable, loving, intimate relationship. His "mother wound" plagues his daily life. He's lived his entire life disconnected from the feminine. He's lived his life as an addict. He's managed to escape the methamphetamines, pharmaceuticals, and heavy narcotics, but the arguably more dangerous, socially acceptable drugs still have a hold on him. The cigarettes, alcohol, caffeine, processed foods, and cheap cocaine (white sugar) rapidly deteriorate his vessel.

My father was incarcerated for four and a half years. Finding "God" seemed to be the golden ticket to eternal freedom. After discovering religion, he reappeared in my life, wanting to be a father once again. My mother, struggling mentally and financially, was eager to have him take me in. I had watched her go through a dozen or more relationships with men. I was fond of some of these men, and some I could have done without meeting at all. When I was young, it was easy to accept these new figures in my life, but as I grew older, I became more closed off. We moved twelve times, that I can recall, switching schools at least five times. I had close friends, but this was before social media or cell phones, and it was difficult to stay in touch. I learned to go deep fast because I might blink and they'd be gone. I became more comfortable with change and uncertainty than with stability and consistency.

I never knew where it would come from, but I always felt loved. Emotional regulation was my job, and my mother depended on me to be stable. My mother endured abuse as a child, though in a different form than my father. She was sexually abused (perhaps more times than I am aware of) and verbally and emotionally abused. Because she never fully healed from her childhood trauma, she often played it out daily with my sisters and me. We'd endure fits of rage as she said things she didn't mean and did things she couldn't erase with an apology. At this point, I don't even know if she was aware of what she was saying. I know this is possible because it's happened to me. She was likely just playing out old traumas after a trigger had sent her into a spiral of fear and emotional pain. There are years of my life and numerous significant details that I have blocked out and cannot remember.

When I was an adult, my younger sister's father recounted the night he decided to leave my mother. "I just couldn't watch her treat you like that anymore." He asked if I remembered one of her frequent, physically abusive fits of rage. I had no recollection of this night. He affirmed that I hadn't been at fault. He painted images with infinite details, and the memory never came into focus for me. "She picked you up and threw you in the bedroom on the bed. Your head hit the headboard, and you started crying. Then she slammed the door so hard that she pulled the door handle off."

We have a rather tumultuous, volatile dynamic, my mother and I (from the very beginning up to now). She'd often say off-the-wall things that would trigger me. She'd accuse people of stealing from her (and often find the "stolen" items later), "backstabbing" her, or slandering her name in some way. I arranged for her to stay with a friend of mine and receive a treatment she'd been adamant about, and just a few days before she was set to receive the ketamine injection, she voiced her belief that the nurse might inject her with something else and intentionally kill her. She'd disliked one of the women working for the clinic, but nothing else would indicate that anyone would do anything that horrific. When she said things like this throughout my life, it deeply disturbed me, and I worried that my mother lived in a very dark place in her head. I've regularly struggled with this mental discomfort throughout my life. It's always been a gut-wrenching dynamic.

It's pretty bizarre how we can recreate these painful scenarios over and over in our lives. It's even more mysterious how things come full circle. My sister's father shared that story with me at a time in my life when I could genuinely put myself in everyone's shoes. There was no confusion.

As a young adult, I found myself in a relationship where I witnessed this familiar dynamic play out between parent and child. It clicked at that moment, and I understood how my sister's father felt. I understood why he stayed to protect me. As he told his story at the kitchen table, I, too, discovered that the inkling to stay was for the same reason. I also understood why he disappeared from my life for his self-preservation. We cannot change anyone who doesn't want to change, and we cannot burn ourselves to save someone from a fire.

I was fortunate to have two incredibly consistent and stable grandmothers. My father's mother was a functioning alcoholic, though I didn't see or understand this as a child. On my maternal side, my grandmother Anita (Grandma K) was the rock in my life. Fortunately, I wasn't left alone entirely—because of her. I had a beautiful example of a strong woman who consistently showed up for me. Grandma K played the primary caretaker role in my life for many years. She also cared for my cousin, Mikey, who was more of a brother for this reason, both in the amount of time we spent together and the type of relationship we had. At one point, we all lived together in a duplex: Mikey; Grandma K; my grandfather, who occupied the lower level (they were separated) with his caretaker, Missy; my four-year-old sister Leah; and my mom. I was eleven years old. Life in that duplex was often intense.

Mikey held me by my ankles over the railing of the stairs after I blasted the volume of MTV music videos on our big screen. He'd always find a reason to torment me. Grandma K yelled, "Now, Michael! Put her down!"

So, he did. He released my ankles, and I landed on my head.

What seemed like a millisecond later, he exclaimed, "Oh shit! Did you hear that?"

I was dizzy and thought, *yes, you asshole, that sound came from inside my body.* He said he heard the pop in my neck from where he was standing. I cried and screamed at him while my grandma went to find her inhaler (she had terrible asthma and had survived seven heart attacks).

There was never a dull moment with Mikey. One could assume that he'd explode into a fit of rage at any moment. A vivid memory I've always been able to access is Mikey chasing my mother out the door of Grandma K's house and around the block with a butcher knife, screaming, "I'm going to fucking kill you!"

How did it begin? He was recounting an altercation with his parole officer while bound by his ankle monitor (a tracking device on his ankle). They warned him that he'd go back to jail. My mother said to him, "You belong in jail." It took him less than sixty seconds to jump up and grab a knife out of the kitchen. The dramatic scenes were endless. Not only did the drama play out in my own home, but my entire social circle also shared this reality. I believe it's nothing short of a miracle that I made it out alive and mentally stable.

In 2016, the *Wisconsin State Journal* described Allied Drive as "the worst neighborhood in Dane County—an isolated, decaying area plagued by gangs, drugs, violence, and battered apartments."[1] The day after I was born, my parents brought me to their apartment, two blocks from Allied Drive. We lived in this area until I was thirteen years old, moving away just to return, again and again. Grandma K also lived just a few blocks from Allied Drive.

The street lived up to its reputation. One night when I was ten years old, I was in a two-bedroom apartment with five of my friends. All six of us were sleeping on the floor in the living room. Just before 7 A.M., we woke up to my friend's mother and her boyfriend screaming at each other. We ran to her room just in time to watch him throw her into the cheap wooden dresser. Her eye was already black, and her arms bruised. She noticed us standing at the door and screamed at him, "GIT OUT! Git outta my house!" We were silent, eyes wide, fists clenched. We were ready to jump in.

He charged out of the house, yelling back at her, "Fuckin' crack-head ass bitch. I'll fuck you up. Fuckin' talk to me like that." My friend grabbed her mom and hugged her.

---

1. Matthew DeFour. "Allied Dunn's Marsh in the Midst of a Rebirth after Years of Decline" (website), *Wisconsin State Journal* (Madison, WI), Sept. 28, 2016, host.madison.com/wsj/news/local/neighborhoods/allied-dunn-s-marsh-in-the-midst-of-a-rebirth/article_140142c2-cbbe-54c8-9aa7-b54bc5eddba4.html.

"I'm okay, baby, just stay here; I'll be back." Her mom left, and we were alone.

"This mothafucka!" My friend ran into the kitchen, yelling over and over, "This MOTH-A-FUCK-A!" She grabbed old, dull steak knives and a butcher knife out of the drawers and handed them to us. She said, "C'mon. We gonna fuck his shit up." We followed her to the parking lot and found his car. She stabbed the front driver's side tire with the butcher knife until it stuck in. We each took a tire while she found a rock to throw at his windshield. I felt a rush of adrenaline, fear, excitement, and victory all at once. I knew cops patrolled this block, and I'd already had a run-in or two. It was the last time I visited that apartment.

While I was in elementary school, the white powders, pills, and weed didn't entice me, even though they plagued my neighborhood and were always at arm's reach. The top of that wood dresser dusted in white powder had no allure. I never thought to inspect, much less ingest it. Simply catching a glimpse of a crack pipe at my friend's house made me feel uncomfortable and dirty. I remember judging my dad, sitting in his little maroon four-door Toyota in Tacoma, Washington, as he sparked a fresh, green cannabis bud in his pipe. The little wooden pipe had a pungent smell of burnt resin that churned my stomach. It always disgusted me. As he inhaled deeply, my father's face went from pink to red to purple in what seemed like an instant before he started choking and coughing. It didn't look pleasant. With little to no emotional intelligence or control of my feelings, I'd felt the rage fill my body as I watched him. While he voluntarily choked himself, I wondered if he cared about me. I couldn't fully articulate it then, but now I know that I felt his lack of love for himself and wondered how he'd be around for me if he did himself in with substances.

At eleven years old, my grandfather lived on the lower level of that two-story duplex on Tudor Drive in Fitchburg, Wisconsin. That home where Mikey dropped me on my head. My grandfather was the president and founder of the American Cannabis Society. He was a freedom fighter and an activist. I was educated about this plant and knew it was an herb—a medicine and a gift from the earth. My distaste began to dissolve. I saw how it soothed and calmed those who lived in pain. I thought these happy, über chill people must know what they're talking about. I would watch my grandfather and his caretaker, Melissa or "Missy," go out every day on their mission to "Free the Herb," as they'd say. She'd pop up the American Cannabis Society stand at eco-festivals and conscious gatherings around the country and display my grandfather's trademarked slogan "Thank You for Pot Smoking." They'd return home with garbage bags of hemp twine, and we'd sit together and knot dozens of macrame necklaces, bracelets, and anklets to sell at the booth. I was grandfathered into the hippie subculture of the nineties. Pun intended.

Unfortunately, I didn't have much of a relationship with my grandfather. By the time I was old enough to cultivate a connection with him, he had developed emphysema and lived with a green oxygen tank at his side. I was closer with his caregiver, Missy, who was eager to teach me about veganism and knotting hemp twine into bracelets. She never once asked me to join her when she smoked cannabis.

Grandpa passed when I was fourteen years old. I remember Mikey being so emotional at the funeral. I couldn't quite understand it at the time. I don't know what I said to him, but it was something like, "Why are you crying?" Like most things I said, this pissed him off, and I can still tap into that horrible feeling in my stomach when he darted back with anger. His inability to receive my sincerity was painful. Today, I believe he may have been so distraught because Grandpa was a legend, and he didn't have an opportunity to get close to him either. The masculine wound runs deep on both sides of my family. We all seemed oblivious to the role of an upstanding father.

Mikey was always eager to get his little cousin high. As soon as the first unsupervised opportunity arose, he introduced me to the two-foot bong. "I'm going to light this bowl, right here, and you're just going to put your mouth on here and suck as hard as you can." The instructions were pretty simple. We were in the backseat of his car; me and my best friend Yanya (Adriana). Her older brothers were friends with Mikey. Lynn, Mikey's girlfriend, was in the front passenger seat. Yanya and I were on one of our shoplifting missions, and Mikey had driven us that day with his plan in mind: He'd drive us, but we had to get high with him.

Yanya took a hit first. Mikey leaned back over the armrest between the seats, holding the water bong. She took it like a champ. Then it was my turn. Within seconds I was gasping for air and flailing my arms. For a few moments, I was sure I was going to suffocate. He started punching my thigh while I gasped in the fetal position, screaming at me to "Fucking breathe!" He was pretty shitty at expressing concern. When I finally caught my breath, I was so high I didn't even know where I was. Yanya had to open the door for me. I genuinely believe I suffer from PTSD from this experience. I was sure I'd suffocate and die for what felt like an eternity in those short three minutes. All I remember of the mall mission was going into Bath and Body Works and attempting to apply eye shadow. A woman was doing the same next to us, and we asked her if she worked there and if she had a Q-Tip that we could use. We asked five times. She finally got upset and yelled, "I already told you *five* times! I don't work here!" This wasn't the first or last time Yanya and I pushed someone's buttons. We made tormenting people our business.

Yanya's two older brothers were named Brandon and Bouk (Jerry). I happened to be in love with both of them. Yanya, Bouk, and their younger sister, Nina, were the children of a very charismatic man from Cuba that I adored after one meeting. I attribute their familial bond and big hearts to their Cuban roots. I deeply loved Yanya's entire family. They all lived together and were close. I was also secretly in love with their cousin Shane, who was like another sibling and often around. This may have been my first introduction to male figures I could truly respect. I'll never forget passing out on the couch in Yanya's basement and Bouk picking me up to carry me to bed. I pretended to sleep in his arms as he cradled me like a baby. This was undoubtedly the moment I fell in love with him. As I remember, both brothers and the cousin were exceedingly respectful toward women. I eventually dated one of them, though it wasn't until years later.

Yanya and I spent our time memorizing 2Pac's *All Eyez On Me* album, getting high on weed, shoplifting, and tormenting Mikey. Yanya was my everything for years. We spent every waking moment together. The day I started my period in seventh grade, I was in the basement of Yanya's house in Verona. It wasn't surprising that Yanya began on the same day. We were only separated once, in seventh grade, when we decided to take my mom's boyfriend's car for a joyride. We were both "grounded" for a month. As I mentioned, Yanya's father grew up in Cuba and had a unique way of parenting. He'd taught her to drive a car so early that she was proficient before we started high school. The vehicle and its passengers were utterly safe during and after the joyride. Our safety wasn't the issue. The fact that we were minors illegally operating a stolen car was the issue, but not until we put the car in park at the exact moment my mom and her boyfriend arrived. Our parents were not thrilled.

We pulled into the parking spot, and Brian, my mom's boyfriend, jumped out of the driver's seat of my mother's car and onto the hood of his car, staring directly into my eyes through the windshield. I wanted to lock the doors and crawl under the seat, but he screamed, "Get the fuck out of the car!"

Yanya's direction was immediate, and I had no time to think about the stupidity of her demand, "Lock the doors!"

It was too late, and Brian had already swung open the driver's side door and yelled, "Get out now!" We looked at each other and deflated, caught red-handed. We were on fire that month. We were evicted from our apartment shortly after. Yanya and I not only stole a car for a brief moment, but we'd also spent countless hours singing at the top of our lungs in the hallway for days on end, at inappropriate hours of the night. That was how we spent most of our time together: singing at an obnoxious volume. Yanya has a voice that penetrates the soul, and singing with her was like medicine. My childhood dream of becoming a globally recognized singer felt real while we belted out "(Everything I Do) I Do It For You" by Bryan Adams at the top of those stairs.

In the last few months of seventh grade, I moved to Stoughton, another small Wisconsin suburb, to live with my dad, leaving my mom's apartment in Fitchburg, where we'd been living with Leah, my sister, who had turned five by that time. I had to leave Yanya and Verona Middle School. I also had to leave Leah, which was painful because I felt I needed to play my role as an older sister and protect her, as I did in our crime-ridden neighborhood. I was devastated and, in my teenage state of mind, I resented my father. How could he just show up and destroy my life?

Before my father showed up, I did my own thing. I would usually have the house to myself. I stayed out late, got high on weed, had groups of neighborhood kids over for make-out parties, and played video games until 5 A.M. When my dad got out of prison and came back from Washington, I wasn't ready to start adhering to his rules. Eighth grade was rough: curfews, getting "grounded," and sleeping at home on weekends. My dad was wary of the weekend-long sleepovers I pushed for only a month after moving in with him. Our dynamic remained the same through eighth grade and into my freshman year of high school, when my desire to rage overrode everything else.

Yanya and I slowly drifted apart. We weren't quite old enough to drive, and our parents weren't excited to make the thirty-minute drive. Everyone was relieved that we wouldn't be causing trouble together anymore. I made friends fast and completely dove into a new social circle. These new friends drank copious amounts of alcohol on the weekends and smoked weed on the train tracks after school. We bonded quickly over blacked-out nights and plastic soda bottle bongs.

Yanya and I had one last hurrah when she came to school with me. We ended up being escorted by the police to my house four hours later. Two girls that already had it in for me saw Yanya's visit as an opportunity to take out two birds with one stone. Yanya and I walked down the hallway from second period to third. I walked into my third-period class, not noticing that Yanya didn't follow me in. I walked back out just as the bell rang. The hallway was empty except for the two girls with the vendetta, Kristin and Melly. Kristin planted herself in front of me.

"Why you talkin' shit, Lana?"

I always freeze when shit hits the fan. I could feel it coming. She swung, and I leaned back. She completely missed my face. Yanya lunged and shoved her into the lockers. Melly slammed Yanya into the lockers on the other side of the hallway, then punched her in the stomach. Kristin grabbed Yanya's hair. Arms were flailing everywhere, and students started rushing into the hallway, hearing the commotion. I was frozen. I watched until the teachers came out and separated the girls. There were clumps of hair in their hands and gashes with fresh blood on their faces. My on-and-off boyfriend, Lee, showed up with his other on-and-off, Megan. Kristin, Melly, and Megan were all best friends. It was all planned. The police arrived. I was suspended, and Yanya was asked not to return. A few weeks later, I had to file a restraining order after Megan's second attempt to physically attack me. Until I graduated from high school, I spent my younger years watching my back from Allied Drive to Stoughton.

Being so far from not only Yanya but also her family was agonizing. They became my family. It was hard to move to a new school again and make new friends as an insecure eighth-grader. I kept smoking pot and started drinking as a way to numb myself and fit in. It was easier for me to do what seemed so familiar instead of completely recreating my identity. I didn't know why I was living with my dad. I didn't have a relationship with him, and my mother never said anything good about him. I didn't understand why she was okay with me moving out of her house and into his. He'd been in prison for years, and his return felt abrupt and confusing. With my mother, I felt free, but with my father, all of a sudden, I had rules and curfews and check-ins, which made me resent him even more. My mother rarely came to visit when I first moved in with my father. She came over one day after school with her boyfriend Brian, the one who jumped on the hood of his car after the joyride. They came into my room and asked me to sit between them on my futon bed.

My mother spoke. "Lana, I have to tell you something." I honestly had no idea what she was about to say. "Grandma K. died last night."

My body instantly became weak and a sharp pain shot through my chest. "No! No! *No*!" I have never felt such a deep sense of grief and anger simultaneously. She continued to explain, and the anger grew more robust. "She was in the hospital for a few days."

I was in disbelief. "Why didn't you tell me? I could have seen her? Why didn't you call me?"

My mother felt guilty, "I know, honey. We didn't know either. I'm so sorry."

The simultaneous desire to strangle her and take my own life became an intense internal battle. My head was spinning, "What do you *mean* you didn't know?! Why didn't you tell me she was in the hospital?" Brian was silent.

It was as if someone had ripped my heart out. I couldn't breathe. My rock was gone. I had no one. I couldn't trust my mother to be around, and I felt utterly detached from my father. It felt like everything I knew was crumbling beneath me.

Stronger and stronger drugs became more appealing and accessible the year my grandmother passed. I didn't have proper support processing the grief, so I latched onto Lee and numbed out with drugs. Lee became my rock. His older brother was a DJ in the underground rave scene. That seed Mikey had planted when he stuck out his tongue with a little square of paper (LSD) on it back when I was in elementary school began to sprout. I was introduced to this world the summer after eighth grade. I'd found a place where I could escape reality, filled with flashing lights, electronic music, and mind-altering substances.

2
THE DARK HIGH

Holly's apartment was across the street from the high school. It was convenient for a lunch-hour smoke session. The stoner posse could walk over, get high, and make it back in time to buy a bagel and cream cheese from the à la carte stand as the bell rang, or we'd just skip fifth period and keep smoking.

One night, Holly; her boyfriend, Stephan, the coke dealer; and at least ten others raged until dawn. Holly's upstairs neighbor had a Percocet prescription, so she had a few pills on hand to go along with a bottle of Jack Daniels, a piss-yellow eight-ball of coke from Stephan, a jar of double-stacked "supermans" (pressed MDMA pills), and a pound of weed. Staying true to my extremist approach to life, I decided to try them all at once.

As the room started spinning, I remember my friend Liz speaking as sternly as she could in her drunken stupor to our friend Levin, in whose lap my head was resting, "Be good, Levin. Take care of our little Lana." I'm sure I was moaning and sensually undulating as I did when the MDMA hit.

Levin was also drunk and high as a kite when he said, "I know, Liz. I know. She's fine. Don't worry." I woke up next to Levin with no memory of removing my shorts. Liz meant well, but she was just as high as the rest of us. She couldn't keep an eye on me. I recall wondering if I was actually raped if I couldn't remember. I left while everyone was still asleep.

I can now see that I disassociated in these painful moments. Without the emotion attached, I also lack clarity of the memory. As an adult, I can see that I became a pro at blocking emotions at an early age. Not only could I let the painful circumstances roll off me like water off a duck's back, but I also forgave the people involved. When my primary caregivers seemed to fuck up daily, the only option was to forgive them early on and become accustomed to people supporting me in a half-assed way. I could not fend without them, and this was their best and the best I would get. The dynamic with my parents somehow wired the story of forgiving people quickly as the only way to survive in the world. Levin didn't know, right? He had his own fucked up story and no good examples in his life of how to respect women. No one would do something like this without their own story of hurt.

That night and questionable experience at Holly's didn't decrease my desire to rage. This underground scene was so full of excitement; it was the unknown. It was a rush. It gave me a sense of identity and strength. I was a bad girl who could get high and still write articles for the school newspaper, ace tests, and keep my name on the honor roll. My peer group was a mystery to my high school friends. They were twenty-somethings who would pick me up from school in their cars on Friday after seventh period. We'd drive to the city for an underground rave in an abandoned warehouse. Only the "cool kids" had older friends with cars. I just wanted to be sought after, loved. Worthy of love—and attention. It was hard-wired early on; I wasn't getting the consistent confirmation at home, and there were a million other ways to receive that external validation I craved so deeply. I dove in headfirst, with more substances, more parties, more electronic music, and less school.

Liz became my new Yanya for a brief period, my new partner-in-crime. I couldn't drive yet, and Yanya was so far away. I still missed her every day. Liz and I spent every waking moment and every delusional moment together. If we couldn't find ecstasy or anything else in pill form, we'd settle for alcohol, but it certainly wasn't our preference. Liz and I took our first LSD trip together. We went to a friend's place at 9 P.M. on a Friday after school. He gave each of us one drop of liquid on the tip of the tongue and sent us home. We spent the entire night exploring the universe of Liz's apartment and tormenting her sleeping mother with our roaring laughter. This was when my obsession with viewing things on a microscopic level began.

We heated frozen French fries in the oven that became a spaceship, and we couldn't bear the thought of consuming them. I looked closely at the plate we'd set on the floor covered in ketchup and the strange sticks of artificial ingredients. Low and behold, it was speckled with tiny fragments of carpet, dust, and whatever else from sitting on the floor for hours while we rolled around next to it, high as can be. I was disgusted with what I saw. I looked at it as if it were a crime scene. How could I even consider putting anything on that plate in my mouth? It was filthy. I vowed never to put anything in my mouth again without carefully inspecting it.

We fell madly in love with LSD and spent countless weekends exploring altered states of consciousness. The galaxy I saw in that kitchen stove window (while the artificial French fries were baked) was one of the most surreal places I'd visited in life at that point. And so began our weekly visits to our friend James's place, searching for new psychedelics. Little did we know we'd find even more mind-altering substances.

James, Kirk, and Chris pretty much lived in the basement of James's parents' house. Sometimes other punk-rock-loving boys from high school would visit, and one senior had an older sister, Darya Lee. One particular visit didn't include Liz. It must have been the stint where she had a boyfriend, and I became attached at the hip with another friend. "Whoa! Do you feel that? I can't move my legs! I'm glued to the floor," Allison uttered in a dazed tone. Little did I know she was my soon-to-be bestie, and we became glued after this moment and literally spent every single day together for months on end.

I responded to Allison in a squeal, "I can't either! Oh my God, this is insane!" I burst into laughter and confessed, "Oh my God. I love it. We need more! James. We need more." We'd arrived in a triad, including Julia, who was Allison's ride or die at the time. Since she was a grade ahead of us, she knew the boys a bit better than Allison and me. The three of us found ourselves in a K-hole on the brown carpet of James's basement bedroom. We were adamant about going back into the hole when we could eventually peel ourselves off the floor. Darya was our ticket back into the void. I kept her number. Allison and I would soon be the girls who kept little baggies of white powder on the top shelf of our blue high school lockers.

A few weeks after the K-hole experience, I called Darya to ask her for more Ketamine. She said she couldn't get anymore, but she had something else. I was alone when she came to my house to reveal this alternative. She offered to bring me to her parents' house where she lived and let me try her drug of choice: "glass." I had no idea what it was; I just knew I wanted to try anything and everything. I jumped in her blue Ford Probe, and we sped off to her parents' house. I immediately fell in love with the music she was blasting, just loud enough that I could still hear her speak, but she had to yell. Her car was filthy, and it looked as if she'd been living in it for the past ten years. Even though that disgusting plate of French fries had changed my life forever, I barely cared at that moment; I was elated to have a friend with a car who was willing to pick me up. She had a pack of Mountain Dew in the back seat and an opened can in her cup holder. The car reeked of cigarettes. Her body odor wasn't any better; fortunately, I had no trouble holding my breath. I'd been doing it for years, growing up in homes filled with secondhand smoke.

I was dumbfounded when I entered her room. Shelves lined every wall, somehow neatly crammed full of clothes. Her room was chaotic, but the clothes were all folded as if they were on display at a department store. There were dirty dishes with half-eaten pieces of moldy who-knows-what. Darya plopped down clumsily on her futon and dumped out the "glass" shards on the mirror of the coffee table in front of us. She used a lighter and a credit card to crush the pieces into powder. There were plastic straws cut into two-inch pieces next to the mirror on the table. She grabbed the closest one and leaned in to snort the line. She handed me the straw while rubbing her nose vigorously as if someone had punched her in the face. There was a much smaller bit of white powder that she'd prepared for me. I leaned in without a thought and snorted the bump. I had already experienced cocaine, Ketamine, and MDMA in this way, so I was no stranger to the method of snorting.

The burning sensation made my eyes water and my nose tingle. My ears started ringing. I glanced at Darya, who giggled, baring her yellow, decayed teeth. "Don't worry; it goes away!" I tried to act cool, like I wasn't holding back tears, and said, "Thanks!"

Dozens of experiences in Darya's room began. She started picking me up daily, not just from my father's apartment; she would pick me up from school during my lunch break. Somehow, I'd always make it back to school, but I completely dropped off the grid on the weekends. During the weekend we drove to Chicago for an underground rave, we had been up for two days, taking a bump of meth (AKA Darya's "glass") every two hours. We headed back to Madison, and even though I could have passed out while standing, Darya wasn't ready to stop. We went to the hotel where her dealer was staying on the Eastside with twenty packs of over-the-counter medication we picked up for him. He brought us into the makeshift lab (the bathroom); the concoction in the bathtub would become a massive supply of meth, basically a big soup of deadly chemicals. We'd brought the missing components to complete the process and would be the first to try it. Darya's goal was to get right to the source. The way to get the cheapest drugs, or maybe even free drugs, was to get them directly from the person who made them. This is yet another one of the many memories I look back on and feel a great sense of gratitude. I'm fortunate to be alive, free, healthy, and sane. I could have died in that hotel room from an explosion, overdose, or left in handcuffs or with an actual mental imbalance. I remember these days that make it easy to count my blessings.

My dad would call on a Sunday after I'd avoided him for the weekend while discovering the process of cooking meth, too high to communicate—days without sleep. Darya and I would find a house party or underground rave every weekend. She seemed to know everyone and was always on the guest list, which meant I was too—more external validation for me. I was in the "it" club. I was young, hot, and ready to dance on stage next to my favorite DJs on the turntables.

Being the life of the party became part of my identity. It became challenging to maintain a connection with most of my high school friends. The "ravers," the dealers, the "candy kids," and the party kids became my close social circle. We were the people who lived by the night and had access to every mind-altering substance. I was usually the youngest, and I loved it. Status. I could hang. Everyone was Darya's age, somewhere from nineteen to thirty years old. We spent a lot of time with Darya's friend Rima, who also loved glass. Rima lived in a fabulous apartment with multiple closets full of expensive clubwear. She had to have been in her late twenties or early thirties. She was a middle-eastern queen in my eyes at that time.

I'd get hand-me-downs from Rima and everyone else but not Darya because she always weighed ten pounds less than me. It was one of her superpowers, at least in her mind. I never once saw her eat a full meal. I rarely saw her eat at all. We'd go somewhere to eat, and she'd never finish her meal. Darya was a bizarre speed addict. She was very interested in health, yoga, and meditation. We visited organic farms, sought out health food stores, and endlessly searched for the highest quality nutritional supplements. She seemed to think all this would somehow counter-balance her addiction to meth. Ironically, it was Darya who introduced me to the practice of yoga. It was subtle and slow, but this first yoga class became the catalyst for the next chapter of my life.

When Brian and my mother separated, she moved to Stoughton to be near me. I'd told her that I was struggling to live with my father, so she moved down the street, unattached to men for that brief period. As a thirty-something, I've come to realize I'd been playing out my mother's story: Following men around the world and allowing the relationship to dictate my every move, accepting that this project (AKA relationship) was more important than my hopes, dreams, and aspirations. No different than my reality at thirty-five years old, my mother wasn't single for long. She'd disappear for days, and when she was away with her boyfriend, I'd stay at her place so I could host Darya and all of my friends who wanted to get high together.

It was perfect timing for my mother to move down the street because my father had lost his temper, and my response was to move out that very same day. A young, close friend of his had hooked up with my girlfriend Sara, and I was appalled for some reason. We were sitting in the living room watching television, and I remarked about his friend being fucked up for hooking up with her. His face turned red, "What the fuck do you mean?"

His intensity shook the core of my being, and I froze. He demanded that I answer him, and instead, I stormed off to my room without a word.

He followed me after setting down his bowl of cereal and confronted me at the door of my walk-in closet, where I sometimes hung out writing poetry. He grabbed me by the neck, "Fucking answer me when I ask you something!" His face was purple as he threw me back at the wall and slammed the door.

Before I'd even noticed that the lock on the door broke, he shoved my bunk bed against the door, trapping me inside. My knees buckled. I sat on the floor and hyperventilated as tears streamed down my face and my heart raced. I was shaking uncontrollably. When I realized the bed was against the door, the anger surpassed the fear, and I stopped crying. As quietly as possible, I slowly nudged the bed away from the door with what felt like a hundred tries. The bedframe was metal, and the bottom bunk was a queen-sized futon. Within seconds after making my way out of the closet, I called Darya and told her to come immediately and park by my window to pick me up. She arrived in less than twenty minutes, and I didn't talk to my father after that day for months. I'd still go to the apartment before school and pick up the lunch money he continued leaving in the same spot on the kitchen table. I guess this was my way of saying, I still need you to be my dad, but I hate you right now. My father often recounts this story to me on the phone. "Do you remember when I threw you in the closet, and you moved out?" I have to tell him over and over that I forgive him and that he can't hold onto it forever. I tell him it's time to move on. Inevitably, the conversation comes up again.

My relationship with Mom wasn't any less challenging at that time. It's difficult to remember precisely what the arguments were about, but some of the events are hard to forget. Sometimes altercations would escalate to physical fights, which certainly played out differently than the fights with my father. One weekend Mom came home early. I think she wanted everyone out of the house. I was upset and said I was leaving too and called Darya on my cell phone. My mom grabbed my phone, and I failed to get it back. "You're not going anywhere!"

I pushed her to the floor and started choking her while I screamed and cried so loud my throat started to burn. "Give me my phone! I hate you! Give me my phone back!" She pushed me off, and I ran into the kitchen, flung open a drawer, and threw every utensil I could find at her.

Not quite a rare occurrence. We weren't always physical, but mental abuse always pushed me over the edge. I can still hear my mom saying, "Oh, you're just fucking gay. That's why you want to spend every waking moment with Yanya." It was the same sort of commentary she'd set Mikey off with that day he chased her around the block with a butcher knife. It was a struggle living with my mother and equally challenging to live with my father, so I tried to escape to friends' houses as often as possible. Darya felt like my get-out-of-jail-free card. I felt like a free spirit with her, like I was on top of the world until I wasn't.

Things started going south with Darya at the Even Further Festival in Northern Wisconsin. It was a three-day festival to commemorate the Merry Pranksters' bus. It was my first. "Furthur is a 1939 International Harvester school bus purchased by author Ken Kesey in 1964 to carry his 'Merry Band of Pranksters' cross-country, filming their counterculture adventures as they went."[2]

Who were the Merry Pranksters? "Ken Kesey and the Merry Pranksters lived communally at Kesey's homes in California and Oregon, and are noted for the sociological significance of a lengthy road trip they took in the summer of 1964, traveling across the United States in a psychedelic painted school bus called Further, organizing parties and giving out LSD."[3] I was thrilled that I could honor this tradition and trip on LSD at a Drop Bass Network party. Darya and I were obsessed with Drop Bass.

We not only knew all of the DJs, we knew all the names of the "production companies," as they called themselves, and promoters who put on all the events. At the Even Further Festival, I knew Yanya's brother Brandon, who was just beginning his career as a DJ. He had come to the festival with Nate Dogg, his best friend (no relation to the famous rapper). Late on the second night of the festival, Darya and I were wide awake after taking a few lines of glass when I ran into Brandon. He was panicking, saying that Nate Dogg had taken too much LSD and had a bad trip. "He tried to punch me in the face because I was grabbing his

2. Dodgson, Rick, *It's All a Kind of Magic: The Young Ken Kesey* (Madison: University of Wisconsin Press, 2013), 132.

3. "Ken Kesey and the Merry Pranksters," Univie.ac.at, accessed July, 28, 2017, https://newspaperarchive.com/madison-wisconsin-state-journal-dec-01-2004-p-39/.

phone. He was calling his mom." Nate Dogg was seeing demons and had run into the woods. No one could find him for a long time.

It was the end for Nate Dogg. He never touched another substance after the festival. He went home to live with his parents and started going to church. I had already heard the horror stories of people having bad trips, never coming down from a trip, getting caught up, or getting thrown in jail. I finally got scared. After Further, I began distancing myself from Darya. She had started to slip away herself. I also started dating Brandon, which meant I had more of Yanya back in my life.

After a week or two of not seeing Darya, she began calling me and leaving bizarre voice messages. When I answered, I wasn't sure if she knew someone was listening. Did she know she had called me? She was "spun out." *Spun* is the title of a film released around this time, and it blew my mind that I was living out this horror film. I started to understand that Darya may have gone too far to come back. The film *Requiem for a Dream* was released only two years prior. After watching it, I developed this eerie feeling of being disconnected from the rest of the world with our substance experimentation. Darya would tell me things like, "there's a cop who lives in my attic. He told me about you, Lana. He told me that you're pregnant." I was so frightened and frustrated by her delusional behavior that I stopped taking her calls.

We'd had a good run, but now she was down to eighty pounds. The last time I'd seen her, she had a scar on her neck the size of a silver dollar. Her story was that she had a worm in her neck, and she'd had to use tweezers to try and remove it, but it made its way back inside before she could grab it. I did not find this shocking. I was disgusted but not shocked.

Once, after being awake for over forty-eight hours, I had a delusional moment with tweezers. I arrived at my mother's apartment believing a hair was in my eye. I sat before the mirror and tried to grab the hair with tweezers until my eye was so red and swollen that I could barely see, and I had to stop. I knew I had a problem. Just writing this over a decade later still makes me feel delusional. I knew I had to stop. I wasn't eighty pounds, but I was damn close. I had no connection with my friends in school, except for the few that would get high with me on the weekends.

I missed Lee, my first love, the one I'd lost my virginity to in eighth grade. We'd been on and off for years, but this was the longest stretch.

After pulling myself away from Darya, it only took a few months before I started reconnecting with my high school friends. Things died down with Brandon, and I started dating Lee again. He forbade me from touching any substance and threatened to end the relationship if I did. I wanted to be with him more than I wanted to get high. However, the white powders and sleepless nights didn't completely disappear from my life.

Mikey and Yanya had started shooting up together. I had to maintain distance from Yanya again. This time it wasn't because we couldn't drive; she was high, and I had no interest in heroin. I had my love affair with uppers, but downers did not interest me. I didn't consider it an addiction because I could live without them. Darya once connected me with a heroin dealer, and after snorting it a few times, I decided heroin wasn't for me. One of the times, the middle-man (a heavy-set black girl from the West side of Madison) came over to my mother's house with her supply. She shot up while I took a line, and she nearly overdosed. I remember her losing consciousness and her face going purple. Fortunately, she snapped out of it, and I honestly have no idea what happened, but it scared the shit out of me. I vowed never to touch it again or allow anyone to shoot up in my house. I had no control over what happened outside of my house, however.

At the end of my junior year of high school, I was dating a sophomore who was an incredible musician. It was time to try on a new identity. Today, I attribute this shift to a powerful psilocybin journey (Matt—did we really eat an ounce that night?). I fell in love with nature and taking care of my body. The dark, underground rave scene was no longer calling me, and I explored what it meant to be a "hippie." I visited Mikey's apartment with my boyfriend, who was awed by Mikey's rendition of Tool's "Schism" on his guitar. After his stellar performance, he sat down and asked me to tie the rubber tourniquet on his arm so he could shoot up. I told him that I couldn't do it and looked away.

Mikey and I had started partying together while I was hanging out with Darya. We did lines of meth together and took pressed ecstasy pills, but I never touched heroin while we were together. It felt so good to reconnect with him, but at that time, I didn't know how to navigate our relationship with his addiction. I didn't spend much time with Mikey after that night. It hurt too much to watch him destroy his life. It all started early on. He was in and out of group homes and foster care during his teenage years. Then it became a vicious cycle of going in and out of rehab and jail. The day his life truly started to plummet was when he nodded out on dope (heroin) while driving and hit a car carrying two older women. One was left with a broken neck. The headline from the Madison State Journal read, "Man, 24, gets 2½ years for drug-induced crash."

Blood test found morphine, codeine and marijuana when he injured two women.

By Ed Treleven
Wisconsin State Journal

A Monona man will spend two years in prison for causing a drug-induced car crash last year that injured two women, one of whom suffered a broken neck.

Michael B. Kundert, 24, also will serve 2½ years of extended supervision for causing the June 30, 2003, crash on University Avenue near Spring Harbor Drive.

According to a criminal complaint, police said Kundert acted strangely after the crash and had needle marks on his arm. A blood test found morphine, codeine and marijuana in Kundert's system, the complaint states.

Kundert received the prison sentence for driving under the influence of drugs and causing great bodily harm to Betty Stasny, 71, whose neck was broken in the crash that pinned her car against a utility pole.

"I think you need to make yourself responsible," Stasny said. "Did I hear you say you're having a child? I wouldn't want what happened to us happening to a child."

Kay Strauman, 62, of McFarland, a friend of Stasny who suffered deep bruises in the crash, said it had a tremendous impact on the active life she lives as a retiree.

"You probably think of me as an old fogy with no life," she said. "I'm a retired psychology teacher with a real life."

She said the only chance Kundert has is to get drug treatment.

"Unless you can lead a drug-free life, I don't want you out on the street," Strauman said.

Kundert also received concurrent jail and probation terms for several charges not related to the crash, including heroin possession, marijuana possession, bail jumping and criminal damage to property.

Kundert's attorney, assistant public defender Robert Burke, said Kundert is ready to make changes in his life and accept the drug treatment he will receive while in prison.

Kundert apologized to the women and said he had made "foolish choices" in his life.

"I'm glad that this is over," Kundert said. "I am ready to do what I have to do to live my life."

The crash was only a year after the night he asked me to tie the rubber tourniquet. To this day, and likely forevermore, I feel the pain of not being able to pull him out of his struggle.

3

HIPPIE STRIPPER

Junior year of high school became my "hippie phase." I had tried out "raver," "goth," "goody-good," and moved to hippie when I looked in my closet one morning and yelled to my father, "Oh my God! All of my clothes are black!"

He said, "Yeah, you just noticed that?"

I went thrift shopping that day, bought a tie-dyed tube dress, and donated my black clothes. I took LSD almost every weekend for a few months with my friend Allison. I'd started writing for the high school newspaper about the dangers of high fructose corn syrup and canned soda. I'd skipped school one day to stay home and read *Go Ask Alice*. This book was pivotal for me. I could relate to the diary of this teenage girl exploring her shadows in the 1970s with substances such as LSD. The story turned a bit dark, but the reality of it hit home for me, and I was comforted knowing that my experiences were not unique. The color was coming back into my life.

One day, my mother took me grocery shopping at a local natural foods cooperative. Among what seemed like a hundred other free publications, I was most captivated by a brochure that read "Why Vegan?" on the front. I loved reading all the literature from the front of the store and figured this would be another exciting find. I was mistaken.

It was a pivotal moment. The images of factory farms were crushing to my naive eyes. I became a bit of an activist after I picked up that PETA pamphlet. They're pros at roping people in with those grotesque images.

Within a week, I checked every label on everything I purchased to see if the product had been tested on animals or contained animal byproducts. My extremist mentality was in full force. It was the perfect starting point for my young, impressionable mind.

Learning about factory farming was a significant catalyst. I started taking stacks of the pamphlets from the co-op and leaving them around my school. I was sure everyone needed to know about this, and I firmly believed they would react the same as me. This burst of radical behavior irritated my family and most of my friends, except for the few that decided to join me. By the time I graduated high school, my father was urging me to get a job at the co-op where I'd found the pamphlet so that I could afford my expensive vegan food and new lifestyle. He supported me by reading aloud the gut-wrenching pages of *Natural Cures "They" Don't Want You to Know About,* a book by author and salesman Kevin Trudeau, who became better-known for the fraudulent promotion of his books and subsequent legal cases. I love the guy for putting this information out there regardless of his supposed scam involvement. My father did his part in exposing me to conspiracy theories and de-mystifying spiritual and esoteric theories that bubbled to the surface on my new path. An activist, conspiracy theorist, and hippie (as friends endearingly labeled me) emerged.

I took Dad's advice, got a job at Williamson Street Grocery Co-op, and immersed myself in holistic health studies. Soon I had moved toward the middle way, a place with more balance and nuance. At five years old, my mother had me swallow capsules of Chinese herbs and attend rah-rah seminars about herbalism and natural healing. The seed had been planted early on. It just needed a little watering (and a sprinkle of LSD on top).

Optimal health became my new drug of choice. My previous love affair with every illicit substance I could get my hands on morphed into a passion for food as medicine, Chinese herbs, and plant medicines. The seeds continued to sprout in my fertile psyche, and undying love was born. The roots of a life mission to explore a holistic lifestyle and natural healing grew fast and deep. My thirst for knowledge led me to enroll in a botany course at Madison Area Technical College, where I took five years of my sweet time earning my associate's degree. The course inspired me to seek an immersive experience in the plant kingdom, and I found myself in France, working on organic farms for four months while furthering my French language studies. I'd always loved French, as my second mom (as I like to call her), Ms. Kelly Christine, was married to an incredible Frenchman. Her two children, Sophia and Jean-Luc, are both bilingual. Christine has always been an influence in my life and was certainly a major catalyst in my French obsession. It wasn't until my late twenties that I found through a DNA test that I have French ancestors. Perhaps the obsession is innate? I wasn't incredibly resourceful at this time in my life and didn't figure out how to make it in France. I ran out of money and went home. I'd also missed my friends.

It only took this short immersion in France to realize that I wasn't aligned with American culture. Europe felt so much more like home. I wrote a long journal entry the week I returned home, ranting about things like toilet paper and how wasteful it is. All of our belongings and possessions. Cups and plates. Why don't we drink out of red bell peppers and eat off of banana leaves? Why are we so wasteful, and why do we consume so much? Why don't we eat better and have more farmer's markets? I wondered what the fuck was wrong with America and why I was born in such a godforsaken backward country.

I came home from France with a feeling of hopelessness. My financial situation was unstable, and employment that I could tolerate seemed scarce. I couldn't go back to the nine-to-five co-op life. I started popping Adderall to improve my forlorn demeanor and shed the twenty pounds I'd gained living on bread as a vegan in the French countryside. Eventually, I got a telemarketing job in which I attempted to sell time-shares to people who clearly could not afford them. I wonder now where the hell these phone numbers were pulled from. Even though I felt like an asshole calling these lonely people, there were a handful of meaningful conversations. I'd get some elderly man or woman who was grateful just to get a phone call and didn't care that I was a telemarketer. They would start telling me their life story or talk about their pets or grandchildren. Some told heartbreaking stories of loneliness. I would listen out of empathy as they touched that place in me where I held the pain of my father and grandmother's loneliness. One older man told me a story that seems etched in my memory for eternity. Recalling his story gets me all emotional and teary-eyed.

He was disabled and lived alone, hours away from any city with a grocery store. He could barely afford to live. He'd never married, had no children. I figured the conversation was about pets when he mentioned rabbits, but then he told me that he ate them. Whenever I attempted to end the conversation, he would bring up a new subject. Because I'd spent an hour on the phone without reading the script or trying to sell anything, I was reprimanded when I disconnected the call. Now, I look back and feel that this conversation was preparation for working at a gentlemen's club. Not that I felt sorry for the men I took into the VIP room, it was more that I could listen with compassion. Many of the men who frequent these clubs are like this man, lonely and seeking the attention guaranteed at the club because they can pay for it. Unfortunately, these men often get *attention* but don't get the *connection* that will begin to heal them.

The night I heard that dismal story was the night I decided I'd had enough. I was getting depressed. Telemarketing felt evil, like I was filling up an energy bank with bad karma. I had to quit. But I also wanted to leave the country, and I needed to fund my travels. I was in a bind. I wanted cash, and I wanted it fast, for my sanity. Desperation had set in. I was ready to jump on literally anything quick and easy. I called Sara, my girlfriend from high school, who had been dancing for almost a year, to confess that I was going insane at my telemarketing job. She responded, "Why don't you just come dance with me?"

I vaguely remember my first night dancing. Sara picked me up, and we drove about thirty minutes from my dad's apartment to Sun Prairie, Wisconsin, arriving at Club Brickle. Winter in Wisconsin is blistering cold. It feels like an undertaking to go anywhere, and the idea of heading out to get naked was comical. Nonetheless, out we went.

I was not impressed with the club. It was tiny and awkward, and you could stand in one corner and pretty much see what everyone in the room was doing. It felt like a typical, dingy Wisconsin dive bar. It smelled of stale cigarettes. Because of the dim lighting, it took my eyes a few minutes to adjust. It was unreasonable to expect something more lavish, considering the size of the venue and caliber of clientele that might frequent such a place tucked away in the farmlands of nowhere. Who would go out of their way to come here?

All too soon, the DJ was announcing my stage performance. "Let's welcome Nicolette to the stage; it's her first night here at Club Brickle!"

Did he have to announce that I was new? *Great,* I thought. *Now I'll be seen as helpless prey.* Nicolette was one of Sara's early names, and we decided it would bring me luck since she had made money using that name. I walked out, shaky and sweating profusely. Fortunately, the stage was less than ten feet from the dressing room door. I immediately grabbed the pole to maintain balance and proceeded to awkwardly clunk around it in Sara's shoes.

That night I learned an elementary yet invaluable lesson: always have the right shoes for the occasion, whatever the occasion might be. These shoes were shiny green pleather. I have never seen any other dancer wear green shoes, ever. The heels were thick, black rubber and less than five inches; a joke for any experienced exotic dancer. But the biggest problem is they were a couple of sizes too large. No one should ever dance onstage in shoes that don't fit. Lo and behold, yet again, my impatience put me in an awkward predicament.

Like the little engine that could, my stage performance went on, oversized shoes and all. I kept my eyes on Sara to see if she had any direction to give me. After one song, she instructed me to get down on the floor. She knew that was easy for me since, growing up, the main style of dance in my life was "ghetto booty dancing." While on that stage, I truly felt that everyone in the club had their eyes on me, and I was not ready for it. Fortunately, only two people were sitting at the stage: Sara and an overweight trucker in khakis, a John Deere jacket, and a baseball cap. He was one of the regulars, which was pretty much the look of most of the clientele at Club Brickle.

I took Sara's instruction. "Get down on your knees. Show us your booty!"

As soon as I could, I was on the floor, doing anything that would get me through the next three-minute song without having to stand again. I did splits and waved my ass around in every possible direction. It was not a piece of cake as I thought it would be. It was a clumsy, uncomfortable first onstage experience. Skilled exotic dancer moves take practice. A decade of ghetto booty poppin' wasn't going to get me through the next (what turned out to be) eleven years of stage performances.

Interestingly enough, I have always loved the stage. I had performed as a tap, jazz, and ballet dancer and walked in beauty pageants as a child. Somehow, I'd always been interested in erotic performance. The idea of women seductively performing nude had intrigued me from a very young age. Perhaps it was that VHS of my mother's I found of a Madonna concert where she dry humped one of her dancers on a bed—on stage. My mother and her cousins idolized Madonna, and I did as well after watching that erotic stage performance over and over and over. I dreamed of performing on stage with thousands of screaming fans as I unleashed my sexual prowess. The thought of it was empowering.

I was only in fifth grade when my friends and I tried to recreate what we imagined was happening inside the gentlemen's clubs. My two girlfriends at the time, Keira and Jamie, were wild. Keira lived on the other side of Allied Drive. I would bike to her house because it was safer to move as fast as possible across that street. We always pushed the limits of what was socially acceptable when we were together. We would shoplift, kiss boys, sing at the top of our lungs in public, and ride the bus as far out of the city as we could. One day, Keira and Jamie came to the duplex (where my entire immediate family was living) to have a sleepover. It was an odd day; no one was home but my grandmother. We took advantage of being unsupervised while Grandma was out for a walk and created a strip club in my room. My queen-sized bed became a stage. A flashlight became our strobe light, and we waved it frantically over the performer as they stripped down and did booty shakes on the stage. I went first since the whole thing was my idea. I got up on the bed, ripped my shirt off, and spun it around my head like a lasso as they screamed for me and pretended to be men catcalling. We were all laughing so hard that we could barely stand up straight.

Keira went next. She was the most developed: huge breasts, tall and voluptuous. I felt intimidated as she slid her sweatpants down. Being a small, petite girl always made me feel younger than the other girls who had a couple of inches on me. And it wasn't only height but all of their feminine curves. As an adult, this inadequacy lingered, especially when I began working in the clubs. My descriptors were "cute" and "small," a box from which I yearned to break free.

Jamie went last. She was the shyest out of the three of us, and she could barely get her first layer of clothing off without falling over laughing. Out of the three of us, she had the most "perfect" Barbie-like proportions yet was the most modest. I remember feeling attracted to Jamie and wondering if that meant I was a lesbian. Until I finished my high school education, I was constantly made fun of for having small breasts. When I saw Jamie's perfectly round B cups, I didn't know if I was aroused or envious. It may have been both, now that I look back. At only twelve years old, I had somehow decided that I knew what perfect breasts were. They were impeccably round with small areolas and perky nipples. We closed our club after Jamie and I did a duo performance, which was us attempting to sensually dance in unison and cracking up while I fantasized about caressing her breasts.

Amid the chaos of my childhood, these memories connect me to the beauty that existed in my life then. I could appreciate and love the feminine form. For most of my youth, I loved my body. My mother never made nudity something to be ashamed of or hide. She walked around the house naked and had a way of holding herself that taught me, from a very young age, that nudity is a natural state. This concept never left me. Often I'd be the girl at our high school parties running around with my shirt off or flashing my friends. Something was liberating about claiming my comfort in being seen without clothes on. There aren't many places in American society where this is acceptable.

Long before Vegas, my first real introduction to the industry was Visions, the only strip club in Madison at the time. I had a fake ID and went with a group of friends who were a few years older. My friends were familiar with the venue and even knew one of the dancers. Within an hour, I found myself bored watching. I wanted to get on the stage. I often get uncomfortable watching performances because they move me, not just emotionally. The emotion doesn't just run through me; it lifts me out of my seat. The many years of my childhood spent performing as a ballerina had trained me to be very comfortable as a performer.

After years of exotic dancing, I discovered that many of these women were once young ballerinas. Many of us had been on a stage as children or in our youth. Most of the dancers at Visions didn't seem like poised adult ballerinas; they seemed malnourished and strung out. A few of them did complex pole tricks, the only moment of excitement I had that night. I left wondering if the glorified clubs featured in rap music videos even existed. If they did, I needed to make my way inside one as soon as possible. Visions was a tease. I wanted to witness women who had devoted their lives to physical fitness and mastery of their art form. I wanted high stages and flashing lights. I wanted my mind to be blown. Part of the allure of dancing in a gentlemen's club was the opportunity to be the one to give that mind-blowing performance. The stage at Club Brickle was utterly disappointing. I was ready to bare all and bask in a standing ovation at the end.

When I stepped onto (more like into) that tiny black hole at Brickle, I felt like I was crawling into a closet. There was no chance of my fantasy coming to life there; no wowing an entire club with my moves and seduction skills. No dropped jaws. No standing ovation. It was by far the most uncomfortable stage I've ever been on, or rather in. It's inside a high bar where crowds of eight to ten people are seated. The setup was such that when a dancer got down on the floor, everyone sitting around the stage would have to look down over the bar at her. It felt demeaning. Every other club I've ever been to has a stage above the crowd; spectators have to look up at the dancer. It would have been nice if it were at the same level, but having them look down at me just felt off. Dancing at Brickle never made me feel like a performer. Despite my detest for that pathetic stage, many dancers made it work for them.

One dancer frequently got the crowd cheering (when there was one). She was a voluptuous woman who appeared to be ten years older than me. She unquestionably had much more experience in the adult industry. She wore cutoff shorts, a button-up shirt that she would tie under her huge breasts, and a cowboy hat. She'd always perform to country music and slap her ass so hard that she lived with a permanent callus. The crowd loved her. She was always smiling and was an extremely loud talker. I found her incredibly bizarre and obnoxious, but I'm sure I could have learned a thing or two from her. Her attitude was contagious. Every time she displayed her hand-stamped buttcheeks to the world, smiling ear to ear, she created raving fans. She never had any difficulty getting someone back to the VIP. She commanded respect.

After my first pathetic stage performance, I spent the rest of the night following Sara around. She did a great job introducing me. However, it was clear that most of the skills would only come from experience. An exotic dancer must learn the art of seduction and develop her multitasking skills. She has to notice who is sitting around the stage, see what customers are wearing, what they are drinking, and evaluate who is ready to hand over cash, who has just entered the club, all while maintaining a seductive presence. Not to mention the attention to her attire: adjusting it skillfully so that she appears to be all put together in an instant and then strategically removing it. She can never reveal the increasing discomfort of a G-string much too snug on the left labia (speaking from experience) or the pain in her feet or back from her heels as she spins, splits, and arches through her performance on stage. There are so many details to pay attention to. Learning the art is priceless.

I walked out that first night with less than $200. I could have made that in a more comfortable situation without being exposed to secondhand smoke and spending the following day delusional and fatigued. However, the freedom to choose the hours and the days and the simplicity of no applications to fill out or timecards to punch kept me intrigued. Not to mention being fulfilled in my desire to perform. With the travel bug pushing me to make money, there was no way I could give up this opportunity. I was hooked, back to living by the night.

4
CLUB BRICKLE

Scarcity mentality is where my parents lived. Hitting $500 in one night took about a week. I had never made that much money in one day. My family operated near poverty, and I had to find my own path to financial literacy. Before dancing, I didn't know I could make that much money without a college degree or some certificate proving I was "worthy." I realized that money and time are much less connected than I had previously thought. It was a significant paradigm shift for me. Why does someone else have the power to stamp a dollar amount on an hour of my time?

I began breaking the chains of my family history. My entire family and peer group had always struggled financially. I was familiar with the saying, "you are who you hang out with," but I hadn't realized that I could also apply this to finances. Time does not equal a certain amount of money; skill equals a certain amount of money. Better yet, strategy equals a certain amount of money. The dancers who had refined their approach made the most money in the shortest time. I learned through experience to "work smarter, not harder." A glimpse was enough to keep me enthralled with this world.

I liked the idea of no longer saying "I'm broke" or "I don't have money for that right now." I had heard these statements for two decades, and I was ready to break free. I knew there had to be a way to do everything my way. I knew that I could make the rules of my reality. Of course, I didn't quite know how to do so at that point, but I loved all the new possibilities. The night I finally hit $500 felt like a completely new chapter. Little did I know, there was so much more to learn about the unsustainable nature of this work and trading time for money. The liberation started here, but I realized there would always be a ceiling unless I learned to make the money work for me and make it flood into my bank account while I slept.

My second night at Brickle was a solo mission. Sara was taking the night off. Walking into that club on my own was a significant leap for me. I felt incredibly naked those first few nights (yes, pun intended). It was like someone had ripped away my security blanket. Luckily, I made friends with a couple of girls who took kindly to a new girl who just didn't seem to have it figured out.

I continued to meet exotic dancers through the years who had their names tattooed on them. One of them, a petite blonde girl whose stage name was Violet, stepped up and took on the role of mentor. It always baffled me that she chose to use a stage name when she had her real name tattooed across the small of her back. I guess she could tell questioning customers it was her sister's name? Girlfriend's name? I always kept these thoughts to myself. Violet led me to the second stage after spending a few minutes at the bar with me, demanding I "make it clap." I failed miserably.

Brickle had two stages: the main and the smaller side stage. Near the entrance, customers would pass the small one to their left before reaching the main stage, and people could face one or the other, not both. Sometimes when it was slow, which was every weeknight, in all honesty, the second stage would be empty, and girls would use it to practice. If we decided to practice while other dancers performed on the main stage, we took a risk. Many girls would be furious if any customers walked in and the girls practicing stole their attention. I can't say I witnessed much camaraderie; quite the opposite. There was always a bit of an edge to the interactions between dancers. There was a lot of competition. Violet made sure we had our little mini-lessons when friendly dancers performed.

Compared to the many dancers I came into contact with within the following years, the girls at Brickle were mediocre in terms of physique. There may have been one or two exceptions, but they were not in great physical shape for the most part. They ate bar food while working, and most drank alcohol and smoked. Brickle dancers didn't look expensive or classy. Cut-off jean shorts and a wife-beater were everyday attire. Elegant outfits were not standard. In Vegas, the dancers wore diamonds and tight black mini-dresses to display their rock-hard abs and glutes; they were shooting for a level of "perfection." There was nothing upscale about Club Brickle. To me, it felt like a dive bar with a few fun girls who happened to like taking their clothes off. I never felt classy working there.

Although I never did anything illegal in that club, I was sure the general understanding was that anything goes. I was pretty oblivious for most of the time I worked there. Sara never let on if anything illegal was going on—I'm not even sure if she knew. Maybe it was a "don't ask, don't tell" situation between us. I figured there wasn't anything shady going on and didn't initiate or give in to anything myself.

I began with and have always maintained my morals around sexual favors. I may have been unclear about the boundaries of the other dancers, but I was clear about mine. I'm not sure how I decided to stick to this way of operating, but I know that one thing has remained true throughout my life—I cannot bring myself to be intimate with anyone I'm not attracted to energetically. No matter what amount of money someone hands me, I can't fake attraction. If I am intimate with you, I'm into you. Money cannot change this fact. Unfortunately, there have been moments where trauma comes into play in sexual dynamics and overrides personal morals. Somehow, I can step into my power—my badass alter ego, Vida—in the club. But outside of the club, I've found myself in a fawn trauma response where the physical interaction resulted from this particular coping mechanism numerous times. It's been a steep uphill journey to override this traumatic mental blueprint.

Upholding boundaries has forced me to climb a steep learning curve. Being "Vida" in the club allowed me to explore a part of myself that was, more often than not, unfuckwithable. The challenge was merging Vida and Lana. In the club, I developed the tactic of grabbing customers' wrists and pinning their hands to their sides when they got too touchy. Every so often, they would seem to think this was a game, and I'd give up and let them touch me. When the time was up, I was relieved to let the money (and the unwanted touching) go. I missed out on a lot of cash for the first year or two while learning by trial and error.

Every night was a lesson in human psychology. Was this man a "major pervert," or was he a well-behaved gentleman who just wanted some good conversation? How could I genuinely decipher this until we were utterly alone in a dark room? There were certain directions one could go based on the specific characteristics of each individual. Since I didn't yet have this knowledge, I stuck with what worked: seduction. Thank you, MTV, for the hundreds of music videos that taught me. I'm confident that the hours I spent watching MTV as a young girl had something to do with my overabundance of seduction techniques. Of course, I must honor that I have always been a sensual, embodied being.

I also watched other dancers closely. I would often tune out the customer before me, completely losing track of the conversation while watching another performer. I encountered this issue repeatedly. I would sit down with someone, facing the stage, ready to seduce and engage, and then one of the dancers whose stage performance I admired would be announced. While supposedly deep in conversation with the customer, I would stare at the dancer, studying her. I would watch how she moved her hands, her feet, every move she made with every part of her body, and the moments she would be still. I would watch how she glanced over her shoulder or locked her gaze on her prey. Sometimes it felt like watching an animal in the wild before an attack. Other times it seemed as if the performer was just performing for herself, deeply enjoying every moment in the spotlight. These were the experiences that resonated with me most.

When I finally began to feel comfortable on the stage (in the right shoes), it felt like worship. I was worshiping my own body. I felt like a true seductress. Later, this morphed into being a goddess, then a dominatrix, and beyond. I quickly learned that however sexy I felt would be precisely how I was perceived. They would respond to what I was feeling. An ounce of doubt or self-consciousness would lead to disinterest. Seduction requires conviction. The men who wanted the classy, confident, seductive girls were the ones who were confident themselves and felt they could play at her level. Often, the ones who gravitated toward the awkward girls felt unattractive and pushed the limits as if it was never enough, as if *they* were never enough. Not to say there weren't always exceptions—it was a profound way of learning and experiencing human psychology.

Of course, nearly all customers are clear on what's advertised and push for more. One of the many memorable experiences I learned from began on a typical, dull night. A dark-skinned man sat at the stage while I performed, watching intently. "Do you want to go to the champagne room with me?"

At this point, a half-hour was rare for me. I was both delighted and shocked. I didn't have to work for this one? I didn't even have to ask? "Of course," I said. "You want to go now?"

From the stage, we went straight into VIP. I wouldn't waste any time. Part of me feared he would change his mind. Later on, in my career, I would walk into the club not only repeating the mantra but owning it: "Every man in this room is praying that I offer them my valuable time." But at this point, I wasn't there yet. This man quickly let me know he didn't want a dance. He wanted something completely different. Do you know that minor whiplash you feel when you stick your head out of a car window at seventy miles per hour? When he told me to sit down and relax, I had that same physical reaction. He asked if he could rub my feet.

What is this? I thought. *My lucky night? A foot massage?* Massage (whether back or feet) was a kind of touching I rarely refused. I honestly didn't refuse much if they didn't go for my vagina or breasts. I am a self-proclaimed touch whore. It's not a sexual thing. I'm sensitive. Kinesthetic. Not to mention, conscious touch is something every human ought to learn. I'm happy to teach. It's my love language and always has been. I have considered walking around in public wearing a shirt that says, "please touch me." Being paid to be massaged was always welcomed if they did it well. The truth: I dropped the ball on this one. The red flags were bold and *very noticeable*. However, they weren't just red flags. This guy was holding up a billboard; I just didn't know how to read the language. I hadn't been in the game long enough to realize that this wasn't an innocent massage.

It certainly seemed like one, though. It was like a boring first date. The man seemed to be running an old script. He caressed the soles of my feet while I endured the small talk. Eventually, he got around to telling me he was a photographer. He said he was interested in shooting me in a couple of yoga poses like what I'd done earlier in my stage performance. I took his card and sent him a text message after leaving work. I was clueless.

I looked him up on Facebook the next day and found that he knew a couple of my friends. I decided it was safe to meet up with him. When I went to his home, we did shoot. I hadn't done much modeling then, so everything seemed pretty normal to my naive twenty-two-year-old self. As the night went on, however, things got a little weird. He asked me to get into positions where I'd have to get between his legs on the ottoman of the chair he sat on. Afterward, he set the camera down and pulled me onto his lap. He stroked my hair and gave me that look, like he was coming in for a kiss. Boundaries weren't yet something I understood, and "no" wasn't in my vocabulary. We cuddled and kissed, and instead of telling him I wasn't into him, I said I was tired, so he led me to a futon, where I passed out. Perhaps I was roofied, or maybe I was just extremely exhausted. Today, it's a blur. I woke up to this man using the soles of my feet to stroke his cock. Did he not realize I was sleeping? My vibe indeed wasn't hinting at even the slightest bit of arousal. The fetish play turned into sex, and I never said yes. I also didn't say no. I didn't say anything. He never asked. I never initiated, but I did kiss him back.

Fawn response.

Didn't he realize I wasn't into him? He didn't care. He was into me. He was a taker. He had no intention of giving. Many of the sexual experiences of my teens and twenties went this way. They just happened. There was no consideration. No checking in with myself. Did I want this? Did it feel right? Did it feel good? None of those questions were asked or answered by either of us. It just happened. Was this rape? How could I say at the time whether it was rape? After our very brief interaction, I fell back to sleep and awoke again feeling fatigued and delusional. The bitter taste I swallowed that night lingered while I ate my cold, flavorless oatmeal at the local diner sitting across from him the next morning.

"I'm hoping I can see you again," he said just before I pushed my bowl away, ready to leave.

"Sure." I couldn't believe I managed to speak anything other than the words of the loud voice in my head, screaming, *NO! NO! NO!* I just assumed I'd never talk to him again rather than confront him and make it clear that not only was I not happy with what had happened, but I had no interest in spending another second with him. I suck at these conversations where I tell someone something I figure they don't want to hear. I'll choose to run instead. I drove away from his house that day and never returned.

Part of me felt flattered that he was attracted to me and wanted to be intimate. *There are hundreds of models he can hook up with,* I thought. But when I look back, the bitter taste in my mouth tells me what's true: I lacked boundaries and he lacked integrity. Weeks, then months later, after the photos never came, I felt even more bitter toward him. This experience didn't immediately teach me to strengthen my boundaries. Many more years passed before clarity came. It's challenging for me to tune back into the emotions I felt then. I didn't fully understand what was happening or how it would play out. I was naive and trusting. I'm a good person, shouldn't I attract the same? I learned later in life that we tend to attract the situations and people we need to learn from, and our wounds are part of who we are.

This scenario played out yet again many years later with a man named Tom in Costa Rica. I thought we were on a short adventure for the day, but as the sun went down, I was lured back to his house by the dark-skinned Latina with big bedroom eyes and plump, heavily glossed lips. She had me in a trance. I felt like a teenage boy with an erection. She and her friend had dressed up in lingerie, and Tom had tied my torso up Shibari-style (decorative Japanese-style bondage with rope) while the MDMA had me melting on his bed. She crawled on top of me, kissing me with her full, soft lips and made her way between my legs. She was the first to give me oral.

"Oh, baby. She tastes good," she mumbled to Tom as she continued to kiss my pussy. I moaned louder.

He beelined to the adjacent edge of the bed and said, "Oh ya? Let me taste."

I was too high to move quickly. I stopped moaning as he aggressively shoved his tongue inside me and violently sucked. I was peaking on the MDMA, and it took all of my willpower to slide myself away from his mouth and announce I had to pee. I managed to stop him before he penetrated me with his cock. I could feel him moving in just before I slid away to the bathroom. She discreetly offered to pay me when he'd left the room, but I refused. I felt I was demeaning her by not taking the same offer she'd accepted. I walked away from that situation with a lot more clarity. My boundaries were weak. There was something I wanted, and he could feel it. Deep down, I wanted to be desired; I wanted nothing more. Was he only acting on his primal impulse, or was I entirely at fault for revealing my desires?

This question arose only a few months later, during a two-week birthday gathering in Tulum, Mexico. Because I was flirty, free-spirited, and labeled a *sex worker*, this was enough to confirm I was open for penetration. Right? Fuck *no*. But no one asked. As soon as the birthday boy and I were alone, he was drunk and pulled my panties off without any conversation. Fortunately, I had enough balls to refuse this time. In the end, I was labeled the bad guy for not having sex with him because I'd been so flirty and sensual. Am I at fault? What role did I play? Yes, I put myself in these situations where I am alone with men after ingesting various substances. Though, I felt safe with them at first. I figured they'd ask, or they'd initiate the conversation. Perhaps it's something I must explore deeper around that childhood wound of being unworthy, stemming from unstable parenting. In my dear friend Destin Gerek's book, *The Evolved Masculine: Be the Man the World Needs and the One She Craves,* he writes that people who have suffered sexual trauma or abuse often have trouble saying no in such circumstances. It hit home.

I never saw myself as someone with sexual trauma because I thought nothing of it when my fifteen-year-old cousin Johnny brought me into the bathroom as a four-year-old and told me to sit down on the toilet seat while he turned the lights off. We were in the living room watching television, and Johnny looked at me and said, "Hey! There are suckers in the bathroom on the back of the toilet. Do you want to come with me, and I'll give you one?"

With excitement and mild, innocent confusion, I jumped up and said, "Yes! Let's go!"

He took my hand and led me to the downstairs bathroom, instructing me to sit down on the lid of the toilet seat. "Now, just close your eyes and open your mouth," he said as he switched off the light. I did as he said and felt him enter my mouth. It was clear this wasn't a sucker, but it wasn't clear why he was putting his penis in my mouth. He pulled out and asked, "Wasn't that good?"

I gave him a weird look and ran out of the bathroom and up the stairs to find my dad sitting at the kitchen table with Johnny's dad, my Uncle Jim. "Johnny put his penis in my mouth!"

His face turned bright red, "*What?*" He stood so fast that the chair fell, crashing to the floor. I recall being confused. Why did Johnny lie about the sucker? Why did he put his penis in my mouth? Why was my dad so angry about the whole thing? Did I do something wrong? Should I not have told my dad about Johnny's penis? Even today, I don't quite see this as sexual abuse, but it's undoubtedly a trauma. My father was so angry that I froze and couldn't speak.

This freeze response happened again when my cousin Jesse and I were playing in the basement playroom of the home of another family who played a mother role in my early years—cousin Lynn. Jesse's family felt like my second family, and he felt like a brother. Lynn was more like an aunt to me. She and my mother were close and had grown up together in my wild, dysfunctional Sicilian side of the family. I had to have been about the same age as during the Johnny incident. We were hiding behind the kid-sized plastic kitchen set, sitting on the floor. Jesse had his pants down, and I tied a long latex "magic" balloon on his penis. You know the long ones clowns use to make those little balloon animals? I have no idea why I was doing this at the time or what I was thinking, nor do I remember how I'd instructed him to pull his pants down. He was younger than me, and I'm sure I was taking the lead, even though I was only two years his senior.

Lynn came down the stairs with her next-door neighbors and spotted us. "What are you two doing over there?" Her voice was playful, but I knew this wasn't something she'd approve of. "Lana! Oh no, Lana. Not again!"

I froze. *Again.* I still can't recall why she repeated it, and I have no idea what had happened the first time and why she was so upset. What was wrong with me tying this balloon on Jesse's penis? He didn't seem to mind, and I actually hadn't touched it; I was simply tying it up. I can remember a few of my thoughts. Even though I had so many questions and so much confusion, it was clear I had done something wrong. A very, very upset Lynn was shaming me.

Were these childhood experiences the root of my trauma associated with sex? Was I sexually abused by my cousin Johnny another time I can't remember? Someone else? Childhood memories are blurry for me, and there isn't much I can remember. Sometimes old photos will provide insight, but many details are missing, and it's much too challenging to make sense of it all. However, how things have played out in my adult life could indicate that sexual trauma occurred early. It's such a weird thing, trauma. Some people go through life seemingly unscathed, and then there are people like me who seem stuck on a merry-go-round with one leg hanging off. If the spinning ever comes to a halt, there's no doubt I'll be jumping off. I can see where I am, I just haven't found a clear exit strategy.

There was another situation where I met someone outside the club, and things went down quite differently. It was less of a trauma response scenario. One night, a Vietnamese man I met at Brickle, who never took me back for a lap dance or spent an insignificant amount of money, asked to take me out to dinner. Sara and many other girls talked about "sugar daddies" they'd met at the club who would pay them monthly or per meeting, which generally meant dinner. This man seemed to be the perfect candidate. Why? I had no idea. It was all still new. It might have helped to pick up a book and study a bit. I gauged him as totally harmless, gentle, and mild-mannered. I had no other gauge. I decided to meet him in a busy, highly visible area for lunch. We had sushi at my favorite place, on the east side of Madison.

As we walked out, he began questioning me. He asked where I was going and where I lived. When I told him I didn't live alone and it wasn't possible for him to ever come to my place, he started telling me when his wife would be out of town. He asked if I could come over to give him a massage. This time it was easier to say no. I was learning and putting myself in better positions. I let him know I wasn't a prostitute and had no interest in having sex with him. He explained that he truly only wanted a massage and I didn't have to worry. Evidently, he was lonely and did not have a good relationship with his wife. As bad as I felt for him, going to his home would never be an option. I told him to visit me at the club again and thanked him for lunch. For weeks, he asked if I'd come over whenever his wife was gone. I guess he finally gave up. I never saw him again. A part of me genuinely felt terrible for not showing up for him because I knew he just wanted presence and attention. Once again, I was seeing my father's wounds in this man.

These are the experiences that make me question myself. The harsher part of myself asks, am I truly that naive? A slow learner? Just plain dumb? This man wasn't a sugar daddy or even a candidate. I wasn't going to get any sort of financial support from him. Or did I just not know how to play my cards right? The more loving, rational part of me sees that I wasn't born a hustler. I was a pure midwestern girl who loved and trusted, giving everyone the benefit of the doubt. I saw a lonely man, felt his longing, and offered myself. Simple. Done. Now I look back and feel silly. I had no idea what I was doing. I missed a thousand opportunities to make money. Was I taking the long route?

Of course, these situations could have been much more dangerous, but the reality is that going to work every night at a club can be just as risky. The horror stories are real. I found myself in much more dangerous situations years later. However, my "street smart" persona came to life somewhere along the way, and I stopped questioning whether or not I was dumb or naive. I was just inexperienced. It is very uncommon to have a "sugar daddy" that never asks for anything sexual. Their support comes with a hook. The female's sexual allure is the bait.

Sara would date guys she met at the club. I certainly wasn't looking for that. I did not meet a single man at Brickle, even slightly intriguing. Exotic men were scarce in the outskirts of Madison. Being paid to give a lonely man my undivided attention and letting him experience my sensuality was my only offer.

As I mentioned, however, I wasn't born a hustler. Sales weren't my forte. I spent a lot of time chatting with customers without asking for compensation. Connecting with people came naturally to me. I could talk to someone for hours, easily keeping them engaged, building rapport without effort. It usually didn't require any flirting or anything sexual. I had sincere curiosity. What do most men love? They love talking about themselves, especially with a woman they find beautiful and fully attentive to their every word. Creating that situation was easy. Still, I didn't realize this was what I was selling.

At first, I thought they could only buy a short, seductive dance. Because I thought of this when I had a lucky night and ended up in the VIP room, the customer would leave after one session. I bored them with the same moves and no sign of sexual favor. I didn't speak much because I feared my words would feel like a distraction. In my mind, there was only my body. I had no clue that 80% of the entertainment could come from conversation. Could I be paid to talk? Oh yes, I could.

Exotic dancers are frequently unlicensed therapists. Some girls are so insanely attractive that their physical appearance alone is enough. They can pull guys into the back all night. Therapy is the superpower for girls like me, who are not runway models with piercing blue eyes and perfectly round breasts. Many men would ultimately open up to me. They might have felt attracted to the external at first, and then I'd keep them for hours diving deep into the dark corners of their mind they'd never explored. Especially not with someone who was a stranger only hours prior. There's also something about being anonymous. I met hundreds of big-name celebrities in Vegas, though I had no idea until the end of our time together. What an opportunity! To meet people without the facade. We're all just humans in the club.

In the beginning, I sometimes felt guilty about taking money from these men, especially in their annihilated stupor. As time went on, I realized they were there for a reason. Whether completely intoxicated or not, they had somehow made it to the club. Which meant there was something for them there; I trusted how things would show up and play out. Why else would it happen that way? Maybe the lesson is waking up to an empty wallet or an empty bank account. Perhaps they yearned for connection. Maybe the reason was something in between or perhaps unrelated. If I was going to send them home with an empty wallet, the least

I could do was offer something they'd look back on fondly. Ultimately, every situation we find ourselves in can be an opportunity for growth. We found ourselves together, and it was irrelevant where—gentlemen's club or the desert of Timbuktu. We could create any dynamic at that moment. At least that's the philosophy that emerged years later.

Brickle was never a massive success for me. The most I made in a night was probably around $600. That was a good night for most of the girls there. The drinks were cheap, the lap dances were cheap, and the champagne room was cheap. It wasn't a classy club. The clientele were generally truckers passing through. On a slow night, dancers would spend hours playing one of the three slot machines in the club. Every so often, one of the girls would make more money from the machine than she would from working. It was such a depressing scene for me. Many dancers had kids and had to leave them at home, sneaking out when they were asleep. I never felt good about it when my mom would walk out late at night and be out until the morning.

A few girls had extreme physical ailments or medical conditions, and some were in abusive relationships. Many of them were in relationships with men who they supported financially. A girl I rarely spoke to handed me a wind-up disposable camera one night and asked if I would go in the champagne room with her. She wanted photos to send to her boyfriend, who was in jail. He was the father of her child. That kind of thing was so familiar. Many of the girls worked at Brickle for years or even a decade. It was simply their life. They would come to the club, drink, smoke, shoot the shit with customers, make money, go home, and come back the next day to do it all again. Their lives were simple that way. It was not a place of dreams. I've always had so many aspirations, such big dreams. I felt empty when I put myself in their shoes—incomplete. My mom always said, "You are who you hang out with." Was I *hanging out* with these women? Really? I'm not judging, just recounting my thoughts at twenty-two years old. We all have unique paths. Who am I to say this wasn't right for them?

Not all of the girls appeared to be struggling. Some of them would only work on the weekends and be in school during the week. It's what I was doing, though I didn't need the money for tuition, just living expenses. I was fortunate enough to have school fully covered through financial aid, which was the only benefit of my financially unstable parents. I needed the money for living expenses and, more importantly, for travel. The quality of my food was also a high priority. My groceries were probably ten times more expensive than the rest of the dancers'. It never occurred to me to spend less money on food. If I didn't eat well, I felt I didn't have the fuel to do the job or succeed. I also had a million supplements to buy each month. Some girls had expensive drug addictions, and I had expensive grocery bills. If my dive bar gig could support that, I was happy.

Overall, the dive bar was a comfortable place to start. It didn't seem like too much drama arose between the girls or staff, and it was never closed down because of illegal activity while I was there. Dancing supported me in upholding the wild persona I identified with, the version of myself that had emerged at a young age and continued throughout my youth. In my social circle, I proudly wore the label of "stripper." It was one of many ways I could invite people to question reality. Question what they believed. Question authority. In what ways do you stereotype sex workers? How does she talk, walk, act, behave? It felt like an opportunity to challenge social and cultural norms in my twenties, even into my thirties. However, it was difficult to bring this persona out of the club.

I hadn't stepped into my power financially, and I settled for living in the mindset of "How can I save enough to travel?" instead of, "How can I afford the life I want." I was living with my father, and it certainly had its drawbacks. I'm a horrible liar, and I'm sure it was written all over my face that I was doing something he would disapprove of. I'd told him about a year before that the girlfriend I was spending a lot of time with was an exotic dancer. He's an intelligent man. He knew I didn't drink, but there I was, coming home in the wee hours of the morning on weekends, smelling like cigarette smoke, washing a bikini in the shower. There was more than enough evidence. We somehow completely avoided the discussion, but I'll never forget when he recited a peculiar joke. Something about, "You know ya done fucked up when your daughta's a stripper!" I was in denial. I decided he was referring to Sara. I wasn't ready to have the conversation. However, I felt the need to reveal my secret to everyone else.

I have the problem of maintaining transparency, even when the truth may not be appropriate to share. Sometimes I felt like I was lying to people if they didn't know everything about me once we'd become friends. What was most important to me was that I felt uplifted in sharing my truth—that it was a story of victory. Stripping was a liberation for me. When I was financially solid for the first time in my early adult years, I sought deeper meaning for my existence. Fortunately, I still have Uncle Jeff, my spiritual mentor, reminding me daily that raja yoga was the path that supported his balanced, stable, healthy life. It only seemed natural to heed the advice of a man who appeared to be in a successful marriage and in optimal health.

5
THE BOLIVIAN CATALYST

When I was twenty-two, Bikram yoga became my solace. I yearned to travel the world, but my strong desire for a college degree grounded me in Wisconsin. The other option was to travel within, to explore the unknown places within my psyche and physical being. Dancing and yoga simultaneously entered my life in full force. I am infinitely grateful to Darya for taking me to my first yoga class. That first formal yoga class brought me the familiar feeling of getting high in a much more sustainable way.

The instructor of that first class was a "seventy-years-young" woman. She was the sharpest, fittest woman of that age that I'd ever met in person. I was intrigued, inspired, and enthralled. I paid close attention to every word she spoke. As I watched her gracefully float into a headstand at the end of class, I made a decision: I would practice yoga for the rest of my life. For the last fifteen minutes of practice, she led us into a "restorative posture," where we used yoga props: bolsters, blocks, and blankets. I fell into deep meditation during *savasana,* the pose designed for integration and relaxation, always done after a proper yoga practice. The music was soft and soothing, and candles lined the perimeter of the room, creating warm, dreamy lighting. For the first time in my early adult life, I felt that deep sense of peace and connection to myself. It lingered for days. After yoga, we had dinner, which was rare for Darya and me. It was a whole new experience: skipping a night of partying, not skipping meals, actually sleeping. I felt myself tasting and experiencing my food like never before!

This profound experience never left me. I only dabbled for the next few years, returning to it with more dedication soon after becoming a dancer. My life indeed became about yoga after reckless sex led to an unwanted surprise. The positive pregnancy test crumbled my world. I was navigating a breakup with my high school sweetheart, which became further complicated when I entered a "rebound relationship" with a guy named Lance. I couldn't be sure whether the father was Lance or Lee. It was a traumatic time. I thought I could avoid a surgical abortion by returning to copious amounts of narcotics and pharmaceuticals. My foolish plan was unsuccessful and gave me additional reasons to take better care of my body. In addition to the damage from the surgical abortion done at a low-cost clinic in central Chicago, I now had to heal from the drug binge. I distanced myself from both the high school sweetheart and the new lover. I wanted nothing to do with either of them. I was projecting my frustration onto them. I was upset with myself for the pregnancy, and I saw Lee and Lance as the evil villains who had impregnated me.

My dear friends, Kendra and Jin, took me to the clinic and cared for me after. Getting high allowed me to numb the pain. Once again, my ability to block emotions served me well, or so I thought. Before the abortion, I didn't consider having the baby—not even for an instant. As for the damage to my body, at that time, I just saw it as an opportunity to learn more about what supplements to take to heal. My friend Brad, who worked in the co-op deli with me, suggested that I begin taking a supplement called E3Live. "You'll heal ten times faster if you double up on this every day and alkalize your body." One of the reasons I loved being in Chicago was the abundance of high-end purist supplement shops, cafés, and restaurants. After that abortion, I spent more money on supplements and products for self-care than ever before. It was as if I'd forced an immersive education in self-care. I could only see this as positive.

Once I was well enough, I moved out of my apartment. It was time to close the chapter of roommate life in downtown Madison, and I moved in with my mother again. While living with her, I found Bikram yoga at the Inner Fire Yoga studio on the west side of Madison. Dancing had given me the means to fund my overzealous ways, so I dove in head-first. I practiced religiously for months. I'd arrive fifteen minutes before class to fully decompress from my full day of courses at the technical college and stay for as many evening classes as I could. I'd take three classes in a row if I had the option. Most evenings, I'd arrive just in time for the last two classes of the day, Bikram followed by Yin yoga. Often when I scanned my key card to check in for the next class, the person behind the desk would be concerned. "Lana, is this your second Bikram class? You know it might be good to slow down . . ." My enthusiastic response let them know it was hopeless, and they'd reframe their suggestions: "At least have an apple before you go back in!" I felt good, and that was all that mattered. Finally, I could connect to that effortless sense of dedication! It nurtured my body on every level, healing the abuse of so many years of drugs and partying.

I had craved that deep sense of peace that I experienced after that first practice with the seventy-year-old instructor, and there, at Inner Fire, I was experiencing it again. There were so many revelations and moments of clarity that came over me during my yoga practice. The instructors spoke of concepts with conviction that urged me to look at the world differently. By the end of almost every practice, I'd be in tears—silent tears I trusted would be mistaken for sweat as I beelined for the showers with my head down. These breakthrough moments were plentiful and profound. I questioned what I was looking for, the meaning of life, and the existential questions that inevitably come when stepping into a new reality. My yoga practice seemed to be the only thing that kept me sane as I kept dragging myself to Club Brickle each week.

After six months of dedication, I was confident that my calling was to become a yoga instructor and utilize my skills as a humanitarian in central Africa. Why Africa? Do you recall ever seeing malnourished African children starving to death on television in between an episode of *Full House* and *The Cosby Show*? I do. My memory was permanently etched with these visuals. So much emotion bubbled up inside me as these horrific images flashed before my teary eyes. How about your parents saying, "Finish your food; there are starving children in Africa!" Okay, so my parents didn't use this one much, but I was familiar with the line. I desired to offer my solace to these children. If yoga could do what it did for me, couldn't it help them?

I'd fallen in love with every teacher I practiced with, but two particular teachers made the most impact: Aubree Saia and Darlene Vander Hoop. It's no surprise that they, as people, were strong characters without the yoga instructor persona. Nonetheless, for me, they defined the life of a yoga instructor. My first class with Lisa O'Connor sparked my interest in Sanskrit and Kirtan music. I began attending weekly Kirtan concerts with local musicians and found Buddhist centers to practice meditation and learn Eastern philosophy. My dream was to go to India, become one of the world's top yoga instructors, and travel the world, bringing yoga to struggling populations. I finished my studies at the local technical college, earned my associate's degree, and applied to the University of Wisconsin, Madison. My course seemed set after applying for the second time.

Once again, a boy derailed my plan as was becoming a theme. I learn the hard way often. I guess I wanted to make sure I would get the lesson without a doubt. I met my Bolivian catalyst after about a year at Brickle. I'm calling him a "catalyst" because everything in my life drastically changed after meeting him. Looking back at old journal entries, I realize we were only together for one month. How could so much have happened in such a short time? But I did everything fast then. Having just finished my associate's degree, I was in complete celebratory mode. I was on fire like never before. I had a disciplined, rigorous yoga practice; I was eating like a queen, meditating daily, and taking care of my body and mind; and I felt financially liberated after a year of stripping. Why would I move slowly? I wanted to escape Wisconsin. Pablo was my excuse, and I loved what he symbolized: A new beginning. And perhaps it was fate because this all became part of the crazy story of how I met the man I was with for eleven years. But first, Pablo.

I'd just graduated. It was April 2008. My yogini friend Erin Slivka accompanied me to the Capitol Square in Madison. The university hosted a party to celebrate an Indian holiday. I gleefully told Erin that I was planning on finding an Indian man to fall in love with at the party and live happily ever after in India. My plan went awry when I met a young man named Pablo with pouty lips and soft dark skin. It turns out he was the one Bolivian man at the bar, out of the hundred and fifty

Indians. Then it turned out he was leaving, heading to Newark, New Jersey, the following month, and then back to Bolivia. Putting my bachelor's degree and a trip to India on hold took little to no consideration as I was hooked. Everything about Pablo drove me crazy. His accent, every word he spoke in Spanish, the way he kissed me with such passion, and the way we made love. I couldn't let him go. I wonder now if the night that Yanya's older brother carried me to bed created a moment that felt so good, I've run my life attempting to recreate it with imposters. Any Latin man with similar features and stature can swoon me with little effort. Regardless of where it came from, I've had a "thing" for Latin men. One took my virginity (his father is Mexican), and many more stole my heart, including Pablo (and then the rebound after Burning Man 2019). Did he also carry the father wound I repeatedly interfaced with? I never found out about that one.

Right away, things got interesting. When we were leaving for New Jersey, Pablo picked me up an hour late, which I had expected, and I scrambled to fit my six bags into his car. He seemed off, but I thought little of it. I tried to pay the first toll, only to find that my wallet was not in my purse. I assumed my wallet was buried in the backseat somewhere. No big deal, I'd find it during our next stop. An hour or so later, we pulled into a rest stop so I could use the restroom and start my search; instead, we made love in the car. Afterward, we continued until I felt my new piercings itching, which led us to a local drugstore for supplies. After a frantic search in the parking lot, I discovered that the wallet was most definitely not in the car.

The adventure continued to get more and more interesting. The whole trip was to return his sister's car to Newark. The plan was to stay with her for a night before flying to Florida. When we arrived, I realized Pablo had somehow forgotten to tell his sister that I would be coming with him. The situation was extremely awkward. She lived in a tiny one-bedroom apartment with her husband and newborn, and Pablo and I slept on the couch.

My situation there quickly deteriorated. I was used to eating good, nutritious food whenever I wanted. Pablo did not eat much, an odd quirk that meant we often didn't eat together. With my wallet gone, I could only eat what his sister had, which, one starving moment, was only a piece of cheese—a miserable moment. And then it turned out we had to stay another night.

On that second night, the shit hit the fan. After waiting an hour, I became curious about Pablo's call and decided to eavesdrop. He was talking to a girl who wasn't happy. I made myself visible, and Pablo disconnected the call. He stuttered, trying to explain that she was his girlfriend before he had met me. However, they weren't together, and his label for her was simply "crazy." She was currently in Germany, her homeland, but the plan was to meet him in Bolivia as soon as he arrived home.

"Is her flight booked?" I asked. He nodded.

I wanted to crawl out of my skin. My face felt like fire. I needed to get as far away as I could. Pablo asked me to come inside, and I turned and walked out into the rain. I walked so far so fast, I wasn't sure I'd be able to find my way back. Hours later, I finally did. I found Pablo sitting in his car in the rain. When he saw me, he jumped out, frantic, demanding to know why I hadn't responded to his thirty text messages or picked up his twenty phone calls, claiming that in Bolivia, they would have called the police after that much time had passed, and he didn't know if I had been raped or murdered. Some sick part of me was glad to see him this way, delighted to see this display of caring. There was nothing to discuss. I told him I had to leave. Being in a part of the country that was foreign to me with someone I didn't trust felt awful. These memories, like many, are a bit of a blur. Overwhelmed with uncomfortable emotions, I made quick, rash decisions.

As it happened, I had a contact—sort of—in New York. A year and a half prior, I was studying abroad in Australia. I was reckless for the whole month. I drank myself into a stupor almost every night of the week. Wisconsinites in college are known for their ability to drink anyone under the table, and we were sure to make our mark in Aussie Land. After a crazy night of drinking, we met a tall bald man with a New York accent while roaming the streets, hungover. We'll call him Ted. He approached us and said, "You kids look like a good time; here's my card. I have a penthouse here in Sydney for the week. Call me." I thought nothing of it but put the card in my pocket. Before doing so, I took a good look at the card, and I guess the guy had a great marketing team because I never forgot the logo. Now here I was, right next door to the city. I figured, why not call him?

I looked up the name I remembered from the card and sent a text. I felt a little awkward. We never ended up visiting his penthouse during that time a year ago, and I hadn't reached out once before this moment of chaos. My text read, "I met you in Australia. You gave me your card. I was with a group of kids from the US. My head was shaved. Short girl."

He said, "Are you sure you have the right guy? Are you a stalker?" He thought I was nuts. Despite his suspicious response, I told him I was in a predicament and wondered if he could suggest a good place to stay in the city. He said he was curious, even though he thought I was a potential stalker. That was enough for me.

After deciding to head to the city, I looked in the pocket of a moleskin journal I had with me. To my surprise, I pulled out a $100 bill I kept as emergency money while traveling in France, and I had a way to flee. I got on Pablo's laptop and found a bus headed to New Jersey, then a hostel that would accept a credit card over the phone. I intended to stay in the hostel until Mom could send me my backup ID and credit cards she'd found at her home. I knew nothing about New Jersey or about where I was then. The flying by the seat of my pants continued.

Buses loop from New York to Atlantic City, all day, every day, for the casinos. Pablo took me to the bus stop at Port Authority in New York at ten that night. Things had settled down between us. We even planned to say goodbye in person at the airport when he left the country. However, I didn't want to tell him I'd found the hundred dollars. I couldn't find out how much the ticket was online, so I went in to pay while he waited outside. When I came out with the ticket, he asked how I'd bought it. In an instant, I came up with a story of how I'd flashed the guy at the ticket window in exchange for the ticket. My intention was revenge. Even though we weren't arguing anymore, I was still hurt. When I heard later on in life that hurt people hurt people, this all made much more sense. It bothered him, and I was glad. It was immature on my part, but of course, at that moment, everything was, so it fit. When I shut the car door, a warm rush flooded my body. I was ready for a new adventure.

New York and the train station felt big. I sat directly behind the driver, hoping I'd get extra support navigating. Everyone on board was either asleep or drifting silently in their separate worlds, except two middle-aged men snorting cocaine and taking shots of whiskey directly behind me. I can't remember how the conversation started, but we began communicating through the crack between the two seats. I was amazed that this was all taking place right behind the bus driver, but an escape from my current predicament had presented itself, and I was all in. Tim, the blond guy, moved up and sat next to me. He offered me a bump of cocaine, and I leaned in without hesitation. I hated alcohol, but I was open to taking a swig from their bottle at that moment. Two seconds after I inhaled the cocaine, my lips started moving without conscious awareness. I explained the whole story about Pablo in detail. I even included the backstory about Lee, plans to travel to India and teach yoga, and my current plans to reach Wildwood, New Jersey, to stay in a hostel.

They went on and on about how crazy I was, thinking it was okay to travel around South Jersey by myself late at night, a petite young girl with an unimaginable amount of luggage. They told me Wildwood was unsafe. The solution they offered was for me to go home with them when they got off the bus in Atlantic City and stay in their house two blocks from the beach for a few days. They were renovating the house, and Doug said that if I helped out and grabbed a paintbrush for a few hours, I could stay. I didn't think twice. Something told me that these men were harmless.

We got off the bus at Bally's Casino, and I waltzed in like a scene from a gangster movie, accompanied by two Wall Street stockbrokers high on cocaine and numbed by whiskey, four bags hanging crisscrossed from my shoulders, pulling two suitcases. My eyes were wide, and my teeth clenched. As soon as I stepped inside the casino, I felt a high simply by being penetrated by the environment around me. I had never been inside a casino in my life. I was already entirely disoriented by the cocaine and alcohol, and the casino blew my mind. The sensory overload was something I had never experienced before. The dinging and chiming of all the machines and loud, obnoxious decor were almost intoxicating. Everyone's eyes were glued to their drug of choice, sitting on the edge of their seat, in it for the win. It was something I'd never seen. Just the size of the building had me in awe. I knew it wouldn't be my last affair with this oddly enticing scene. Little did I know that I'd be swimming in the thick of it just a few short months later.

In my small world, casinos were only in movies. Not a thread of my being had ever desired to gamble, which was quite astonishing considering my upbringing. I watched my grandparents drink themselves into a stupor while chain-smoking Marlboros and playing cribbage every week for the first seven years of my life. They would willingly share their secrets, but their game faces were intimidating. I felt much more comfortable with their lax attitudes during a fair game of war or crazy eights. Cribbage, surprisingly, never became second nature. I associated a deck of cards with the nausea of secondhand smoke and the putrid smell of booze, slurred words from the lips of my elders, and crude commentary from the peanut gallery. Casinos had never appealed to me, but in May 2008, a cat-like curiosity came to light, seeking to investigate the world of bright, flashing, blinking, buzzing, and dinging lights all night long. But that would have to wait just a little longer.

We took a taxi to Doug's home. When we walked in, the party began. The house felt like a bachelor pad, but all of the bachelors seemed older than they should have been. I ate my first piece of South Jersey pizza that night, and with this small dose of the East Coast, I instantly fell in love. Tim and Doug had told me that they were both stockbrokers on Wall Street on the bus ride. Tim also claimed to be the owner of the big nightclub. Did I believe it? Why not? I figured it was a fun story either way. I had never met anyone labeling themselves as such. I told them that I had been stripping for about a year, and Tim boasted that there were terrific dancers at his club in New York, and I could dance there anytime. We all fell asleep just as the sun came up. I was happy, sure I'd made the right decision in coming with them.

When I woke up that afternoon, everyone was ready to start working. I managed to paint for a couple of hours, then they thankfully let me off the hook for the rest of the day, and I got to spend a few hours calling my mom, Kendra, and a few other close friends to let them know where I had ended up. No one was too surprised, but a few were concerned. Pablo was completely shocked. He couldn't believe I'd decided to stay with some strangers I'd met on the bus. He was even more upset that they happened to be men. I gave my mom Doug's address to send me the credit cards. It was already late in the day by this point, and everyone was winding down.

After taking a shower, Tim slid into the bathroom. He knelt in front of me and slid my panties off. Then he slowly brought his mouth up between my legs. I'm not sure why I let him get so close, but I felt a burning sensation as soon as his tongue made contact with my clit, so I pushed him away. He pressed a fresh, red piece of cinnamon gum between his front teeth with his tongue. I'm sure the look on my face let him know I wasn't into it. I questioned, in my head, who told him this trick was a good idea or what sick female truly enjoyed it. I used my favorite excuse: I was on my period. Not a thread of my being was into Tim. I had no attraction to him. Pablo had my heart. My blinders were on (or so I thought). I wasn't honestly bothered or threatened by the situation, but it made it more urgent that I figure out where I was so I could continue on my way to Florida to meet Pablo.

A woman named Kim arrived just after this bathroom scene. I was so pleased to see another woman. Kim was fascinating. She spoke a bit of French with me and told me she had spent half of each year in Morocco for the past ten years. After listening to my whole story about how I had ended up there, she insisted I stay with her. She had an extra bedroom and no roommates. She cared for her mother-in-law and lived in the lower level of this large house that belonged to her late husband's mother. Her husband had just passed away. I left my luggage at Doug's and headed to Kim's with relief. Kim and I stayed up all night sharing stories about travels while sharing Moroccan olives and French cheese. We also dove into the subject of yoga, and she offered to leave her favorite yoga video, David Swenson's primary series, out for me to practice in the morning on my own. She invited me to visit her at her home in Morocco a few weeks later. Buzzing with excitement, I laid down, my mind racing with thoughts of what was unfolding. Kim said to let myself out to return to my belongings in the morning.

When I woke up, I attempted to follow David Swenson's primary series in the video but was uninspired to complete the practice. It was the longest I'd gone without my beloved Bikram practice. I headed out to find the beach that Doug and Tim had raved about to practice Bikram there. Kim's home was even closer to the beach than Doug's. I could see the shoreline from the sidewalk in front of Kim's house. It all felt like a dream. It had been way too long since I had seen the ocean. When I was younger, my mother had me travel to Hawaii and Florida, where I'd fallen in love with the sea. I don't know how she managed it, but we'd travel often. She'd make enough money for a flight and just make the rest work somehow. And thus, I'd always yearned for the warmth of white sand and sunny skies. I was elated when I found myself a block from the shoreline that day. I walked over to the beach in my maroon Victoria's Secret yoga pants that I lived in during that time, wild with anticipation.

Once I reached the beach, I was so happy that yoga didn't feel like a priority anymore. Taking it all in was a practice in and of itself. I just plopped down on the sand and watched the waves roll in. I didn't understand how I had ended up where I was, but I was thrilled to be there. After about an hour, I walked back toward Doug's place to get my bags. I was about a block away when I heard someone calling my name. "Lana! Hey, Lana!" I didn't pay attention the first time. I didn't know anyone who lived in the area, and I was pretty sure that Doug and Tim couldn't have known I was coming back from the beach. It also didn't sound like a familiar voice.

All these thoughts ran through my mind as the stranger called my name twice more. I finally looked back and saw a man on a bike. The bike was an old cruiser, pink and tacky. The man riding the bike looked like a typical buff surfer dude. He had long hair and was shirtless, tan, and toned, wearing sunglasses. He looked like he was in his mid-thirties. I later found out he was approaching his fifties. He rode up and said, "Jump on my handlebars." I looked at him like he was out of his mind. He had to be if he thought he wouldn't need to introduce himself before I just jumped on his handlebars. And what made him think I felt comfortable riding on handlebars? In response to the expression on my face, he continued, "I'm going to take you over to my house." He explained that Doug's wife was on her way home and had heard I was staying there. She was unhappy with the two "bachelors" having picked up a random girl from a New York bus station and feeding her cocaine and whiskey. The man on the bike introduced himself as Jim, "a good friend of Doug's." He said I could stay with him for a few days until my package came. I told him I needed my six bags from Doug's place, and he said, "I'll go get them for you. Shit's crazy over there." I was looking at him like he was crazy again. I asked if he thought he would pick up everything on his bike. I could hear his South Jersey accent now. "No, I've got wheels. Just get on my handlebars!"

I jumped on, and off we went. Jim dropped me off at another house only two blocks from the beach at his place. He told me to make myself at home. I immediately beelined for the kitchen, the best way for me to get to know anyone. I fell in love with Jim immediately. His kitchen was full of herbs, vitamins, and food that I loved. I thought to myself, "Clearly, this man is a hippie. This is my vibe." I saw instruments, guitars, and cat food dishes. When he returned with my bags, I exclaimed, "You have all the herbs I take!" He responded in that same matter-of-fact way. "Yeah, I know all about herbs." This East Coast fast-talking tickled me. I loved it.

Jim told me we would go out for dinner, so I needed to get ready. I took a shower, and when I got out, I started asking if he had anything for my new piercings since I saw that he had one nipple pierced. He said, "Of course." I had the hang of it by then and expected this response. He had told me earlier that he was a bodyworker. More dreams were coming true. When he offered me an adjustment after the shower, I didn't hesitate one bit. I came out in my towel, revealing my raw, red piercings, and sat on the edge of his bed.

I figured he would have a remedy for me. He walked around, grabbed a few things, and came back to me. He ordered me to lie down with my head at the foot of the bed. I tried to keep myself decent with the towel, but he grabbed it and tossed it to the side as if he had no concern. He doused my nipples with ointment and began spinning the barbells. I was screaming in pain within moments, ready to jump up and slap him. He told me to take a deep breath and relax because this was what I needed to do. As I got to know Jim, I learned that this was the way he always did bodywork. It certainly wasn't relaxing. Not quite the style of bodywork I had in mind. He called it "surgery without the knife." Even though it wasn't relaxing, it was healing. Jim was a true healer, and I felt it the first day we met.

By the time we finished my nipple torture session (which Jim had proclaimed healing), Ed, his son, had arrived, and Jim left the room to speak with him. Jim dove into a tense conversation with Ed just as they greeted each other. It was clear there was a situation at hand and that Ed was in the wrong. Ed had just been caught with prescription medication and was experiencing intense withdrawal symptoms. I knew this situation all too well. I'd watched my cousin go in and out of rehab, juvenile detention centers, and jail for years. A deep sense of empathy welled in me, almost bringing tears to my eyes. I had to meet Ed. Jim must have felt it because he opened the door and said, "Ed, meet Lana." Ed's bedroom door was open, and he was sitting less than ten feet away, at the foot of his bed with his head in his hands. I felt a magnetic pull the moment I saw him. At that time, I had no idea if it was attraction or empathy urging me to nurture him somehow. I wasn't entirely in tune with who I was or what I had to offer at twenty-two. I knew, deep down, that there was nothing I could do. My understanding of the recovery process was rudimentary. However, I thought I could comfort him in some way.

A few hours later, I decided I was genuinely attracted to him. Part of the attraction may have just been my longing for Pablo. Or to forget Pablo? Maybe it was the whole "bad boy" persona that hooked me. Years later, I've connected the attraction to that same father wound. I wanted to heal him. Of course, I could only choose what it was for myself and believe what felt right for me. I can't say for sure why the desire to connect with him was so strong. Perhaps it was that absence of threat. Somehow that feeling of safety he emitted was palpable. Whatever it was, I thought about him all night while Jim and I went out to have fun.

We left for dinner. Jim took me to Wonder Bar, which was on the bay. It only took one sip to have me feeling the buzz. Fortunately, this wasn't where we were eating dinner, so I had time to compose myself. After chatting at the bar for thirty minutes, we decided to have sushi. I was a sushi fiend, so our next adventure exhilarated me. Since this was one of Jim's spots, he insisted on ordering for me, a new experience as

I was considered the sushi-ordering pro in my friend circle. I was clear about not eating red meat or chicken. While I had broken free of my extremist vegan ways, I was confident I would never go back to eating red meat. I had never ordered red meat from a sushi menu, so I didn't realize that he had ordered beef tataki until it arrived at the table. As soon as it came, he grabbed one of the thin, blood-red slices from the plate and gobbled it up. He moaned, smacked his lips, and looked into my eyes. I knew what he was going to say. "You have got to try some." I was appalled and refused, but Jim had a way of speaking and doing things. It was a matter-of-fact, this-is-how-it's-going-to-be, my-way-or-the-highway kind of declaration. Also, the sake was on his side. I let him feed me a thin slice without much of a fight. I chewed with a disgruntled look on my face but was pleasantly surprised. I liked the flavor, even though the texture was that familiar flesh-feel I had divorced.

Jim was full of pride and satisfaction. "See, isn't it good?" He was the ultimate salesman, regardless of what he was selling. As we sat and playfully flirted and joked, Jim went through his contacts and called close friends. It seemed I had brought in fresh, new energy that may have been rare in his usual circles. To Jim, I was a "crazy gypsy from Wisconsin, super cool and smart." I suppose, for a small-town girl, I was worldly and had some understanding of cultural diversity. I was down-to-earth but able to hold myself as a sophisticated woman or quickly turn into a wild vagabond. I was right on the cusp of *becoming,* and he enjoyed every moment of my company. He called friends and said, "I'm out having sushi with this cute little gypsy from Wisconsin I just met. She's super cool; say hi."

The third or fourth call he made was to Josh. Before calling Josh, he pre-framed: "Josh is amazing. He had a kid in high school and took full responsibility by getting a full-time job, becoming a realtor, and buying his own home. He drives a Lexus and is intelligent and ambitious. He did well for himself."

Jim explained that it was all a miracle, considering Josh's upbringing. His father left him at a very young age and later committed suicide. His only brother had also recently killed himself. He didn't have a stable upbringing, but that never held him back from success. Jim dialed Josh and told him the story: "Josh. It's Jimmy. I'm here with Lana. She's from Wisconsin, and she's just passing through. She's a cool girl, and we're here at Miyako having some sushi and sake. You should come join us."

Jim handed me the phone and told me to say hi. I was pretty intoxicated at this point, and the voice on the other end couldn't quite grab my attention. It was challenging for me to hold up my end of our conversation at the table. I went along with Jim's game, said hi to Josh, and asked if he could meet us at Miyako.

Josh responded, "I wish I could come out and meet you guys, but I have my son tonight, and I just put him to bed."

I told him that was too bad because we were having a fabulous time, and it was too bad he couldn't join so maybe next time, then I handed the phone back to Jim.

He said, "You're missing out!" and disconnected the call. I was still thinking about Ed, even in my drunken state.

After our extravagant meal, we headed back to Jim's place, laughing and joking the whole drive. We ended up in his bed. It wasn't sexual, but it was awkward. I kept asking about Ed, and Jim kept telling me I could just go into his room if I wanted. My attraction to him was apparent. Eventually, I opened Ed's door and jumped on his bed. He was watching TV and was startled. He asked what I was doing in his bed. I told him I wanted to say hi and know how he was doing. Laying by Ed's side and wrapping myself around his trembling body, I started kissing him, eventually crawling on top of him.

Ed was slightly confused and much less interested than I'd expected him to be. I had never experienced intimacy with someone going through withdrawal, and I had no idea what to expect. I thought I could distract him in some way to ease his pain. I don't think I was much help. After we had fumbled through disconnected sex, he fell asleep. Before we passed out, he asked, "What's wrong with my dad? Why are you in *my* bed?" I told him I thought his dad was amazing, but I saw him as just that, a dad, and there was no physical attraction. I wanted him in my life as a friend or mentor. I didn't fully understand why I'd decided to make that move on Ed at the time, but it certainly shifted what was to come the following morning.

We awoke to Jim at the door, telling me it was time to go. "The dynamic here is just not going to fly." He was right. Not the right environment for me. He told me to get ready, and he would drop me off at one of the bus stations before work since he knew I was still planning to get to Florida to meet Pablo. Timing aligned, yet again. Ted from New York had been messaging randomly throughout my trip out here, and a text came in that he was set to arrive in Atlantic City in an hour. I sent him a message to let him know the location of the bus station where Jim would drop me. He responded right away and asked me to meet him at the Atlantic Palace.

Riding with Jim felt like we were in a video game, racing down the streets by casinos and dodging odd little blue buses. Jim came to a screeching halt at the entrance to the bus station, told me to call him later to let him know that I was okay, then kissed me on the cheek and said to get out because he was late for his appointment. I was glad he felt responsible after rescuing me from the bachelor pad.

I called a few friends and waited at the bus station for about an hour before another text came in from Ted. He was close. He'd brought a girlfriend named Shea for support in case I "tried to attack him." Now, I think that any sane individual would not have met with someone after pinning them as a potential *attacker* or *stalker*. I figured he was some superstar in my naive state of mind, and he had stalkers. It didn't cross my mind that he may have been living in some delusional state. Perhaps he needed to protect himself. I could have been a crazy fan, right?

Asking random people on the street, I managed to find him and Shea in the hotel lobby. He took one look at me and realized I had no intention of attacking him. We went up to his room. Shea's boyfriend lived in Atlantic City, and she got on the phone with him and became rather distant right after introducing herself. I didn't notice anything going on because I was in complete awe, staring out the window. Our room was on the twenty-fourth floor of the Atlantic Palace and overlooked the ocean. It had been raining earlier that day, and the sky was full of dramatic colors. As I stared, feeling those familiar waves of gratitude, Ted and I got acquainted in an incredibly unconventional way. He asked what I was doing and what my plan was. I told him the truth. I didn't have a plan, and I felt that I had been stuck in New Jersey by mistake. Just as Shea got off the phone, he asked what drugs I wanted for the evening. She was unimpressed. "You don't even know she's like that. Why wouldn't you ask her that first?"

I laughed at his response: "She's an exotic dancer; of course, she does drugs." I told him that, funny as it might sound, I'd never gotten high while at work, and I hadn't used in years. It was a phase during high school and was of little interest to me, despite the random coke binge with Doug and Tim. It was merely a means of connection, as in, "sure, I'll try your drugs. Want to be friends?" I told Ted that he could indulge all he wanted and I would pass. I was more into yoga classes and beach meditation. Ted taught hip-hop dance, and Shea was a good friend and fellow dancer. We could dance instead.

That was Ted's solution. "No drugs? We'll dance." He got the music started, and we began dancing around the room. With the music blasting, he told me his idea. "All right, you seem like a cool girl. Here's the plan. We're going to go out gambling tonight, and if we win money, you can keep it." He was offering to start me out with a couple of hundred dollars. I knew nothing about gambling and let him know that his idea was a complete joke, but he had faith in his teaching skills and assured me I'd do fine.

We left the hotel still dancing in high spirits, and they introduced me to the Atlantic City Boardwalk. I felt like I'd walked onto the set of a film. The scene was unlike anything I'd ever witnessed. There was an energy to the boardwalk that was new and exciting. The casinos were these forbidden adult amusement parks that felt mischievous in the most delightful way. My two new partners-in-crime started singing as soon as we hit the boardwalk, dancing in unison as we moved forward. Soon they called me to join in, and we began making a scene. We laughed, danced, and sang until we walked into The Pier. Shea's boyfriend was waiting for her inside, and they disappeared after a quick introduction. Once again, I was in awe. What was this place? It was so glittery and flashy. It was a shopping mall, but not like the mall you'd find in any random American city. The Pier was a high-end mall.

Ted and I walked around for a bit since he seemed to enjoy the flashy mall. We had sushi for dinner across from a restaurant with a massive golden Buddha statue visible from the entrance. I saw Buddakan after the sushi restaurant and made a mental note to return the following day and order the Edamame Ravioli.

I felt a rush of excitement as we headed toward the exit, and my eyes became fixated on the shoes. The shiny Steve Madden store drew me in. The black leather boots on display lured me in, and I tried them on somewhat reluctantly. I've never been one to spend an excessive amount of money on anything designer. I was more ready to book a trip to an exotic destination with my modest funds. I fall out of love so quickly with most of my clothing and possessions that I can't rationalize spending much on any particular item. However, I've always been mad about shoes. If my feet aren't comfortable, I'm not a happy girl.

Smirking, Ted said, "If you want the boots, baby, just ask!" I had no idea this was the type of relationship we had.

Was Ted buying me shoes from the high-end mall? Did I just find my sugar daddy? "Of course I want them!"

He motioned for someone to come over and box them up for me. He handed over his card to pay. I was in such disbelief that I didn't even think to say thank you. I slid my hand through the bag's handle and left standing a little taller. When we left the mall, I was so excited to wear my new boots that we had to return to the hotel room so I could change. I made it quick because Ted had tapped his watch repeatedly, letting me know it was time to gamble. It had been weeks since I'd been out of my yoga attire, and I felt like I'd put on a superhero outfit when we exited the hotel this time. I was flirtier and more playful in this new outfit, like I'd stepped into an alias. As we walked down the boardwalk, I felt like an infant with my eyes darting to every sparkling sequin glittering on the countless belly dancing costumes. When Ted noticed he'd lost me, he turned and said, "You want that too?"

I was honest and told him I loved the baby blue costume I was caressing. He pulled a hundred out of his pocket and handed it to the Indian man standing there, eager to sell. My amazement grew as he bagged up my new costume, and we continued on our way. Our first stop was the Taj Mahal. We went into an area that seemed detached from the main floor. Ted and I sat down at a table for a game that was foreign to me. To this day, I couldn't tell you what it was. I knew nothing about gambling, and I had no idea what was in store for us that night.

I watched the dealer put the cards out on the table. Before picking up the cards, we each had a shot of Patrón, the chosen poison of my early twenties. Ted quickly learned that *favorite* did not mean I could drink a lot of it. I was already intoxicated when Ted whispered a few options into my left ear and instructed me to put the first card down. I had no idea why I'd chosen what I did, but it was right. Onlookers cheered a little, and Ted gave me a high five. Another Patrón shot came. I downed it and chose another card, and I hit again. Still, no idea what I was doing or what was actually happening. It felt like hours had passed. Eventually, Ted said, "I think it's time to quit; what do you think? We're up $4,000." My jaw dropped. Did I win $4,000? I couldn't believe it. I told him it was good enough for me and that I needed fresh air. The feeling of being trapped in a giant pinball machine had come over me.

My intoxication was brutally apparent when I tripped and fell in my new Steve Madden boots on the wet boardwalk on the way back to the Atlantic Palace. I blamed my lack of coordination on the rain, then confessed that I couldn't handle more than one shot of Patrón. Ted was drunk as well. The path to the room is a blurry memory. Fear may have granted me instant sobriety because I remember everything after Ted asked me to give him a shower show. It all became clear. Ted had me trapped in a box he'd constructed in his mind, with a big fat label that read "exotic dancer!" To him, it meant a girl who would pleasure her client sexually in exchange for his money. Whether that was the general exotic dancer stereotype or he had mistaken me for an escort, I knew what he wanted. Fortunately, everything seemed to be in my favor, including the layout of the room. Right outside Madison in a small city called Juneau, one of the clubs I'd worked at had a similar setup for "shower shows." I told Ted that I could certainly give him a "shower show," but he wasn't allowed to enter the bathroom while I was performing, as it would interrupt my routine and ruin the show.

I was apprehensive. Fear welled up inside me, and I wondered if I was setting myself up to be raped or for a situation like I'd experienced with the foot fetish photographer in Madison. I stalled as much as possible as this is how we really draw out the duration of the time in VIP. I told him I wanted copious amounts of bubbles, and he called the front desk to have them send up as many shampoo bottles as possible. I asked when Shea would meet back up with us, and he exclaimed, "Oh, it's just you and me, baby; she's with her man tonight." I cringed. I'm sure he was so drunk he didn't even notice.

The bubbles arrived, and Ted filled the tub and dumped in four shampoo bottles. The bubbles overflowed in only minutes, and I chose my outfit for the performance: A white cotton thong and white tank top. I figured that, with white, I wouldn't have to remove them, which would somehow add an extra barrier for safety. Despite my apprehension, the plan seemed to work. Ted stood on the other side of the glass while I played in the bubbles, forming a mountain in the tub. I slowly submerged myself in the water and began dancing seductively, tugging at my wet panties and shirt while pressing myself against the glass barrier. He begged and pleaded for me to remove them, and I told him he'd have to tip. He continued begging, and that sense of power fired up inside me again. I was so naive in the world of erotica and oblivious to how I'd been dominating him. BDSM 101: Tease and Denial. All I knew was that it felt good to have him begging instead of touching. I finally gave in and slipped off the panties and pressed my backside up against the glass. He slipped off his bottoms as well.

When I spun around and noticed him shirtcocking, I was disgusted. He was touching himself, but not as if he was trying to get off. He was rubbing himself against the glass and moaning. It became comical after a few minutes. I'd never experienced a man becoming aroused in this way. I couldn't imagine he could achieve an orgasm by rubbing himself against the glass. He began begging for me to touch myself as well. At this point, I thought, what the hell, why not? I slid my hands slowly between my legs and found myself utterly numb. It would be purely a performance.

Just at that moment, Ted's phone rang. Saved by the bell. He had to leave immediately. A limo was coming to pick him up within the next thirty minutes to send him on his way to a meeting in Asia. He pulled his pants up, hugged me, and asked me how much money I wanted from the $4,000 I'd won. I'd never fully practiced the art of asking for what

I truly wanted, so I stuttered, battling a voice in my head saying it was dirty money. The voice won. I asked for six hundred. Ted immediately counted it out and set it next to the TV. He told me it should be enough, and he would also book the room for a second night as he passed by the front desk on his way out. I was delighted he had to leave. I didn't think to ask for anything else or make any plans. He told me he had a great time and was so glad he'd come down. He did a line of blow and rushed out the door. I was so happy he'd left but torn about being alone again. What the hell was going on? Where was I? The only thing I was sure about was that I was on a wild adventure, and I didn't want it to end. I also knew for sure that I didn't want to be alone. I didn't realize it at that time in my life, but I avoided pain. The pain of the abortion. The pain of my seven-year relationship with my high school sweetheart ending. Being alone meant I had time to think and feel. I wanted a distraction. I wanted to feel pleasure. To be soothed. Often, I'd take the distraction in any form.

6

CLOSURE WITH PABLO

The moment Ted left, I called Ed. I knew it was completely inappropriate, but he was close, and I didn't want to be alone. When Ed didn't pick up, I called Pablo. He asked where I was and what I was doing. I told him the whole story. Before I could even finish the story, he began shouting. He was drunk. "You whore! Why are you with all of these guys? What are you doing with them?" If only he knew. Did he honestly think I'd slept with all of them?

I didn't give him the details. He knew nothing about the bathroom scene with Tim or the shower show with Ted, and I didn't even mention Ed. I didn't think I'd be able to hide from Pablo my deep desire to reconnect with Ed. But why did it fucking matter? He had another lover in his life, so how could I feel shame for connecting with other men? It wasn't until I started writing this story that I realized his reprimand made no sense. I truly felt bad, but the feeling was shadowed by a sense of gratification, knowing he was jealous. Perhaps it was my way of testing. He still wanted me! Everything inside of me knew it was wrong. I was still upset with him, yet I craved him. I had a habit of turning my sorrow into anger. That moment of pain when Pablo told me he had another lover had dug deep into my heart.

Pablo was mid-sentence when I disconnected the call. I surrendered to being alone yet again and tucked myself in at 2 A.M. Unable to sleep, I sent him a message on Facebook. It was May 17, 2008, exactly one month after we'd first met. At 3:10 A.M. I hit send on a message:

> I think I'm realizing how much I really do love you right now. The really, really, hard way. I have only slept about one hour. I can't sleep. I woke up in tears and they won't stop. I don't want to make you feel bad but I can't make them stop, I just keep crying. I just want to be with you. Everything in my life seemed perfect when I could open my eyes and you were right next to me. To not have that, to not be able to wake up next to you is impacting me more than anything has since I realized it was really over with Lee.

This dramatic message went on for paragraphs as I professed my true, undying love for this young man who was a stranger only a month prior. I cried myself to sleep.

Drawing the curtains the following day to reveal—yet again—this reality that felt so surreal, I took in that breathtaking view of the Atlantic. The sun was shining, and all I could see was the vast ocean. My next move was to go on a calling frenzy: Ed, one more time. Then four of my close friends. I demanded that they book a flight or take a road trip over. This place was full of excitement, and nothing stopped me from staying longer. I had no one to answer to and no clock to punch. I truly had no obligations or responsibilities at this time in my life, and it was exhilarating. I knew I could strip anywhere in the world and all I had to do was choose a club and walk in. I could work as little or as much as I wanted, and if I needed more money, I'd work smarter. I had at least a week before Pablo would fly out of Miami. Somehow, I wasn't deterred and still wanted to see him off despite our harsh exchange the night before. I planned on booking a flight as soon as possible. Since I hadn't eaten my usual organic, locally-sourced vegan fare in days, I went on a mission, thinking I'd find it in such a happening city. I assumed the high-end mall would have some options and headed over in my brand-new boots, hoping I wouldn't stand out too much. I had no idea that it wasn't even possible to stand out. Atlantic City is a big mess of people from every socioeconomic class and culture. There were homeless people, crack dealers, and prostitutes on the same block as wealthy business owners and entrepreneurs visiting AC to gamble for the night.

Taking my time in the mall, I tried on the idea of "window shopping." I was so relieved to be free from the ordeal with Ted that everything seemed appealing. I laughed to myself. I'd made it out of all of this unscathed. I waltzed into Juicy Couture to try on a pair of jeans and left without purchasing them, still questioning the rationale. Did I need a pair of $300 jeans? I settled on a much more reasonable purchase: a newsboy-style hat from Bebe. Just as my blood sugar plummeted and I began to feel faint, I found a small market in the back of the mall. It was in the perfect location, near the windows facing the ocean. Organic specialty items and a salad bar—I finally found the gold. Feeling relieved that I'd found something familiar and nourishing, I sat down to enjoy a huge salad, staring out the window at the view. I was daydreaming about meeting Ed again, greeting him in my hotel room. We cuddled in the bed and fell asleep. My phone woke me from my daydream. It was an unknown number with a New Jersey area code. Could it be?! "Hello?" The voice on the other end was male, but I could barely make it out. My cell service was shit. I ran out of the mall.

Back on the boardwalk in front of the massive candy store, my phone got reception, and it rang again. I answered again with butterflies in my stomach. "Hey, Lana. It's Josh. Jim wanted me to give you a call and make sure you're doing all right." Dammit. It wasn't Ed. My high crashed into the boardwalk beneath me. However, I was thrilled by the thought of a new friend. The emotional rollercoaster continued. Josh asked where I was. I told him that I was at the designer mall.

He responded, "Oh! The Pier! I'm about ten minutes away. Do you want to meet somewhere? Maybe we can have lunch?"

I responded, "Oh! I just ate, actually," kicking myself as I said it.

"Okay, that's fine. Maybe we can just get a drink then." I was so nervous that I didn't realize until after disconnecting the call that I'd committed to a drink. I didn't even want a drink. I wanted a friend. He must have intuitively known and suggested tea. Why was I so nervous? Did I look okay? Did he know I had given Ted a shower show the night before? Did he know what happened with Ed? Did I even know what happened with Ed? It wasn't until years later that I understood I couldn't relieve his pain by taking it on myself. My empathic nature and lack of energetic boundaries allowed me to soak up his suffering like a sponge.

My attempt to absorb it showed up as an invitation to penetrate me physically.

After the surprise phone call from Josh, I waited while imagining what he might look like and his reaction to meeting me. What had Jim told him? Did he think I was nuts already? Jim certainly did. I was so unsure of myself. I had spent seven years in and out of one relationship and just finished another with an abortion. My experience with the opposite sex was chaotic. I didn't know how to behave. It didn't help that I had been drinking or getting high every night since I'd found myself in this new city. I was disconnected, ungrounded, and disassociated.

Josh appeared in front of me, sporting a white tee and gray running pants, with messy wind-blown hair. He was wearing Burberry sunglasses on his head and looked nothing like I had expected. I was awkward. I didn't know where I wanted to go or what I wanted to do. Josh suggested Buddakan. The magic began. We sat right next to the epic view of the Buddha. After only a moment of studying the menu, Josh knew what he wanted and announced it was the edamame ravioli.

I sipped the lychee martini I'd mindlessly ordered and squealed in excitement. "That's what I wanted to order yesterday!"

He said, "Perfect, we can share."

I have this unique relationship with drinks of any kind. Basically, I can never have too many; a martini, juice, and a cup of tea felt standard. My drink game is still going strong today (minus the booze). The table was tiny, and the alcohol made me clumsy. I knocked the fork off the table, followed by a spoon, and later by another spoon. He pretended not to notice, and I took his lead, hoping that I could hide my bright red face by staring at my plate.

We chatted about our life experiences and somehow dove into the topic of psychedelics, specifically LSD. Quite typical for me; for about ten years after my first acid trip, the topic would come up at some point and shift the direction of the conversation. I was fascinated by the places I'd explored. I was instantly intrigued by the experiences and could converse for hours if anyone could relate. Josh felt the same way. I remember asking him if he had random hallucinations every so often. He said yes. Time stopped as we gazed into each other's eyes and felt the chemistry spark at that table, recounting our LSD journeys. We were fully engaged, then Josh's Blackberry vibrated, shaking our tiny table. He apologized and answered the call. I guess I was startled because I dropped my fork again. This time, I decided not to drink any more of my martini.

It was a quick, formal conversation. It was clear he was missing an appointment. My heart sank, fearing that our time together was coming to a close. He explained that he was missing a Board of Education meeting. I found myself even more fascinated with this man before me. Board of Education? He explained how he had become a board member and was also on the Zoning and Planning Board for the city of Mays Landing. I'd never met anyone involved in politics in this way. I was so curious about him. I could have listened to him talk for hours.

We were interrupted again by his Blackberry ringtone. It was Molly, his son's mother. His frustration was more obvious this time. Her request was urgent; she needed his son's clothes for karate within the next two hours. He hung up quickly and announced he had to leave immediately. I was relieved when he invited me to come along. I was deeply enjoying this new connection. Josh was so different from anyone I'd ever met. I accepted his offer with one caveat—a quick stop at my room. We took his car over to my hotel a few blocks down. I heard Jim's words ringing in my head from our dinner at Miyako. Josh did indeed drive a shiny, gold Lexus.

All of my fork throwing must have rubbed off on Josh. When he backed out of the restaurant, he bumped into the car next to him. His face didn't turn red, but he was embarrassed. After ascertaining he hadn't done anything too significant, we fled the scene. When we reached the Atlantic Palace, I ran up to my room alone, changed out of my new boots, and slipped back into my usual—the maroon yoga pants, a tank top, and DC sneakers. My desire to look presentable had dissolved. I was comfortable with Josh. No need to put on a show—I could just be me. I honestly wasn't loving walking around in heels all day. It was a playful persona I was trying on.

I was relieved when we pulled into the parking spot in front of Josh's townhome. I was no longer alone in an unfamiliar city. I was with a friend in his home, deemed "the safe house." While transitioning, a handful of

Josh's friends cycled through the house. His home felt safe and inviting. He ran upstairs to get his son's clothing together, and I sat in the living room on a plush leather loveseat and waited.

Within minutes there was a knock on the door. Remembering my childhood, I visualized a young boy standing on the other side of the door, ready to grab his belongings. My mother always told me to "run in" when we stopped somewhere or "grab your stuff, quick!" I opened the door after about thirty seconds of knocking, figuring it was only appropriate since I was sitting less than ten feet away. A little boy with a red, furry stuffed animal wandered in, followed by a short, slightly overweight woman. Josh walked down the stairs as she entered, leaving him standing two feet before the front door. She greeted Josh with, "Who is this bitch?!" I was never one for confrontation and was relieved when Josh motioned for me to go into the kitchen where Tony was.

I could hear Molly and Josh bickering at the front door, but Tony started questioning me before I could tune in to what they were saying. "Are you my dad's friend? My name is Tony. This is my toy. My mom says he looks like a devil." He was comical, personable, and witty for a six-year-old. I wasn't surprised because he was Josh's son, after all.

Molly interrupted our conversation about the furry devil by shouting, "Tony! C'mon, let's go."

I said goodbye, and Tony went on his way with his little stuffed red devil. Josh apologized for her behavior, and I apologized for answering the door. He assured me it was okay and told me she wasn't used to seeing girls in the house. She'd only moved out a year ago. Ten minutes later, there was another knock on the door. I decided not to answer this time.

A man named Ruby let himself in and beelined for the computer desk in the kitchen. I wondered if he had some business to do, as he didn't even say hi first. The kitchen was like an office, so it wasn't entirely inappropriate. An island created a separation between the desk and stove. The large wooden "L" desk had two monitors and a laptop. Next to the desk was a table. Josh and I sat at the table, and Ruby sat at the desk in Josh's leather chair. He was downloading music. Ruby asked me where I was from, and when I told him, he joked, "Right, because they don't make girls like you in South Jersey." Ruby was likable. He was witty, always joking.

It didn't take long to get onto the topic of my new career as an exotic dancer. This time I was asking for advice. "Is there anywhere good to dance here?"

Josh and Ruby answered in unison: "Bare Exposure."

Josh joked and said, "Ruby *loves* Bare," which Ruby affirmed by confessing that he liked to go to Bare after gambling to spend his winnings. What a new concept, I thought. They explained that in Atlantic City, the dancers do well because the gamblers who win at the casinos spend their thousands at the club. I'm not sure how we moved from there onto the topic of medicinal mushrooms. Still, for some reason, Josh pulled up a video on one of his three visible computers about mycoremediation. I was proud of myself for keeping up with the video. I had just finished a phenomenal botany class at Madison Area Technical College, and the fungus material had my full attention. Josh was pleasantly surprised by how much I knew about the subject. Yet another spark ignited between us.

Besides having a seemingly innate desire for allure, my body was often in motion, stretching, searching for physical pleasure. As we conversed that evening, I found creative ways to use the countertops and furniture to assist my yoga postures and stretching. Blocking the kitchen entrance, I extended my arms and torso to the edge of the island, forming an L shape with my body. As a not-so-subtle gesture to get me out of his way, Josh lightly placed his fingertips on either side of my ribs, which was unexpected and made me jump slightly. Was he flirting? Yes, he was. I didn't have a strong physical attraction to Josh. My obsession was/is exotic men from abroad. My detest for America extended to my intimate relations. Josh was born and bred on the East Coast, which doesn't exactly make him exotic. However, he was worldly, and spiritually connected, and he roused me to the core of my being with his mind and unique ontology.

He asked me to sit with him in the living room on the leather loveseat where I had been sitting a few hours earlier before answering the door.

He slid in next to me, and I allowed myself to sink in close. He opened his left hand in front of us to reveal two capsules. I asked, "MDMA?"

He said, "I've been waiting almost a year to take these. I've had them in my freezer, and I've been waiting for the right person to come on the journey with me. You said you like ecstasy . . ."

I said, "Yes! Let's do it!" I explained that I'm particular about the way I take it. "We have to get organic orange juice, fruit, and a few other important items. Also, I want to do it in my hotel room." I don't know what it was, but I insisted on using that room. Perhaps it wasn't often that I had the opportunity to appreciate such a view. He agreed to do it my way but clarified he liked to sleep in his bed at home, so he couldn't promise we'd be there long. We said our goodbyes to Ruby and left him there, glued to the computer.

Our hunt for the essentials took us to multiple grocery and convenience stores in Atlantic City. I bought a Vicks inhaler, incense, and copious amounts of water. I knew that the little shop in The Pier would have what I wanted, but it was past 10 P.M., and they were closed. I was crushed. Josh had a lightbulb moment and said there might be something at Tropicana. He used to work there and was familiar with all of the shops. I went a little nuts at Zeytinia Gourmet Market. I bought fruit, drinks, nuts—anyone would have thought we might be in the hotel room for days. I knew it would be an undertaking to go out, and this one store—the only store in the entire city with what I wanted—might close soon (I was still totally naive to casino hours). I thought we had only one shot at getting everything.

Armed with our supplies, we finally made our way back to the hotel room. Because I started at fifteen, I thought that I was a total pro when it came to MDMA, and I declared that the best way to do it was to insert it rectally. However, these pills were not pressed, they were capsules, and I'd never tried "plugging" with a capsule. We opted to snort half and swallow half because my "plugging" theory seemed out of the question. Before ingesting MDMA, I would always explain to everyone joining me that we'd lose 40% of the substance in the digestive tract. We had to either take more or find another way to get it in. Josh had never snorted anything. Part of me was honored to be making history with him, regardless of the story. At twenty-two, I had an interesting perspective of what it meant to create a memorable moment. There had to be a risk mixed with danger and rebellion. He wouldn't forget this night; I was sure of it. That was enough for me to celebrate. I aimed to create memorable moments with everyone I met. Getting high or anything that involved risk was a commonly chosen route for me since it was relatively surefire. We peeled the big juicy orange we'd bought at the market and poured some of the MDMA on a slice. It wasn't a brilliant idea. I'm not sure what the logic was because it still tasted like a bitter, vomit-inducing substance. Oddly enough, a part of me later grew to enjoy the repulsive flavor of MDMA. I associated it with euphoria.

It hit quick. Thievery Corporation's album, *The Cosmic Game,* became the soundtrack for the entire experience. Josh picked up the book I'd been lugging around, *Man's Eternal Quest* by Paramahansa Yogananda. I wandered into the bathroom where I had apprehensively performed the shower show the night before. I filled the bathtub with bubbles again and slid into the hot water. After what seemed to be about twenty minutes, though it was probably much shorter, Josh ran into the bathroom and professed to me, "I love you," as he walked in.

In my euphoric state, I announced, "I love you too! Get in the bathtub!" He stripped off his clothes and cautiously climbed in. The water was hot. It was a huge tub; we could fit comfortably, sitting facing each other.

We dove into a deep conversation about metaphysics and the meaning of life, future aspirations, and our wildest dreams. We covered how the president, George Bush, simply needed a warm embrace. We co-created a vision of directing the American people to the website we created in our minds, "Hug Bush." The site would be famous, so everyone would want to be featured on the home page. If someone got a shot hugging Bush, we'd put that photo on the homepage as the winner of the Hug Bush contest. We talked about helping our friends and family in need and moving to the Ananda community together. We were not physically intimate, but it was the most intimate conversation I'd ever had. It felt as if the water had amplified the electrical current between us. We were vibrating in that tub, exploring realms of our consciousness together, speaking aloud the complex geometry of our minds for the first time. It was one of the most profound, intense experiences of my life.

Josh and I spent the entire peak of our MDMA experience in the warm bubble bath. When we finally noticed the water was freezing, after we'd both cried and confessed all of our sins, we managed to escape from our portal. I wanted comfort, so I crawled into bed in my towel, straight from the tub. Josh didn't follow this time. I didn't want sexual interaction, but I did want a physical connection. He must have picked up on it as I lay on the bed with my chin lifted, yearning for an embrace. He gently kissed my lips, saying nothing. My way of conveying satisfaction was to roll into the comforter and curl up into a ball. He sat on the ledge next to the window. I later learned that Josh had a thing about wet skin and bedsheets.

As the sun rose, I fell into a dream state, not quite sleeping but not awake. Josh crawled into bed next to me and joined me in this waking dream for a few hours. I awoke to him sitting up and adjusting the comforter. He told me he was ready to be in his bed. He followed this statement with a question: "Wow, did I tell you that you could move in last night?" I could barely verbalize my thoughts but affirmed, "yes, you did," with a smile. I vaguely remember telling him I needed to pack, but I remember the daunting process. He tried his best to help, but I had wholly unpacked and arranged all my belongings around the room. I knew I was going painfully slowly, but eventually, I had everything jammed back into the six bags, and we were out the door.

The drive back to Josh's place felt like a waking dream. I was still high; I was happy, in a calm, Buddha-like way. We were moving in the afterglow, and it was peaceful and slow. He helped me carry my bags to the third floor when we arrived, telling me this would be my room. The agreements we had made in the bathtub still raced through my mind. He had simply asked that I support him in developing a more holistic approach to nourishing his body and keeping the house clean, and in exchange, I could live there for free for a month or two until I made my way to India. I spent the entire day unpacking and arranging yet again. I made myself at home without any effort. It was hard to believe things were working out this way. It felt so good to call someplace home, yet I was unclear how I had chosen this place. It was a quick decision, and I didn't think it through, which is probably why the dynamic shifted within days.

Hours later, after napping, I found Josh in the kitchen. He had prepared fish and brown rice. Dinner was quick, as he had to run out, but I was invited to join him. We were becoming glued. We went to a mall that was three minutes from his place. I set my focus on finding supplements. I hadn't been consuming the usual organic, whole-food goodness I was used to, and I felt depleted. I discovered the Vitamin Shoppe that was closing down. I was in supplement heaven. Everything was dirt cheap, and I went a little overboard. I left with a huge bag filled with more supplements and "healthy snacks" than I could have used in a year. Josh seemed pleased when I unloaded them back at the safe house on the kitchen counter. He was open to learning about health in any form. I popped open a few bottles and gave him a handful of capsules. He only asked what they were after swallowing them. This trust never faded.

A day later, we went through the entire kitchen. He asked me to take out everything that wasn't healthy. The fridge was pretty empty and the most accessible place to start. I poked around and put a few things on the counter, and I wasn't impressed by any of them. I ended up clearing pretty much everything out, down to the condiments and spices. After about an hour, the counters were full, and the cabinets, fridge, and freezer were empty. We agreed to put a few items in paper grocery bags to give to friends since they weren't horrible, but I certainly wouldn't eat them. We realized we were hungry, and it wasn't possible to make food at this point, so we headed out to dinner at Tomatoes Restaurant in Margate for sushi.

Josh and I took our first photo together at that table. Josh was wearing his geeky argyle zip-up sweater. I had the hat I'd bought at Bebe during that lonely day at The Pier. I had a martini in front of me, and my expression was fierce. Josh was sticking his tongue out to the side and wearing glasses. Josh sent Jim the photo. I still hadn't heard from Jim since he'd dropped me off at the bus station a few days prior.

When we woke up the following day, it was time to restock the kitchen. I searched online for a co-op or store with organic produce and spices, to no avail. There was absolutely nothing in the area. I knew Whole Foods Market was our best bet. At that time, it was one of my favorite grocery stores when I was away from my beloved Willy Street Co-op in Madison. We drove an hour to get there. It was Josh's first visit to Whole Foods. How odd, I thought. I'd never been so far from a Whole Foods Market in the US! South Jersey is a bizarre area for many reasons, notably the lack of healthy food options besides Pamela's Health & Harmony in Margate. Thank God for Pamela's. In 2008, it was a feat to get quality food. We bought the basics and checked out with an $800 balance. No surprise. We were replenishing an empty kitchen. My priority was replacing spices; the requirement was high quality, organic, and non-irradiated. The condiments would spoil in a year or less instead of five or ten. The staples also needed to be organic and ethically sourced. We threw in a few Himalayan salt rock lamps to create more positive vibes in the house. I was elated. I'd never had so much fun grocery shopping in my life. We shared a deep culinary love.

Something felt different as I got ready for bed that night. I crawled into my bed on the third floor and felt lonely. I walked downstairs to Josh's room, finding him sitting up in bed, reading. I asked, "Can I sleep in your bed tonight?" He didn't hesitate to make space for me. I crawled in, and we cuddled. It is a blur, but it was undoubtedly a moment of comfort. I didn't sleep in my bed on the third floor again after.

I made Josh a green smoothie with all our new goodies in the morning. I wasn't big on cooking, and I didn't know what I was doing, but I was inspired to teach Josh everything I knew about health and nutrition. He whipped up some eggs and toast for us to accompany the smoothie. We discussed documenting our adventure. We went to Target to pick up some kitchen utensils and picked out a journal together. It was a bit more expensive than the rest, with an earthy look we both liked. It looked official. We went home, and I poetically wrote our love story: how we met, how we felt, what happened in the bathtub, and our life goals and dreams. We had so much fun recounting our adventure and reliving that pivotal evening.

Despite how much I enjoyed myself with Josh, I still had a crazy impulse to see Pablo. Josh helped me book a flight the following day. It wasn't easy to decide since the trip to visit Pablo had never made sense in the first place. We figured a ten-day visit to South Florida would suffice.

The weird feeling that came over me when I saw the ticket confirmation might have been excitement wrapped up in discomfort. I was going to be away from my new best friend. However, I felt so deeply connected to Josh by this point that I had no fear of losing what we'd created. He promised I'd still have my room when I returned. I left for Florida on May 24, five days after meeting Josh. I wanted closure with Pablo, and I'd committed to seeing my grandfather's old caretaker, Missy, who lived in Tampa at the time and had a new baby.

Missy had been an essential figure in my life back in the days when we made hemp macrame in our duplex. She'd taught me about the vegan lifestyle. We planned to spend a few days together before I flew to Miami to see Pablo off. After realizing at the last minute that I had the dates mixed up, I spent only one night in Tampa before going to see him. I jumped on a Greyhound bus to Orlando that bothered me so much that I took a black limo from the bus stop to meet Pablo at Vanity nightclub to shake off the feeling. I had a secret plan to meet my friend Sara, who had moved to Orlando to work at Disney World. She knew of a few good strip clubs in Florida that I wanted to try out. I felt the freedom of being an exotic dancer and the desire to have an extra thousand dollars to enjoy my trip.

I allowed myself to fall into a dream state, imagining that I had stepped out of the limo and onto a red carpet. Fans and smiling faces waited to greet me. Why not play out the fairy tale? Who said it was an excellent idea to let go of a child-like imagination? It was fun to try on this celebrity role, and I exited the limo like a star when we pulled up in front of the club. It felt so real. I'd messaged Pablo, and he was waiting right at the entrance with his group of friends when the limo pulled up. Stepping on the red carpet after my driver opened the door for me was the icing on the cake. The club was huge and packed. Pablo and I kissed and flirted, entering hand in hand. My heart was racing. Making a spectacle had me high on adrenaline. His friends were eyeballing me and whistling, which thoroughly annoyed him and pleased me. I resented and loved him all at once. Determined to make a scene on the dance floor, I walked into the massive crowd of swaying bodies.

Pablo wasn't into dancing, so I asked him to hold my purse and a few articles of clothing so I could get right next to the stage quickly.

Within seconds I had a circle of young, sweaty, fist-pumping Latin men surrounding me, pushing their way closer, a few close enough to grind up against me. I pushed back with a playful grin, incorporating the push into my dance routine, but not fast enough. Pablo rushed up to me and handed me my purse. He gave me a disgusted look and rambled in Spanish before uttering, "Slut!" I didn't expect that reaction, though I realized that Pablo was an angry drunk. He stormed out of the club. I followed him.

"What's the deal?" The rhetorical question didn't impress him or diffuse the situation.

"You're a slut!" he responded. He was in a mental loop.

By this time, all four of Pablo's friends had found us and chimed in, advising him in English and Spanish that he was going too far. "C'mon, man. Stop talking to her like that," one of them shouted as they grabbed his arm and leaned on him. "Pablo! Man, you're drunk," his friend pointed out—who wasn't any soberer. The four intoxicated boys begged and pleaded for Pablo to calm down. I hailed a taxi and jumped in. One of his friends, Evo, grabbed the door before I closed it and asked where I was going.

When I said back to Tampa, he grabbed my hand. "No, no. Come with us. He's just drunk. Don't let him make you upset. We're gonna take my car." Evo also had a sexy Bolivian accent. He carried my purse and wrapped his arm around me. Evo opened the front door of his white BMW and insisted I get in. The three others continued their drunken rambling in Portuguese, crammed in the back seat. It was clear they were still reprimanding him. I was pleased and bothered, all at once. While waiting at a stoplight, Evo told me to take his number in case I needed anything. He spoke the digits aloud, and I called him on the spot. We reached the Greyhound station within minutes, and I jumped out of the car.

Pablo followed me and continued the one-sided argument: "Who were all of these guys you met in New Jersey?"

I found his concern comical and replied, "You have a girlfriend, Pablo! She's coming to live with you in Bolivia in a matter of days! Who cares?"

Evo stood between us and took my hand to lead me back to the car. "Just come back to the house with us. He's an idiot. He's drunk and doesn't know what he's talking about. He's going to regret it later." I reluctantly got in the car, reminding myself that this was what I had intended to do in the first place. I wanted to see him off the next day. I *would* regret it if I didn't follow through. It was unlikely I'd ever see him again. Ending on a sour note would leave me suffering from heartbreak. Even in that moment of intensity, I was able to think ahead and make a wise decision on my behalf.

The car ride to the apartment was much quieter. I think they were ready to pass out after a crazy night of drinking and rambling at the top of their lungs. I didn't know where we had arrived, but I followed them inside. By this point, the sun was up, and I always struggled to sleep once the sun rose. Pablo and I lay on the couch together, and eventually, he sobered up. We snuggled, which ultimately turned into lovemaking.

A few hours later, Pablo shot up and grabbed his phone. He had missed his flight to Miami. Even though I felt utterly delusional from lack of sleep, I managed to come up with a solution. I had just been introduced to Spirit Airlines while in New Jersey with Josh, and I knew we could jump on a cheap last-minute flight, especially since it was less than an hour south. Just a few weeks ago, this option wouldn't have even crossed my mind.

One of the hungover Bolivian boys woke up and gave us a ride to the airport. With confidence, I walked up to the Spirit ticket counter and asked for the price of two seats to Miami. It was less than $100 for the two of us on the following one-way flight from Orlando to FLL. I handed over my credit card. Pablo finally exhaled a sigh of relief, and I felt like a superhero. We arrived at the airport in Miami and made our way to the international terminal. We had a long goodbye with a lot of tears. Looking back, it all seems completely melodramatic. I might have loved Pablo, but it was simply for his role as a catalyst in my life. But really, why was I so sprung on Pablo? The sexual chemistry did have me hooked. That first kiss ignited the fire. I knew that I would never see him again when we said goodbye.

However, I reached out thirteen years later to tell him our story would be in this book. I could not have foreseen how deeply healing it was to receive his words. “Oi Pablo! It’s been a reallllly long time. I have a really quick question. Because you’re in my book and I’m adding some details.” I figured he would be cold and the interaction would be short.

“Hey, Lana! Yea, it has been a really, really long time. I have to say; I am quite surprised. To be honest, I never thought I was relevant enough to be in anyone’s book besides family members, maybe. I really don’t know how you feel about our experience, and I hope I didn’t bring anything negative to your life. May I ask what and in what context you speak of me in your book?” His words were anxious.

“Very simply put . . . if it weren’t for meeting you and landing in the state where I eventually met my husband. I mean! I have to tell our story. Don’t worry. I won’t use your real name.”

I figured that would be the end of the conversation, but he slowly opened up. “I’m married with a child now, and I can’t risk this coming back to haunt me.” He was direct and clear.

I was ready to end the conversation. “No worries, name changed. I’m happy that you’re happy. We have no mutual friends, and I’m sure this book will never show up in your life.”

He felt me leaning back and tried to smooth it over. “I really wish you well, and I hope you understand.”

I felt his pull, drawing me back in. “It does make me sad to know that you’ve lived with a lie. This type of shadow can’t be serving you well.”

I felt my heart melting. I had loved this man intensely in another life, and it pained me to know that he had to hold this secret from the mother of his child for so many years. “Please don’t worry, though. I will conceal your identity.”

We began to present ourselves back to that time. “It was something unforgettable for me too. You may not believe it, but I still recall the very first time I saw you. You were the most beautiful girl in that club, and I knew right away that I would be chasing you that night. I was so amazed by the way you danced.”

I begged for more. “Pablo, my memory is so blurry. I’ve blocked things out, and I don’t remember what we really talked about or did together. I just remember how I felt, and you were so passionate, and I melted when you kissed me, and the lovemaking was surreal. But honestly, though, what did we talk about? Can you tell me anything?"

He didn't hold back. "I think what connected us the most was our differences. Not only culture but our personalities too. You introduced me to so many things. I was in love with you for sure. Your body. With your passion for yoga. I still remember the Bikram class you brought me to. I felt so comfortable with you. And yet uncomfortable with you and your friends getting high. I never really did drugs."

I chimed in. "I still don't consider cannabis a drug!"

He retorted, "Yeah, it just wasn't my environment. But it didn't matter. I just wanted to be with you. I really struggled for a long time with just feeling comfortable and happy."

I felt my current self stepping in to bring clarity to the dynamic. "I felt that you were struggling, and I just wanted to be there for you. This had so much to do with why I was so attached. I felt your pain, and I just wanted to take it from you."

He didn't seem to connect with my words. "Yeah, fully. I'm sure it was that, but I was so in love with you. The thought of just clicking the fuck it button and living with you crossed my mind a thousand times. For a guy like me, that says a lot."

I dove back in as my heart sank for that twenty-two-year-old Lana that felt so betrayed. "Okay, Pablo, so why? Why didn't we stay together?"

He paused and didn't have much to say, "Looking back, I'd say it was loyalty to her." It didn't matter, and I didn't need any more explanation. "But really, Lana. You were the girl of my dreams. You know, when I first heard your voice again after all this time, I could actually smell you. It was shocking." I felt a chill run through my body, imagining him having this experience. "You are my favorite story to tell when I'm out late, drinking with friends."

Slightly appalled and somewhat amused, I laughed. "Really?! You talk about me at bars while you're drunk?"

He boasted, "I tell them how I once conquered the girl of my dreams, and we had wild, amazing sex, and you were so hot. How you got me to do all of the things I didn't have courage to do on my own."

I laughed harder. "I'm still confused as to why we didn't stay together if this is true."

I could feel him pulling out of the fond memory into the darkness. "It was my insecurity after some time. I thought you'd slept with my friends, and that really hurt."

I was baffled. "What?! I didn't sleep with any of your friends! You and Evo weren't friends."

He seemed relieved. "Oh, I'm sorry I misjudged. Evo and I had just met and we weren't friends and never spoke again after that night. It was truly what I had to believe to hide my insecurity. You know, just before I boarded the plane that last day, you said that you'd marry me if I wanted to stay in America with you. I carried that close to my heart. Hearing you offer that kind of commitment made it so hard to leave you. I'm so sorry. I'm getting emotional now. My wife would kill me if she knew we were talking."

I reminded him that she'd found me on Facebook a few months after he'd returned to Bolivia and confronted me, asking if we had sex without a condom, if it was more than once, if I'd known about her, and how she had to ask me because Pablo "lied often." I'd asked her why she stayed with him if she really thought this. She reached out again months later and apologized for being so aggressive. We didn't want to relive that part of the story. "This has been so healing for me, Pablo. I never really understood how you wrote me off so easily, and I do think it's unlocked something inside of me now. There were so many memories I couldn't access while I masked the pain. I loved you so much. I think I still do. Love never dies. You'll always hold a special place in my heart." At this point, I couldn't hide the tears and didn't find it necessary.

"Talking to you felt really good for me too. I have to go take care of my son. I don't mind staying connected. I'd actually like to. I feel that same comfort now that I felt when I was with you. I'm so happy for you, and I hope your book sells thousands of copies."

I knew it wouldn't serve either of us to go any deeper, "Goodnight, Pablo. Go take care of your son." He signed off, and I cried for that younger version of me that was so in love and so deeply hurt, feeling that it was unrequited, and I cried tears of joy for releasing that story.

When Pablo's plane took off, I dried my eyes, ready for Miami. I was prepared to let loose. I couldn't let myself feel; it wasn't my practice then. I wanted to go wild. I was single; even though Josh and I had connected, we hadn't committed to any labels. The only person I knew who lived in Miami was an old boyfriend of my mother's, Arthur. He'd known my mother for decades and had thought he was my father for a split second. I thought I'd visit him. He lived in a gorgeous place overlooking an inlet, not too far from the ocean. His family was from Venezuela and relatively wealthy. He was a race car driver for many years. It was the perfect way to get acquainted with Miami. I instantly dropped into that South Beach vibe and wanted to stay as long as possible. It was good that I had to leave in a few days.

Arthur dropped me off at a hostel in South Beach the next day. I dropped off my belongings and headed straight to the beach. When I got back to the hostel, three girls had checked in and were staying in the dorm room that had been empty when I'd arrived. They were hanging out by the pool and invited me to join them and share a bottle of wine. I grabbed coffee mugs that would serve as our wine glasses, and we started having fun. We drank and laughed and chatted about travel. One of the girls was an au pair in Northern New Jersey, and we made plans to meet up as soon as I returned from my Florida adventure. Before we finished the bottle, one of the girls called the group's attention to a young man who passed out in a chair ten feet from our table. We figured we'd try to help him out. One of the girls went over and tried to wake him up. No luck. The next girl went over and gave him a shake and asked his name. No luck.

Here was a golden opportunity to put on a little comedy show for my new friends. I marched over and sat on his lap, whispering in his ear. I figured he'd surely regain consciousness. No response. Roaring with laughter, the girls took photos, and I posed, calling him my "hot date." Our last hurrah for the night ended there, and the girls headed to bed. It felt like the right time to call Josh and check in, so I stayed outside. Starting with a video felt appropriate at the moment. I was pretty buzzed from the wine, and the video became a continuation of the scene with the unconscious guy.

It felt like a typical Tuesday in Miami when I ventured out the next morning. It was the moment I had been waiting for—South Beach was calling my name. I claimed my spot on the sand, undressed down to my bikini bottom, and attempted not to pass out from the blazing heat while reading my issue of *Yoga Journal.*

Before long, a short, dapper man with a Spanish accent approached me. "Hi! How are you? My name is Roger." I wondered if I was sitting in the wrong place, and his next words would be asking me to move. I sat up, somewhat alarmed, without bothering to cover my bare chest. He continued while I struggled to gather my belongings. "Can I take you to dinner?"

I was in disbelief. "Dinner?" He explained he had noticed me while walking along the beach and figured that since he was going to dinner and thought I was very beautiful, inviting me couldn't hurt. He must have been waiting to be sure I was alone.

A train of thought raced through my head. *Well, I am hungry. Dinner will be free. We are in public. He's a petite guy, and I could totally take him.* "Sure, but I'm vegetarian, and I only eat organic."

He chuckled and said, "Of course. We can figure something out." He offered to help me carry my bags, and we walked back to his hotel. At first, I didn't fear walking into his room with him. After a few minutes, though, I felt uneasy and told him I had to go back to my hostel to get my things and move to a new hostel. He said we could just get my bags and bring them to his room. It seemed easier to go along with his plan. In my head, I was already coming up with creative ways of letting him know I'd need my room and would not be staying with him. I didn't resist, and I just went with the flow.

We went back to my hostel in his rental car, grabbed my bags, and brought them back to his room. Before we left the hostel, I told him I was starving and needed to eat immediately. I figured this would rush things along once we dropped the bags off at the room so we wouldn't have to go in again. When we got there, we did go into the room again just to leave the bags. Before he swiped his key card to unlock the door, I reminded him I was utterly famished. He assured me we were definitely going out to dinner, and he was also ready to eat. We went for a short walk to a quaint street with high-end boutiques and white-tablecloth restaurants with outdoor seating. I chose an Italian restaurant. Roger agreed without hesitation.

Roger seemed harmless. He was just a lonely man on a business trip. There was no way I could be mistaken for an escort. My nails weren't done. My breasts were real. My lashes were natural. I wasn't manicured in any way. There was a slight chance I could have passed for the least-manicured escort of all time, but the chance seemed really, really slim. Did he think I would have sex with him just because he bought me dinner? He couldn't, right? The thought crossed my mind, but I rejected it, watching him smile at me innocently. We savored our meal together, and he taught me some Spanish words and phrases. We giggled a lot. It was a surprisingly enjoyable experience. He insisted I stay with him in Mexico City to live in his home and teach him English. He offered $500 per month with all living expenses paid. We spoke about this idea for over an hour, and I fantasized a bit. There was no way I could settle for $500 a month, but it was fun to consider a new opportunity. I told him I would think about it if he would consider paying more.

When we left the restaurant, we strolled down the street and entered a boutique with belly dancing costumes. Another dream of mine was to become a master belly dancer and travel the world performing and teaching workshops. My thoughts came out in words, and before I could stop myself, I offered Roger a performance in exchange for the costume. Realizing the glass of wine at dinner wasn't working in my favor, I confessed I wanted the costume, but I wasn't ready for a solo performance. I figured I'd done my part not to lead him on, yet he still bought me the costume. It was black fabric with silver coins. I was so in love with it I wore it for the rest of the evening over my dress, shimmying and shaking my hips as we walked the streets of South Beach.

Being playful, carefree, and spontaneous and letting anyone in who was ready to play the game was the supposed exotic dancer persona I'd constructed in my mind. It didn't feel wrong or manipulative, because I was genuinely enjoying myself, yet there was a voice in my head cautioning me to be wary. The sun set while we were still in the boutique, and the posh Miami nightlife began feeling like the enchanting song of a snake charmer and I the snake. Conditioning seemed to be the culprit, as I reflect. Darkness meant it was time to work. It was time to find a club. Roger was down for anything. He hailed a taxi from where we stood, and within moments we were at the entrance of Club Madonna on Washington Avenue. I wasn't super impressed by the girls standing in the entryway, but I figured I could step into the limelight, and it would all be worthwhile.

The club was pretty empty and unimpressive. I'd been in the business long enough to know that the only way to get attention from one of the dancers outside of the VIP was to "make it rain," so I asked Roger to get me a stack of $100 in ones. After three or four stage performances, I started losing hope of showering my favorite dancer with one-dollar bills. Fortunately, after about thirty minutes, a playful dancer came out and pulled me onto the stage. Ready to perform at the drop of a dime, I slid off my dress and arched my back as I lay on the stage. I had my black lace panties on and nothing else. I noticed a couple moving up to the stage as I walked back to my seat next to Roger. As I put my dress back on, the girl approached and asked if I'd like to go out and dance with her. The couple had moved to the stage to get a closer look at me. I asked her if she was a dancer and what she was doing at the club. I had completely turned my back to Roger now, all my attention on my conversation with the couple.

The petite Latina, Lily, was about my size, and the man with her was a tall, muscular black man named Daren. Their clothing was flashy and expensive, and they spoke in absolutes. She leaned in close to me and asked, "Is he paying you?"

I laughed, "Who? Roger?" I glanced back at him. I shook my head and asked, "Why?"

She said, "Well, if he's not paying you, you should come with us."

I was attracted to her. It felt like she'd put a spell on me, and I simply had to obey. She had soft, dark skin and long curly hair. Her jeans seemed to hug her curvy body in a way that made me think they were custom-made for her. Her bright yellow shirt was unbuttoned just enough to reveal her white lace bra. Her accent was light but just enough for me to adore her every word even more. She had me hypnotized.

Lily informed Roger that our time had expired and I'd be gathering my belongings from his room. Receiving the news, he seemed caught off guard. He asked if I knew the couple. My response was that it wasn't any of his business, and we needed to leave immediately. I felt a little bad but also knew we would end up back in his room, and that's precisely what I didn't want to deal with. Lily insisted I ride with her to Roger's hotel, and we would follow him in Daren's black Escalade. Despite the opposition I heard in his voice, he seemed intimidated by Daren and agreed to the new plan. Lily asked me a million questions during the ten-minute ride to the hotel. When we arrived, she told Roger through her open window that he could get my bags and bring them to the car.

I felt guilty for the way they treated Roger. He had been delightful all night and hadn't made any moves. Not only was he respectful, but he was also generous. I believe the dynamic between us would have remained neutral because his ultimate goal was to persuade me to live with him in Mexico City. Either way, I didn't want to risk ending up in an uncomfortable situation with him, and somehow this situation seemed safer. How? I have no idea. I didn't know Lily or the man with her, who likely was not a boyfriend. She just happened to be the epitome of beauty for me.

Roger brought out my six bags, and we sped off. I had no clue where we were going, but Lily did seem to be giving me options. "Do you want to stay with us tonight? We have an extra bed in our room." I felt more at ease and reaffirmed that I was safe and the couple was harmless. We didn't go out dancing; we headed straight back to their hotel, which was utterly glamorous. Collins Avenue runs parallel to the Atlantic Ocean, and I knew right where we were when we arrived. My hostel was down the street, only a block away. I thought, *well, isn't this an interesting turn of events.* From a hostel with massive cockroaches only one night prior, to finding myself on the other side of the street, only a block down, in a posh hotel with this intriguing couple. It was surreal. Lily's relatively silent counterpart, Daren, asked if we wanted anything from the store.

The situation felt even more comfortable when just Lily and I were in the room. She told me I could shower to relieve myself of the Miami heat. In the shower, my thoughts ran wild. What was Roger thinking? Was he calling the police, reporting a kidnapping? What was I going to tell Josh? I didn't even know these people. What was Pablo doing? Was he with his girlfriend now? What was going to happen when I got out of the shower? Would they be sleeping? What did they want from me? Why did they invite me to their room? I turned off the thoughts when I opened the door to the bathroom to find them lying on the bed watching television. He told me that there was Vitamin Water on the nightstand for me, and I could order room service if I were hungry.

I came out of the bathroom and lay on the bed in my panties. I grabbed my phone to text Josh. Lily came and sat next to me. She ran her fingers through my hair and asked, "Do you like girls?"

I looked at her and put my phone down. "Yes, why?"

She said, "Well, I do too."

She slowly moved closer and came in for a kiss. I just let it all happen. I kissed her back, and she slid down next to me. She asked if Daren could join us on the bed, and I agreed, with one stipulation: I could leave my panties on because of a yeast infection. It was true, but I was surprised when they respected my request completely. Lily responded in her sweet accent, "That's fine, Mami. He doesn't have to touch you." I felt relieved and continued kissing her while he came over and undressed her. She asked if I'd go down on her, and I didn't hesitate. Feeling rather dominant, I gave her a look, grinned, and went for it. She'd lathered herself in coconut oil and hadn't missed an inch of her body. She was shaved, except for a landing strip. I wasn't highly experienced in feminine oral pleasure, but I knew what I liked. Assuming it wouldn't last long, I exhaled the anxiety of performance.

Lightly pressing my teeth against her clit, I let my tongue moisten her labia. She started uttering words in Spanish and then switched to English, moaning to Daren, "Mmm baby, she's so good. She's so good. Mmm! Baby . . ." She repeated herself over and over while he caressed her breasts. Eventually, she sat up and started sucking him. I didn't watch intently, but he came quickly and asked if he could take photos of me. It seemed harmless, so I agreed.

He took out a disposable camera, which I hadn't seen in a while. I posed, and he snapped away. Lily went back to her bed and watched, mumbling how sexy I was while he took photos. When he finished, I was surprised at how quickly it happened. He hit the lights and crawled into bed with Lily, and they said goodnight to me. I thought, "That was it? This night sure worked out well."

I woke up to Lily kissing me on the cheek and saying goodbye. She knew that home was New Jersey for me. We had spoken about her place in New York during that rapid interview on the ride to Roger's hotel. She said she worked as an exotic dancer at a nice, upscale club and made thousands of dollars every night she worked. She insisted I try it out because I would do well, just like her. "Call me as soon as you get home. You can come up and stay with me." They left and told me to sleep until housekeeping came to clean the room and refuse to leave for an hour or two more because I was waiting for my driver. I couldn't complain. The bed was luxurious. I had nowhere to go, no one to answer to, no obligations whatsoever. The door shut, and I sunk into the fluffy down comforter and exhaled.

Still in my black lace panties, feeling sexy, I grabbed my phone to snap a set of photos to send to Josh. I also texted Evo because he'd asked how I was doing via text the night before. He was flirty, saying he wanted to see me again. He reiterated that I could text him while I was in Florida if I needed anything. I sent him a selfie with my lips puckered in a kiss. He'd say kisses after every text, and I knew this was just the Bolivian way of speaking, but I wanted to invite more, so I flirted back. I attempted to explain the wild evening I'd had the night before to him. He replied, "Naughty girl!"

Josh seemed relieved to hear that the night had gone the way it did and I was safe. Roger had already messaged me to ask if I was all right. I told him everything was fine, and he said he was flying back to Mexico City and was looking forward to my arrival. Part of me still found this idea somewhat enticing but not enough to accept his offer. Lily had left an impression. Roger became a client, and the whole dynamic shifted. Some part of the game, or so I thought, was ordering him around how Lily did. Perhaps she knew how to be a sugar baby? After they left, I figured my new sugar daddy could take care of me again for the day.

Distracted by the messages coming in from Evo and Josh and still preoccupied with thoughts of Pablo, I dropped the ball with Roger.

Feeling complete with Miami, I booked an evening flight to Daytona to visit Sara. She had just finished working at Disney World for the summer. I pinged Roger a few times before departing, though we never ended up meeting for a second time. The insanity only continued for a few days, just long enough to paint a picture of where my mind was. I was shooting from the hip, moving without a clear goal or intention. There was no skill or strategy with the connections I made. I was naive in the underground world and sex industry. All I knew was my superpower was being sexually liberated, young, and attractive, despite my lack of confidence. I continued to dive in, head first.

Next stop: Daytona.

7
NAKED BUSINESS

Sara was on a short, romantic getaway with her boyfriend, Jerry, visiting for a week from Oceanside, California, where he was stationed in the army. I took a taxi to their hotel from the airport and arrived as they were heading out for dinner. I joined them. We took a detour on the way so Sara could point out a club she'd worked at a few times called Lollipop's. She said it was a great club, so I inquired and was told I could come the following day to audition. I could get in a few nights in Daytona to fund the rest of my adventure in Florida.

Sara wasn't as wild as she'd been during our Club Brickle days. She was content with her man, so I didn't expect to stay up all night having another sexcapade. I was wrong, of course. We all had a few drinks at dinner and ended up on the moonlit beach skinny-dipping. Skinny-dipping in the warm Atlantic Ocean was erotic and sensual, and our intoxication dissolved all inhibition. I had my hands all over and inside Sara while her boyfriend took photos and cheered us on.

When we finally rolled out of bed and stumbled down the stairs onto the sand, it was afternoon. I felt jittery thinking about working at Lollipop's that night, so, unable to relax and enjoy the environment, I announced that I'd be going on a mission to find a store with exotic-dancer apparel. I had to get creative. I was running extremely low on cash. I noticed a man sitting on a beach chair a few yards away. I told Sara I would talk to him and asked her to keep an eye on me. She didn't think anything of it, just turned her head so she could see where I was walking.

"Hey! Do you want some company?" The only thing that came to mind was the same approach I used in the club.

"Sure. Take a seat. What's your name?"

I gave him my real name without much thought. I guessed he was in his mid-to-late forties—brown hair, balding a bit, somewhat overweight, a Florida accent. I sat next to him and engaged in small talk, just long enough to lead into my proposition. "I'm super hungry. Do you want to go to lunch? I have to work tonight, so you can drop me off at the shop to buy new outfits after."

He seemed excited, "Sure, what do you want to—"

Mid-sentence, I held up one finger to signal I needed a moment and ran back to Sara to tell her I'd be going with him to buy my outfits for the evening.

She looked at me in disbelief. "What?! You're going where?! With who?!"

I realized she had been half-asleep when I told her I would talk to him in the first place. I explained again until she finally loosened up. She told me to be careful and text her along the way so she knew I was safe. I pranced back to Bill and said, "I'm ready for our lunch date!"

We walked over to pick up his car at the hotel valet on the beach. When the valet driver opened the passenger door of the Mustang, I felt little butterflies in my stomach. Score. I'd led with honesty and offered nothing more than a lunch date. At lunch, after he bored me with his monologue about the shuttle launch that day, I asked, "So why are you here? Where are you from?"

Bill had a slow southern Florida accent, and it made me anxious. "There's a NASA Space Shuttle launch here in Daytona this weekend."

I pretended to be interested because he was extremely enthusiastic, and I waited until he took another bite of his steak before I made another proposition. "Do you want to take me to get outfits? We can have a little fashion show, and you can help me pick out what to wear tonight at Lollipop's!"

He said he wasn't really the strip club type. "I don't think I'll be visiting you tonight at work, but you can call me after you get off, and we can go out for a drink. How about that?"

I had no intention of offering any sexual favors and assumed he wouldn't ask.

Bill happened to know just where to take me and said I could pick out what I liked. "Just promise you'll come back to my hotel tonight and give me a little show."

Fuck. I was wrong again. Somehow completely oblivious. Of course, he expected something from me. "Remember, Bill?! I told you that it was my first night. I can't just show up. You can come to see me there."

He reminded me, "I don't do strip clubs."

After a bit of back and forth, he seemed to understand and again asked me to promise to visit him after work in his hotel room. I agreed because I wanted to get my outfits and get away from him at this point, but I realized my plan wasn't as simple as I'd expected. He wanted more from me than I had initially offered. I hoped it would work out in my favor if I gave him a good show while I tried on the outfits. I picked out a few and playfully peeked out from behind the dressing room curtain as I slipped out of my swimming suit and into BodyZone bikinis. He seemed to enjoy my performance and asked if I needed anything else as we checked out. The total was just under $300. I bought clear plastic seven-inch platforms and three bikinis. Mission accomplished. I walked out of the store feeling satisfied.

Bill dropped me off back at the beach to meet Sara after I promised to contact him after work. I thanked him with a kiss on the cheek and hopped out of the car with my bags. Sara and Jerry were just getting dressed in the room to head out for dinner as I giddily walked in. I announced my success and threw my bags on the bed as I entered. "New shoes and thongs, baby!"

Sara laughed. "You're crazy!"

Of course, I now see this situation as manipulative and would not have operated this way today. I have come to a point where I take pride in men walking away from our interaction better than when I'd met them. I don't believe this was the case with Bill. Though I'm sure I added a little excitement to Bill's life that day, I'm sure he didn't feel great afterward. I do believe that I was conscious back then, but I also thought I was playing a role. I had an idea of what strippers are—what they do, and how they make money. I hadn't yet come to the awareness that I can create my own version of reality, and I don't have to play the role of anyone or adhere to any label, no matter what industry I'd chosen.

I didn't want to cause any tension between Sara and Jerry, so I held back the thoughts running through my head. I knew she'd done the same in the past. My three outfits and shoes didn't compare to the shopping sprees she'd been on with her clients. I grinned at her and playfully slapped her butt. They wished me luck and left the room. It was their last night together, so I didn't plan on seeing them again. I had been chatting with Evo, who I'd met during the volatile argument with Pablo just a few days earlier in Orlando. Evo wanted to visit and had booked us a room to spend some time together in Daytona for the weekend. Not fully understanding why Evo was pursuing me, I went with it anyway, appreciating that I still had some sense of connection to Pablo.

I wasn't used to the scene at Lollipop's. It was huge compared to Brickle, and the poles were the highest I'd ever seen. Intimidated by the whole scene and wary of new dancers, I kept to myself in the dressing room. Coincidentally from South Jersey, a girl named Star introduced herself to me, noticing I was new.

She said, "No one fucks with me here because I don't do drama, so you can just tell everyone that you're my cousin."

After telling her my new home was in South Jersey and felt like home because I'm Italian, she took me under her wing. Star was Italian too, born and raised in South Jersey. She'd come to Daytona for bike week and did so well that she figured she'd stay a while longer. I was relieved to have a friend. With my guard let down, I walked onto the stage with a confidence boost and a red Blow Pop in my mouth.

I had no intention of attempting to whirl around next to the ceiling on the poles, so I employed my seductive floor-work skills to entice the crowd. The Lollipop's DJ was adamant about playing my song choice, "Lollipop" by Lil Wayne, which just happened to be number one on the top-forty playlist that summer. It seemed appropriate to play off the theme and perform with a Blow Pop in my mouth for the first set. A couple that genuinely looked like the real-life version of Barbie and Ken enjoyed my performance and ended up with my Blow Pop by the end of the second song. I crawled over to Barbie on the stage, dove into her lap, and blew on her cleavage. Ken opened his mouth as I came up to ask for my sucker. Lightly tracing his lower lip first, I slid the wet Blow Pop into his mouth, then rushed offstage to spend half an hour with them in VIP. So began my first official encounter with swingers.

As soon as we sat down on the couch, Barbie started kissing me, and Ken pulled her perfect, fake breasts out of her white, low-cut tank. He slid his hands into her blue jean booty shorts and was soon fingering her. Assuming they frequented Lollipop's, I played along, hoping this wouldn't get me fired on my first night. After about ten minutes and no bouncers, I stopped worrying. Barbie and Ken must have noticed the tension leaving me because Barbie's hand moved closer to my inner thigh. Ken begged me to suck on her pierced nipples, and I did (willingly, as I'd already accepted that this was my week of sex with women). I straddled Barbie, who clearly enjoyed it, taking it a step further by sliding my bottoms to the side and fingering me. My initial reaction was to stop her, but Ken had kept his hands off me the entire time, and I was enjoying it, so I let her continue. They were both pretty intoxicated based on their aggression and lack of coordination, but they still knew they were into me and the VIP session wasn't satisfying enough for them. When the bouncer knocked and peeked in to tell us our time was up, they asked for my number. I gave it to them without hesitation, and they invited me to stay with them after work. I considered it and then remembered Bill and Evo were expecting me. Bill was still on my mind because I knew I'd be getting a call from him, though I had no intention of visiting him that evening or ever again. If he'd asked for another lunch date, I probably would have considered it, but he was hunting for more, and I had no intention of going there. Not with him.

Four hours into the night, I'd had enough. Leaving with about $600 was satisfactory. Evo picked me up, and we headed to a hotel on the beach. I told him about my encounter with Barbie and Ken and got another, "You're crazy!" It felt good to hear, and I wanted that validation. I didn't want to hear how I was so calm, relaxed, or collected. I wanted to know that everyone thought I was wild and reckless because it translated to fun to me. I'd take anything opposite of dull. Unfortunately, after two nights of drinking, I couldn't uphold the naughty girl persona, so I told Evo that we had to sleep as soon as we hit the sheets.

The following day, we woke up and drove back to Orlando. I planned to return to Missy's in Tampa, where I'd begun my Florida adventure. Missy and I hadn't spoken since I'd left her place in a rush, and there was a bit of tension between us. I'm a horrible communicator in uncomfortable situations, and it didn't feel right going back to Missy's, so I stayed with Evo again. This time we stayed in his home. I met his sister and his parents. It felt a little odd, knowing each other for less than a week, and I had no interest in starting a relationship with him. I was still mourning Pablo's breakup, and I missed him even more now that I was with Evo. Feeling vulnerable and wanting comfort, I let Evo get close—really close.

We had sex that night, which temporarily distracted me from missing Pablo. The sex with Evo was empty and felt like a performance on my part. It was solely a distraction, so I didn't have to feel. By morning I was already thinking about Pablo again. I asked Evo a slew of questions. "How did you meet Pablo?"

He seemed disinterested, "I don't really even know him that well. I'm just friends with the guys he came here to see, and I met him a few days before that night we met at the club. I don't really like him, though. He was kind of an asshole to you, right?"

I figured that he had to know something more about him. "Do you know where he lives in Bolivia?"

He seemed perplexed. "Like I said, I don't really know him, but I know that his family is pretty wealthy, and they run a successful company there where he's from in Santa Cruz."

I figured as much and asked a more daring question. "Are you going to see him again?"

Apparently, Evo was patient. I admitted to myself that the only reason I was in contact with Evo was to keep the only tie to Pablo that I had. I called the driver who had taken me to the club to meet Pablo and hired her for a ride back to Tampa that night. After two nights with Missy, I headed back to Jersey.

Josh picked me up from the Atlantic City airport with a warm embrace and a huge smile. He was happy to have me back in his arms. I was pleased to be back with this man I had bonded with so deeply just weeks before. I was grateful to have had the Florida adventure, but I was ready to create a home with Josh. We had discussed our relationship before I left Jersey, but I knew we had to re-evaluate when I returned. I told him I didn't want a committed or serious relationship because my big plan was to go to India for a year and immerse myself in yoga training. I didn't want to plan what would happen from there. I wanted to be free to explore my options as they unfolded. I walked into the house and saw Josh's good friend, Nicole, waiting for him. I felt her disapproval as I entered the room and defaulted to my usual reaction when I felt rejected: How could I get her to like me? I knew this was one of Josh's dearest friends, and I wanted her to love me as much as Josh did. Josh must have wanted her to like me as well because he asked me to make her something unique from our fully-stocked kitchen. She seemed to loosen up as I served her.

In the following days, Josh and I slipped back to where we were before I'd left for Florida. We were experiencing that playful puppy love, where anything goes and nothing else matters. Equally dedicated to my dream to study in India, Josh knew this meant getting me working as soon as possible to fund the trip. Josh knew the value of getting me in the right headspace to audition at the new club, so we went to see his stylist in Ventnor: Omar Lopez. I immediately fell in love with Omar and the salon. He had Mariah Carey blaring when we walked in, singing at the top of his lungs. The salon had funky, modern decor and a Hollywood vibe that made me feel like a celebrity when I sat down in his chair. I asked for bright red highlights and told him to surprise me with the cut. It was the most enjoyable salon experience I'd ever had. I left feeling ready to grace the stage at Bare Exposure. We made a quick stop at an exotic dancer's apparel store for a few new outfits before I went in to audition that night.

When I walked into Bare, the lights were all on, all the staff moving about prepping for the evening. I didn't get a feel for the club since it wasn't opening for a few more hours. The manager happened to be seated at the door and asked me to come in so he could take a look at my ID. He glanced at my ID and took a look at me. "Do you want to work tonight?" I felt my heart start fluttering and thought, *It's that easy? I'm in?* I barely took a breath before blurting out that I was ready.

My first night at Bare was wild. The girls worked fast and hard. They dominated in every sense of the word. They were ready to chew up and spit out anyone who walked through the door. Most of the girls were Latina, many from Philadelphia or New York. Only a few lived in South Jersey. Most of them were incredibly beautiful. They were ten times more manicured than the girls I'd seen in either Daytona or Club Brickle. They all had big, round bottoms and full lips. I felt I fit in well with my round bottom and mistakably Latin features. I made friends with a few Russian girls that first night after discovering they also spoke French. Bare had makeup artists for hire and a small boutique attached to the back of the club for dancers and their clients to visit during the night.

I was in awe of how fast the cash rolled in. I'd step onto the main floor and get nabbed for my next lap dance in less than five minutes. We had chipped plastic cards, resembling credit cards, to track the dances. The card was attached to an obnoxious, coiled neon cord that most girls wore around their ankles or wrists. To clock in for our shift and track our dances, we'd slide the card into the reader mounted on every chair in the lap dance room. I loved this way of tracking the dances because there was no ambiguity. When the dance began, I'd slide my card in, the light would go on, and we'd start. If the customer had only paid for one dance, the light would blink when we had sixty seconds left and went off when the dance was over. I ensured that the customer knew about this timer so there would be no question when our time was up.

The dancers of Bare Exposure thrived on this hive-mind mentality of dominating the customer. In the lap dance room, there was a strict no-touching policy. If a bouncer noticed a customer's hands moving from the armrests, he'd yell out, "Keep your hands to yourself!" The bouncers were on point at Bare, which felt so good. I loved it. I felt safe.

Bachelor parties were the norm at this BYOB strip club. Groups from the entire stretch of the East Coast would come in for the special occasion. The public humiliation was a major selling point for Bare, which aligned with the dancers' domination vibe. The party would pay for a stage show where the bachelor would be the focal point of the performance. It was called the "hot seat;" this meant that either the club or the group would choose one or more dancers to go onstage with the bachelor and put on a show that consisted of the dancer (or dancers) slamming their pussy into his face, dropping down onto his balls from the top of the pole, pulling his pants down and whipping him with his belt before or after splitting his boxers down the center and pulling the elastic band up over his neck, and then eventually riding him around the stage while he was on all fours. I'd never put on a show like this before.

When asked to do my first hot seat, I was lucky enough to go up with a pro. I stood back and watched her in awe, fearing I'd fuck the whole thing up if I stepped in. She put the belt in my hand and directed me. The crowd was screaming behind me, and my knees were shaking. My heart felt like it was going to beat out of my chest. I held onto the belt with a white-knuckled grip and swung my arm forward with all the force I had. It barely made a sound, and the crowd screamed for more. I took a deep breath and swung again. The belt snapped against his red, welted ass cheek. When I heard the cheering, I went in again and noticed the man tensing up and leaning away. I felt his pain. For a blip in time, the room fell silent. It was like a bad dream. I didn't like it. I dropped the belt and backed away. The other dancer took over and pushed him down to the floor. When I backed off, I stopped holding my breath and exhaled in relief, having made it through the performance.

After that first go, whenever someone asked me to do a hot seat, I always felt anxious butterflies in my stomach. One time I had a customer approach me and ask if I'd do a hot seat alone and handed me the money. I wasn't having a particularly lucrative evening, so I accepted. The club wasn't so busy, and I figured I could get away with a subpar performance. When I was called up to the stage, I was followed by a very handsome, muscular man who must have been almost seven feet tall. He was big. When I took my shoes off, all five feet of me quivered as I stood next to him while he signed the waiver. I wanted to give him a typical lap dance; sensual, seductive, slow, and erotic. No part of me wanted to humiliate this man, and my intuition told me he didn't know what he had gotten himself into. I was only about halfway through, and I could feel his agitation before noticing his expression. I dropped down on his lap for the second time from five feet above and felt his grip tighten around my waist. He threw me off of him (rather gently), jumped down from the front of the stage, and walked straight out the door. His friends booed, and one of them ran after him. I was still on stage, and a small crowd was watching me, so I played along and shrugged my shoulders with an innocent look on my face.

My detest was affirmed. I hated the hot seat. I'd only do it if it came with a huge tip, and I had other dancers to take over if I froze. Once in a while, a group would let us know they planned on tipping well, and I'd accept the offer, but I generally refused and said I'd never given a hot-seat dance. This was confirmation for me.

Yes, I pretended to be the girl who could dominate and emasculate men because I'd somehow understood it was the mentality of the highest-earning dancers, but it wasn't me. Lily's power dynamic with Roger had taught me a lesson, however. If I wanted to make money, I had to adopt her demeanor, even if it meant going against my nature. If I wanted to maximize potential, I had to have multiple "sugar daddies," like Sara, and there was a particular way I'd have to deprive these men of their dominance. None of it came naturally to me. I'd try it and end up feeling horrible about myself. I would go home from Bare and tell Josh, night after night, how I hadn't made much money because I'd spent hours talking to someone because he was "just a nice guy." Building rapport and connecting came easily. My girl-next-door persona was natural. I didn't innately have the *hustler* mindset some girls seemed to possess naturally.

Unfortunately for me, weekends at Bare in the warmer months meant hot seat after hot seat, sometimes with a line stretching down the sidewalk and wrapping around the corner. The club was right on the corner of Pacific Avenue in Atlantic City, across from Trump Plaza. The typical clientele were men from Connecticut or New York, down to Atlantic City to "have a good time" gambling and visiting Bare Exposure. Even more common was the bachelor party group. They usually went to gamble first and arrived at Bare to spend their winnings on the girls. If they weren't coming in with money they'd won at the casino, they were looking for a distraction from the hundreds or thousands of dollars they'd lost that night. The girls would know a gambler had really lost a lot when they came in stumbling drunk and alone.

Big, rowdy groups at Bare were generally big spenders. They weren't quiet and hiding in the corner because they were broke and embarrassed to be at a strip club. There were always a few stragglers who were shy, but it didn't mean they didn't have cash. Some younger guys would come in, but they were only good for one or two lap dances unless they were in the service. Military men would spend every last penny. If I wanted to take it easy on myself, I would approach a younger guy, and I'd know he would come back for a dance without much convincing. That was my strategy at Bare. One lap dance after another. I didn't try to go for the thirty-minute VIP because it was a whole ordeal. The process wasn't streamlined like it is in Vegas.

I didn't understand how it happened or why it was acceptable, but there was a dancer who just sat by the door of the champagne room entrance. She was at least one hundred pounds overweight and wore the same outfit and wig every weekend. When a dancer brought a customer back to the room, she'd ask if he wanted more company, referring to herself. They'd either be caught off-guard and not know how to respond or immediately refuse. Sometimes I wouldn't see her by the door, but she'd end up in our room halfway through and push herself on the customer. They'd almost always say no unless they were so drunk they were barely communicating in the first place. I only encountered this scenario a few times. I always felt like she was stepping on my toes. I would have spent more time with the customer and ended up with more money if she wasn't coming in and asking for him to split what he was willing to pay. It didn't feel right. On the rare occasion she wasn't working, I was more likely to ask a customer to spend a half-hour with me. The customer would pay $200 for a half-hour in the champagne room, and I would have to give the club $50. The lap dances were $30 for the customer, and the club took some random amount like $11 from the $30. It felt like I had to do less work if I just did seven-lap dances instead of a half-hour in the champagne room. Since I wasn't offering any sexual favors, I found it difficult at that time to ask for a large tip after VIP.

My love for the quick, one-song lap dance began at Bare. I had a few moves that would awe him during those three minutes, making the dance worthy of a nice tip. I would usually make about $30 in three minutes. That's $600 per hour. Realistically, it's about $400-$500 per hour since I'd have to walk out and find someone new after a dance or two. I could live with that. Obviously, after a few songs, the customer gets more and more aroused. If, for some reason, I could get him to be more interested in conversation than in being seduced, we could spend much more time in the lap dance or champagne room. Seduction came naturally. The conversation was the actual work, so one or two songs in the lap dance room was perfect.

When my customer sat, I would step back to determine what I was working with, and that first moment was such an adrenaline rush. The clock was ticking, and it was time to perform. Sometimes I'd get nervous, and sometimes I'd feel dominating; sometimes, I'd feel purely seductive. I would play off their energy.

My techniques for dealing with different men had also evolved and adapted to the new space. If he was touchy, repeatedly trying to put his hands on me, I would move quickly and aggressively. I'd prop myself above him, straightening my arms and hovering over him, using the sides of the booth. Each lap dance chair at Bare was like a tiny stall. The sides of the chair were just tall enough that the customer's head was a foot or less from the top. I loved propping myself up above them so I could dangle my legs. I'd bend my knees and pin my touchy customers against the chair a few times so he knew I was not afraid of being aggressive. If someone was too much, I'd perform half or more of the song on top of the chair so he would have to look up the entire time, which is somewhat disorienting for the customer. They were less likely to reach up than sneak a hand onto something in front of them.

For two and a half weeks, I went hard at Bare. Josh turned me on to Robert Kiyosaki's book, *Rich Dad Poor Dad*, and the concept of financial literacy. We listened to discs of Tony Robbins, and I read Tim Ferriss' book *The 4-Hour Work Week*, which Josh had given me. Slowly I started wrapping my head around what it meant to build wealth and the opportunity I had as a young dancer. The realization that dancing was neither sustainable nor an end-game left me daydreaming of something bigger. Lily's enticing proposal was also lingering in the back of my mind, so we visited NYC at the end of June.

Molly, a girlfriend of mine, had flown in to meet up with us in NYC. It was a sweltering day in the city, over one hundred degrees. When it cooled down in the evening, we met with Lily and Daren at a nightclub on the lower east side. They rolled up with a crew of six drop-dead-gorgeous Dominican girls in short bodycon dresses and Bordello heels. I felt like we'd landed in the scene with Taz's angels. Daren was playing the same role I had witnessed in Miami, easily mistaken for a boyfriend, yet unquestionably in a different role than the other three men with the girls that evening. Josh filled me in after having a private chat with Daren.

Lily was an escort. Daren was not her boyfriend. He managed her, the five other girls in her crew, the money, and the clients. Daren asked Josh about my earning potential. I was naive. Perhaps at some point, I'd given this all a moment of thought, but I have no memory of it now. We all took shots and danced. Josh's car was parallel-parked on the street outside the club in front of Daren's. Lily's sister flirted with Molly, attempting to convince her to get in their car to keep the party going and sleep in her bed. Lily reminded me she had space in her apartment for me, continuing our conversation that began in Miami. When the sun came up, Josh and I were huddled by our vehicles, being seduced by five of the most attractive females I've ever come into contact with.

I have a vision etched in my mind of Molly's outstretched arm reaching toward me, with Lily's sister on the other side. They were cooing, "Come with us!"

Josh was standing by his car, looking at me in disbelief. Even though he was utterly silent, I could hear his thoughts. "Are you really going to go with them?" His look of disapproval had me frozen. Josh warned, "You can go with them, but I'm not interested, and if you get in their car, I'm not following you."

Deciding between the two felt more complicated than running from both parties. Why couldn't I have it all? Of all the moments in my life when I wanted to become invisible, this may be on the top of the list. The escort life seemed glamorous and fulfilling on the fleshy, human level. All my desires to indulge in intimacy with women were available, finances would be a breeze, and every day would bring a new thrill, all while living in a city I'd always longed to be in. The rational part of me knew it wasn't truly an option. I got in Josh's car. I told them we'd follow. When we lost them two blocks later, Josh announced we were going home. The stars (and Josh) didn't align for me to become an escort that night.

8
ULTIMATE CONTRAST

Josh and I were soon on our wild adventure together, and it wasn't hard to forget that blurry night in NYC with Lily and her crew. Less than a month after that night, we found ourselves in Essaouira, Morocco. I was baffled that Josh had never left the country because he seemed so worldly to me. I couldn't imagine being without him for this big adventure, and I certainly couldn't imagine leaving his son in Jersey while we were having the trip of a lifetime. We brought six-year-old Tony along and spent a few days in London and Spain on both ends of the month-long journey.

It's been said that traveling with someone is the best way to get to know them. We catapulted ourselves into the most uncomfortable situation possible. Tony asked if I was his stepmom and didn't seem too sure of the dynamic between Josh and me. My state of mind was unbalanced on its own. I didn't have clarity about who I was or what I wanted. The trip became tortuous, witnessing a man I'd thought was an incredible father disciplining his child in ways I disagreed with. I decided this wasn't a person I could spend my life with, especially raising a child. If he treated his son like this, how should I expect him to treat me differently? I justified traveling without them to the Sahara with a Moroccan man named Ahmed and proceeded to engage with him intimately for the last week and a half of the trip. I completely swooned the moment I laid eyes on Ahmed. I detailed our poetic love story in a message I'd sent to a girlfriend at the time:

On the 2nd of August 2008, I left Essaouira (ie: ex-hippie paradise of the '70s), with one of the most beautiful humans that I have ever laid eyes on. He's a twenty-one-year-old Moroccan boy. His body is perfect. He has skin the exact color of yours (no lie); the darker the better you know. Ha! I love dark skin. He has thick, dark curly hair. Everything about him is perfect. I feel like a horrible person. I have completely betrayed Josh. I have totally fallen for this boy. We have had interactions I cannot convey in words. I can't wait to tell you in person. It's just craziness. I can't stop thinking of him. Simply gorgeous. Intelligent. Talented. Yup.

I met him at his summer job here in Essaouira, where we are staying. He works in a jewelry shop, selling ancient wonders from all over Africa. There are masks, statues, scarves, mirrors, knives . . . it's incredible. We visit there often, just as a hang-out spot, and sit on pillows or the floor and laugh while drinking copious amounts of the best of the best Moroccan mint tea. I think I am addicted to it.

It is simply breathtaking. This is a magical, mystical land of snake charmers, belly dancers, dancing monkeys, elegant and tribal fabrics so pleasurable to touch and wrap around my bare skin moistened by the oil of the Gods—rose and Argan (both specialties of the region here in Morocco).

Heaven of Sand. Not a noise to disturb the rhythm of my heart as it synchronized with the galaxy of stars above. The blanket of darkness lifts as the moon illuminates the vast Sahara. The evening departs, inviting in the blistering sun. The heat of the sun has only the intensity of your own interpretation. Thousands of years have passed as the nomadic Saharouie tribes took a liking and comfort in its medicinal effect. Any ailment one may endure or encounter seems as such—ceasing to exist, after the rest of the gods—the slumber of the privileged among the dunes. One night of restful, peaceful sleep in the immaculate dunes can cure any worry—internal, external; all that is purely self-inflicted. I can label this experience as the most enlightening in my life thus far.

As for the parts not so poetic. We rode in on camels to one of the four (permanent) campsites. Ahmed (the gorgeous boy's name) and I rode in relatively close to—well actually, just as—the sun set. Just him, the guide, and me. They spoke the native tongue for the entire one-hour journey into the Sahara with a bit of French every so often so that I could understand.

When we arrived, we were treated like royalty. A native Moroccan magic carpet was laid upon the sand to rest upon; nourishment and musical entertainment were provided and instruments to play. Of course, I have no skill with such things and I didn't attempt. However, Ahmed is a Saharouie. He is from the Sahara, born in the beige powder, softer than the finest silk, and inherently does things with these drums that puts me in a trance. He plays the drums like no other. He joined in with the three guides.

Hearing the music from afar (we left the camp to put on our own show), the sounds of these tribal drums must have carried for miles. They called me back to them. The dunes vibrated with the rhythm that stole my heart that night. My soul was soothed as

> I engaged in conversation with a Persian man, husband of a beautiful Indian princess, perched upon a dune next to three beautiful children; young Moroccan girls sat across from their mother, a native of the Sahara; she sat directly next to her husband who was placed next to the Australian wife of the man from London. A happy little bunch we were! Under the stars, we enjoyed the dream of nomadic Saharouie life together. And then I woke up. Sweet departure.

Looking back thirteen years after this saga played out, I now see that I am strongly attracted to some specific physical features and most definitely men who play instruments and grew up in magical, mystical geographic locations. I almost can't believe the distinct similarities between *four* of the men I fell madly in love with. How can it be possible that I found doppelgängers in Northern Africa, Costa Rica, the Philippines, and Bolivia? Hey, it's worth mentioning. I'm on an internal adventure here.

The rationale for hooking up with Ahmed was that I didn't want to be with Josh. I was appalled by his parenting. I didn't think I could be in a relationship with a man who treated his child that way. I was—and still am—extremely sensitive to any inevitable ugliness in parenting due to my traumatic childhood. But of course, this was secondary. I get triggered watching strangers in a random grocery store displaying undesirable parenting. Communicating that to Josh would have been a better plan. Instead, the whole affair turned into an explosion that left us with a mess to unravel over the years that followed. Josh was so hurt and angered by my choice to run off with Ahmed and sleep with him that he truly never forgave me. I haven't fully forgiven myself for staying in a relationship with someone I didn't align with, attempting to transition and not sticking to it. When I left for India just two months after returning to Jersey (September 2008), Josh and I had space to get clearer on what our connection meant and where it would lead.

Many obstacles arose before departing, one of which was the unexpected death of my cousin Mikey. He had left me a voicemail a few weeks before his death saying he was excited to share how much he enjoyed practicing yoga. He was eager to get his life together and be out of jail. Out of jail meant access to his poison: opiates. He'd been clean for some time and, in my understanding, didn't take into account his decreased tolerance. He overdosed. To this day, I have not fully processed Mikey's death. I know that I could not decide his fate, but I carried the heavy weight of guilt. Believing I could have saved him has hung over me like a dark cloud for more than a decade. I still feel my heart sink and find myself breaking down, unable to hold back the tears when I hear any song by Tool or Nirvana that I remember him playing on the guitar. Another man in my life that I couldn't save.

Josh and I had made a pact in a bathtub on May 19, 2008. Following through was the only option. Mikey's funeral was scheduled for the same week as my flight to India. My presence wasn't going to bring him back. I was initially torn but made peace with leaving instead of attending the service after a long phone session with my Uncle Jeff. India was in the cards long before Pablo appeared, and the overwhelming flood of love chemicals aborted the mission. Someone advised me against going to India, becoming an unsuspecting oracle, warning me that my leaving would complicate matters further.

We had Sunday dinner with Josh's extended family at his grandmother's house in Cherry Hill. His grandmother was a witty, often strident woman who lacked a filter when speaking. To me, she was hilarious. To this day, I laugh, remembering her whimsical commentary. Instead of chairs, there was a bench at the round kitchen table where three people could comfortably sit next to one another.

After dinner, she sat down next to me with her cup of coffee and glared at me over her right shoulder. "When are you leaving for India?"

Mind you, this was only a week and a half before my departure, "Really soon. Just over a week now. Flying out of Philly."

I could feel her piercing gaze through her thick glasses after she took another sip of coffee. "Don't do it. Don't go. You'll regret it."

My stomach turned, and I tried to play it off with a smile. "What? Why? I'm going to come back."

Whether she ruined my trip to India or my subconscious was simply unable to un-hear her words, the trip to India was challenging. There were moments when I regretted leaving Josh and South Jersey, especially when Josh called to tell me he couldn't be in a relationship with me any longer and it would be best for him if I didn't return to Jersey. I had no solid plan to leave India, but I wanted nothing more than to return home when that breakup call happened. I had never felt so lonely in my life. My best friend had cut me out. This massive country was full of strangers that couldn't fill the void.

The beginning of a dark time began there. My drive to explore and experience India dissolved. It felt like I was going through the motions with the yoga training, my guru's ashram visit, New Year's celebration in Goa, and a Sikh wedding in Chandigarh. It was all so incredible and new but heartbreaking to experience alone. It left me feeling even emptier. I wanted nothing more than to tell Josh about every waking moment. All the sorrow led to binge eating, which led to a depressed immune system. Much of the experience was somewhat traumatic. I met up with a random Indian guy on Facebook, whose bed I ended up in after a night of partying and too many drinks. Another Indian man promised me a way out of a congested area of Goa during the winter holidays, only as a bribe to lure me into his hotel room. I left India with new scars, and the yoga training certificate never felt worth it.

In January, I was back in Wisconsin with Hepatitis A. I gained thirty pounds and lacked any drive to maintain my health. Josh and I began spending four to six hours on the phone every day, but he still wasn't open to the dynamic we had before I left. He was bitter about Ahmed. Grandma had been right—there was a period of regret. I'm still processing the lessons learned during that four-month rigmarole. The biggest lesson was the missed opportunity to change my state, create my reality, and leave fond memories. My angels must have guided me because I arrived back in Wisconsin just in time to ride out the horrible experience of Hepatitis A with my entire family as my support system.

After getting fed up with being back in Wisconsin, I moved in with Sara in Fallbrook, California. Living with her and her partner only amplified the loneliness. One month was more than enough time for me to run back to the other side of the country to live with Evo and his immediate family. Somehow, I thought I could trick myself into thinking Evo could take Josh's place or at least distract me. Perhaps my worst decision yet.

Every move I made seemed to cut deeper. Being preoccupied with Josh and feeling consumed by guilt while questioning whether or not I pushed him away kept me in a constant state of unrest. I'd sold my beloved little forest green Honda Civic to help fund my trip to India and eliminate a potential headache. I was too depressed to be resourceful, and I felt stuck. Mentally I was just that—*stuck*. I tried working with Evo's family at an airport car rental company in Orlando. It was painful, attempting to integrate back into a system I'd shunned.

I quit after a few weeks and went back to what was familiar: stripping. There was a dive bikini bar close to Evo's home in Orlando, close to Disney World. Not a great location. Dancers were required to wear pasties, the place only offered $10 table dances with minimal contact, and there were no private rooms or opportunities to upsell. The most I ever made in one night was $300, barely worth inhaling secondhand smoke and assaulting my eardrums for six hours. Only a half-mile down the street from this club was an upscale club where girls were required to wear gowns. They only offered me the dayshift, and it wasn't an option to borrow a car during the day.

Two girls from the club became acquaintances, and we plotted to work in another city for a weekend, feeling dissatisfied with our weekly dive bar earnings. Nikki and Sam were not typical dancers, if there is such a thing. Sam was overweight and older than most dancers at our home club. Nikki was new to dancing and somewhat awkward in social situations, a bizarre character trait for someone whose income depends on social skills. Out of the three of us, only Nikki had a car. She picked us up on a Thursday morning, and we drove from Orlando to Tampa. We planned to work at any club that would hire us for the weekend. Tampa is full of gentlemen's clubs, and I figured it would be a breeze to walk in and get hired on the spot, which had never been an issue for me.

We gave up after being rejected at four different clubs. On our way out of the infamous Mon's Venus in Tampa, we picked up one of those shiny magazines full of advertisements on the way out, the ones for the guys who still hadn't gotten quite what they wanted at the club. I flipped through the pages, praying I'd get inspired to try one last club, and was surprised to find what looked like another option. "Lingerie Shows" were advertised on the back few pages. I dialed a number from one of the ads, and a man named Josh with a New York accent answered.

"We're hoping to work tonight. What's the hiring process?" Knowing I wouldn't get a clear answer to my question over the phone, I asked for the address and said we would be happy to meet in person.

Josh sounded like a character from *The Godfather*. "Come on over, and we'll see what we can do."

We pulled up to a three-story house tucked in the corner of a neighborhood only a few miles away from the cluster of gentlemen's clubs. Apprehensively, we pulled into a dark gravel lot behind the house with one other parked vehicle. Fortunately, the porch light was on. We rang the doorbell. A girl with long, dark hair, heavy makeup, and a red satin robe answered the door. She didn't seem enthusiastic about the three women staring back at her from the other side of the screen door.

She mumbled, "follow me," and turned around. She led us past a large living room with five women in lingerie sprawled out on couches watching television, up two flights of stairs, down a corridor, and into Josh's office on the third floor.

"Have a seat," he said, without turning from his computer monitor. Making a swift quarter-spin with his chair, he turned toward us. His eyes widened. "Oh! There's three of ya," which had been the issue all night. No one wanted to hire three girls at once. Not just three girls, but three girls who were not *tens* in the sex industry (fake boobs and Barbie bodies would have changed the game significantly). Sam and I were overweight and out of shape, and then there was Nikki, in all of her awkwardness. The three of us were not making great impressions.

There was only one chair on the opposite side of Josh's desk. I took the seat directly across from him, and the girls took the couch five feet behind me. Josh listened quietly and patiently while I explained our grand plan. He could tell we had no idea what we were getting ourselves into. He began with, "Let me tell you, ladies, how it works here." Like a man who had written the book on communicating with law enforcement while running an illegal operation, Josh laid out the entire "Lingerie Show" business in cryptic detail, never mentioning the word sex or even alluding to it. "They just close the door, and whatever happens between two consenting adults is none of my business." Then he said, "My best girl leaves with over five thousand every weekend." His only hint at illegal activity was in these last two sentences. Our eyes lit up. I felt myself leaning closer as he rattled off numbers. He wrapped up his spiel with the caveat—he couldn't hire three girls on the spot because he already had a full house, and it wouldn't be fair to the other girls. We could work the following day and likely not all at once. I wrote down my number on a post-it and told him he might see me tomorrow.

After this almost-not-quite rejection, we had enough of a spark to try one more. Nikki chose this moment to confess she didn't have enough gas money to get us back to Orlando, which left us with no option but to keep trying anyway. A man named Charles answered the phone. Before we made the same mistake for the fifth time, I explained there were three of us and we needed to work tonight. Charles said it wasn't a problem. He gave us an address that took us to a house a quarter the size of Josh's mansion. Charles answered the door and took us upstairs to his office. This house had only two rooms on the lower level; one with two girls watching television and one right next to it with nothing but a black leather couch and a lamp.

Charles sat behind his desk and gestured for us to sit across from him. He didn't waste time. He said, "So, the three of you want to work tonight?" We looked at each other and nodded, dumbfounded that we'd finally heard the magic words we'd been waiting for. "All right, we have to get the ads up on craigslist. Change into your outfits, and we'll go downstairs to take photos."

There was no need for an explanation. I'd already told him over the phone before we arrived that we needed to work and were familiar with lingerie shows. We took photos in the room with the couch and went upstairs to upload them to the site. Charles explained the process with his eyes glued to the monitor. "Usually, someone calls within ten or twenty minutes. When someone calls, you'll just answer the door and take them into the room. You don't have to do anything you don't want to. It's just like the club. You can just give them a little show or a lap dance." Somehow I believed him. I wanted to believe him. I didn't want to hear that I'd have to have sex with anyone who answered my ad.

While the girls chatted with Charles about their craigslist ads, I texted my ad to Josh. He answered right away. He asked what I was doing. Somewhere in the forefront of my mind was a cry for help. I wanted nothing more than to be back in South Jersey with Josh, living our carefree, adventurous life together and working at Bare Exposure. Josh said, "Lana, there are other things you can do for money. You don't have to do that." Using what Charles had said, I assured Josh that I didn't have to do anything sexual. We could talk to the customers, just like at the club. After all, sex wasn't mentioned in the ad, listed under "erotic services."

Just five minutes after Charles had posted the ad, someone rang the doorbell. He seemed startled but recovered and instructed us on what to do. "Just answer the door and take him into the room. Have him sit down and let him see you. Give him about one minute, then give him your rate for the hour." My heart started beating out of my chest. The four of us ran down the stairs and hid on the opposite side of the door. Sam opened the door and led a short Latin man into the room. Less than a minute later, she said, "He asked for another girl." Nikki went in next and came back out ten seconds later. It was my turn. As I went to open the door, the man walked out of the room and headed for the exit. Sam attempted to redirect him but he refused: "I'll come back later."

My angels must have been watching over me because I didn't end up "modeling lingerie" for any strangers that night. After that, Charles and I kept a text thread going for an entire year. He told me I was intelligent and gorgeous and he could help me make money another way. He offered me a room in his house in Tampa and a job selling ads or assisting him with one of his many endeavors, all within the sex industry. He made it clear I wasn't a fit for lingerie modeling, but there were more lucrative opportunities. It was his way of saying he had a thing for me and would much rather pursue a relationship with me than support me in his "lingerie modeling" side business. Charles was a hustler and was adamant about teaching me his ways in return for my companionship. We never met again in person, but I maintained our connection for a sense of security if I ever found myself so pressed for cash again.

After returning to Orlando unscathed, I promised myself I would go solo on any similar future endeavors. I was sure that if I'd gone to Tampa alone, I would have been hired at a gentlemen's club and never gotten to test the waters of "lingerie modeling." So later, when I called Feng, a man I'd met in the club in Orlando, I decided to keep my plan private, only to wish I hadn't after it was over. Feng invited me to accompany him on a business trip to Daytona. I figured I could use the trip to go back to Lollipop's and make money with a few weekend shifts.

Feng picked me up from Evo's Friday afternoon, and I introduced him as a new friend I'd be staying the night with. The plan was for Evo to pick me up from Daytona on Sunday evening. The short drive from Orlando to Daytona was painless. Feng seemed a perfect gentleman. He took me to dinner when we arrived. Our conversation was light and playful. He managed to sweet-talk me into an impromptu photoshoot under the street lights during an evening stroll. When we checked into the hotel, I asked for my own room. He said he'd get us a room with two beds if I were okay with it. I enjoyed Feng's company, so I figured it wouldn't be an issue. The only room available had one king bed. Once in the room, I made it clear to Feng that we were not having sex, reminding him it had never been on the table. Requesting that a pillow remain between us while we slept, I got into bed, giving Feng the benefit of the doubt. He'd had four cocktails during dinner, and I could smell the alcohol wafting from his body as I lay next to him.

Later, who knows how long, sweaty palms caressed my waist, rousing me from a deep sleep. Peeling his hands from my sides, I inched toward the edge of the bed. I felt the hands return seconds later with a firmer grip. The warmth emanating from his body and the smell of alcohol lingering on his breath churned my stomach. A familiar feeling came over me, followed by a flood of memories—an officious man in India, an aggressive girl in middle school, my cousin Jimmy, an intoxicated boy in high school—all of the people who'd touched my body without asking for permission. This pushing and inching toward the edge of the bed continued for hours. Why I allowed this to go on as long as I did will forever be a mystery.

When the sun finally rose, I jumped out of bed and sat on a chair next to the window. Crossing my arms, I leaned over and rested my head against the round plastic table. Feng rolled out of bed on the side I'd left empty only two minutes later. He seemed surprised that I was no longer in bed next to him. With guilt in his voice, he said, "I hope you are not upset with me."

I lifted my head to give him a dirty look. "I'm tired," I said and returned to my slumped position.

He said, "You're so beautiful. I'm sorry. Can I take a photo of you?" He lit up a cigarette and grabbed his camera. I had nothing to say to Feng. I didn't end up working at Lollipop's that weekend, and I never saw Feng again.

Because Josh and I had continued speaking every day since I'd left India, he heard about my experience with Feng and warned, "You have to be careful. You don't even know these people." I had no plan to repeat the experience.

Fortunately, all temptation dissolved when Josh invited me to meet him in Miami a few months later. I had been living with Evo for four months. It had felt like the worst four months of my life. I'd wallowed in depression longer than I ever thought possible. Suicidal thoughts became the debilitating norm. The promise of reuniting with Josh restored my faith. I had a reason to live again. The one and the only person I wanted to spend every waking moment with would soon be within arm's reach, and I could finally stop holding my breath. Not only would we meet, but I'd also return to South Jersey with Josh for a week and fly out just in time for my dear friend Kendra's wedding in Chicago.

The moment we embraced was one of the most gratifying moments I'd experienced as a young twenty-something. We made love two days later, diving right back into the romance we had shared before I left for India. Things were different. I was scared. I couldn't fully let him in. What if he decided it wouldn't work out? What if we were just having a brief affair? It seemed too good to be true. How could I be sure it was real? After spending only a week in the home we'd played house in for nearly a year in the past, I left Josh and South Jersey. Even though he has said he wanted to pick up where we'd left off. We discussed our new life and laid out all of the priorities, one of which was getting me a car. Going back to Wisconsin meant getting back to the grind.

I had to start getting financially stable after almost a year of earning little to no income. Josh was back in my corner where he'd always been, though I was reluctant to acknowledge it. I also knew in the back of my mind that unhealed wounds (from the unstable first few months together) would perpetuate our volatile dynamic. I moved in with my friend Erin, who also wanted to make as much cash as she could as fast as she could. Together we committed to working every night until I could buy a car. We started at Club Brickle. Having braved the clubs in Florida and Jersey, I had a new sense of confidence as I circled back to where I'd begun. Josh bought me a book called *Strip Success in a Few Steps* by Jenna Smith and coached me on upsell and the importance of mindset in a sales position.

Something in me had shifted. Erin and I worked almost every single day for an entire month. After completing the book Josh bought me and private email coaching from the author (an exotic dancer herself), I broke through the ceiling. It was a Saturday. Operating outside my usual M.O., I took a man who was betting me that I couldn't "get him off" to the VIP. Because I was willing to do more than usual to make as much as possible, as fast as possible, I said "fuck it" and accepted his challenge. Recalling the advice from the *Strip Success in a Few Steps* book, I blew hot and then cold. I made it seem as if I was attempting to get him off, and he was winning. Because he was winning, we had to extend our thirty-minute VIP session to one hour, then an hour and a half, and eventually two hours. At $200 per half hour, that bet moved me up to almost $1,000, the most I'd ever made in one night.

Everything fell into place. I bought a car just a few days later—another little '98 Honda Civic for $2,000, and considered using it to make another few thousand and buy a nicer car. Dancing was feeling more liberating than ever. Shifting my way of thinking became effortless. No longer would I have to say, "I can't afford it." Now it was, *how many nights do I have to work to afford it?* I began playing a game with myself: If it usually takes ten nights to get there, could I do it in eight nights or five? I felt so empowered. All right, so money can't buy happiness, but it sure helped pull me out of depression. Stripping was the training ground. As I grew, I could offer more to my clients. Mindset is crucial. It was time to get my mind right.

9

UP-LEVEL

Less than a week after Josh congratulated me on purchasing the new car, he showed up on my doorstep. He'd taken a one-way flight and asked me to drive back to Jersey with him. I was surprised and flooded with emotions. He came for me. It was such a romantic love story that played out that year. I wanted to return to Jersey with him, yet I was torn. The resistance only lasted a moment before I packed my six bags again. It caught me off guard; I was ready to grind for another few months in Wisconsin.

Bare Exposure in Atlantic City was a whole new world now. I was armed with sharpened sales techniques. No more sitting with customers for hours talking without getting paid; no more lap dances or VIPs without a tip. Old habits and patterns snuck in often, but the difference was that I had a stripper coach who helped me reroute, thanks to Josh. Jenna Smith, an exotic dancer, wrote the stripper success book. I began our three-month-long email thread on July 13, 2009:

> Hello Jenna,
>
> I have so many questions I don't know where to start! First off, it is a bit strange to be asking a complete stranger these questions since the business is a bit hush-hush and at times, even though I'm doing absolutely nothing illegal, I feel compelled to ask everyone if they are authoritative figures! Having said that, is our communication secure? My first question—the problem I encountered last night for the billionth time—I have a lot of trouble leading the conversation. I tend to talk too long because I cannot redirect the conversation from friendly to, "Will you take me in the champagne room?"

Last night I spent almost an hour talking to this one guy who said finally that his friends only brought $200 collectively and he could not afford it . . . But would come back tomorrow as he didn't ever carry a card on him and the banks were closed being that it was a Sunday. I have no problem with conversation just with the direction. The club was pretty empty, so I figured I could sit and talk with him longer, but then again, I didn't know how to go about putting a price on my time. My second question is regarding the stage. We are required to remove everything by the end of the set, and I believe this kind of takes away from the allure. I believe also that pole work is what draws the most intrigue, which I have in no way mastered! Any tips on that? I'll leave it to that for now! Thanks!
Lana
Sent from my Verizon Wireless BlackBerry

Oh, how I've changed. "The business is a bit 'hush-hush.'" Here I am, writing a book about my time as a sex worker. Where did I get the idea that I had to be private or secretive? Why did I think I was doing something wrong or undignified? I've done so much work. Jenna's email response seems logical to me now, but then, it was part of a massive learning curve. I had to change the way I thought, my old useless beliefs, my shitty self-esteem, and my fear of rejection and unworthiness.

Hi Lana,

Thank you for your email. I am glad you have written and have so many questions. It is my pleasure to answer all of them.

Firstly, let me reassure you. I have taught over 200 girls mostly in America, and they have all had really great results. Also, everything we talk about is 100% strictly confidential, and only I get to read and see your email. Our communication is completely and 100% secure, you have absolutely nothing to worry about.

I am a dancer myself and not many people in my life know, so I understand about the hush-hush . . . Your details are totally safe, you can even use a fake name if you feel better. Just let me know of the situation and I will support you.

After a couple of emails, you and I won't seem like strangers. As you will start knowing me as a friend, I hope you can open up to me . . . after all, you will probably never see me, so you can ask anything you want. By the way, have you read the book yet?

Okay, the first problem you have about not redirecting the customer, I had for 3-4 months when I started . . . I would talk and talk feeling I was being polite and sweet and not ask the customer to spend money. Let me tell you what happens when you are doing this . . . It creates problems for everybody . . . firstly to the customer . . .

1) The customer gets you to talk to him so he is feeling great . . . but after 10 minutes or so because he can feel your tension, he is not having a lot of fun anymore . . . also there is nowhere it is going, so it goes stale and uncomfortable . . . Don't think the customer cannot feel your own battle within yourself. There are some customers who will take advantage of that, and others who will wonder why they are not having fun with you . . . both lead you not to make money . . . so the customer needs to follow a path that leads to his enjoyment

2) Now, what you are doing to the club and other girls . . . When you are sitting there giving away your time and effort for free, the club where you work is not making any money as the guy is not letting loose and spending money in the VIP . . . This is not a bar where you are a girl who they can try and chat up . . . Guys know when they come to a club like this they have to spend money . . . that is a given . . . You don't want to be the Freebie they think they have been lucky enough to get, do you?

Also, you are letting the other girls down because if you are giving it away for free, why should they pay? The club and the girl's value decreases . . . this is not a good thing . . . so please don't do this

3) Next . . . what it does to you . . . You approach a guy really sweet and having fun, the guy feels attracted to you, you are getting along, but after 10 minutes you know this should be going somewhere and you are more worried about what you are going to say to him about spending money than giving him a great time . . . If you have read my book, my no. 1 priority is to give the guy a great time . . . so that is not happening. You are feeling uncomfortable, and he can feel this . . . You feel like it is becoming harder and harder to do this and end up feeling like crap . . . You finally leave the customer and approach the next one feeling like crap because of the last customer and end up in the same circle . . . am I right?

I have been there so don't worry . . . you just need to change your beliefs on some things. If you think about the best situations in life, they are win-win. Well, if you are doing your job properly, it would mean you approaching the guy, giving him a great time, getting him to spend money, your club makes money, and you make money . . . everyone wins. Do you think if you look at it like that, you will feel more comfortable asking and redirecting the customer? Before you approach your customer, you need to put a price on your time. It costs ____ for 1/2 hour and ____ for an hour. Always approach your customer with it in your mind that you are going to spend an hour with him in the VIP room and that is how you will approach him . . .

Just because it is quiet in the club, doesn't mean you have time to talk to him . . . you need to get him to spend more . . .

If you haven't read my book yet, you will know what to say to customers, but more importantly, I need you to change your beliefs about why it is a good thing for you to get money from your customer. Have I done that yet? I agree that removing everything on the pole takes away from the allure . . . do you have to do that?

About pole work . . . Some clubs put a lot of emphasis on that and others do not. Do girls who are good on the pole get tipped well? If not, don't worry if you are not great . . . I am not so good. I just scan the room and look sexy and make eye contact when I am on the pole. I see it as a time to hunt, but different clubs vary. If in your club you earn more, it would be worth you taking a few pole dancing classes. They are everywhere now.

I hope what I have said has helped and I will speak to you soon,

Jenna

The email thread with Jenna went on until September, and I didn't reach out again for three years. I couldn't have predicted at the time that her coaching would not only support me in making more money in the club but would also give me the tools to be more confident and adventurous in all of my endeavors. Shifting belief patterns to make more money as a dancer sounds so small. I was shifting belief patterns to step more fully into my power as a dancer and as a woman.

My next endeavor was as a yoga instructor. It was a fundamental concept. I had to believe I was good—truly believe it—or no one else would. Josh and I went to an immersive, month-long yoga teacher training in October, just a few months after I moved back to live with him in South Jersey. During the training, dancing faded into the background.

Once again, the dream of becoming a world-traveling, humanitarian yoga instructor moved to the forefront. In 2009, Kripalu Center for Yoga & Health offered a profoundly transformative two-hundred-hour yoga teacher training. As if I was ready for another opportunity for transformation after an entire month-long, immersive, on-site training, I jumped into the first of many workshops to explore sexual energy.

The weekend following the training, Josh and I enrolled in a beginner's level Tantra workshop with the founders of TantraNova Institute. I had been fascinated with Tantra since a girlfriend told me her best love-making experiences had been with a guy who was a student of this philosophy and practice. We had worked together at Willy Street Co-op. We were in our early twenties, and this idea intrigued me. My relationship with my high school sweetheart, Lee, had always been on and off, with a few random, casual encounters with other people. Since I'd lost my virginity at fifteen, there were no riveting stories of mind-blowing sexcapades. With what we'd learned in the yoga teacher training and the TantraNova workshop, a whole new world of possibility opened up for me as a female, lover, and sex worker.

After that first weekend, Josh and I were hooked. We continued to work with Freddy and Elsbeth, the founders of TantraNova. We were so inspired by the Tantric practices and the magnetic teachers we'd found that we began moving toward becoming teachers ourselves. We started assisting with the weekend and week-long workshops. The practices started becoming second nature. Freddy and Elsbeth became close friends. I would tell Freddy each time we met that I was still dancing to make money, and he'd always have genius ideas of how to get creative in business and give up my stilettos (or make more money in them). When I started webcam modeling, he suggested teaching Tantric practices to my viewers. I figured it couldn't hurt to bring these ideas into the clubs. It certainly worked out well from behind my computer screen.

The Gold Club in San Francisco was the first club I tried in Northern California. The dancers received little pink Caboodle boxes as purses. Somehow it was legal to demand that we carry these boxes with a thin slot cut out of the front to slide in cash. Dancers were not allowed to touch money or we'd be "fired" (yet another quasi-illegal practice), so customers had to place all cash inside the box through the thin slot. The "house mom" would lock zip ties on the boxes so that the girls couldn't open them before checking out, and they were cut open at the end of the night. That was when the money was counted, and 40% would go to the club on top of tip-out for the staff. I played the game for less than a month and felt like an indentured servant. We were forced to carry these boxes, developed a fear of handling cash, had to schedule in advance, and were required to take three slow nights or day shifts each week as new hires.

My inability to adhere to their strict policies forced me to seek other options, and I found Cheer's Gentlemen's Club in Sunnyvale in early 2012. Once again, I wasn't impressed with the scheduling options (or lack thereof), and a month later, I received a text from the manager that read, "You don't need to come back." Although most exotic dancers are "independent contractors," they are rarely treated as such and are often managed like employees, except in Las Vegas. I felt I had no option but to travel to that exotic dancer mecca.

I'd heard girls rave about Vegas since I first started dancing. Josh came with me on that first trip and accompanied me on the crazy mission to get my sheriff's card and a business license and find a club that would hire me. This wasn't an issue, as we found out. All the clubs had a revolving door and were always hiring. Sapphire was my first Vegas club. Arriving at this massive venue made me feel like a star. The private rooms resembled upscale hotel rooms, with elevator access from the main floor. Not only did the sheer size of the club shift my perspective, but I was also given special treatment only one day after being hired. The owner's son managed the club and invited me to go out on "promo," which meant lavish dinners at casino restaurants with a few other girls to promote the club. We would have dinner, then walk around the casino in our sexiest, shortest black dresses to rouse some interest and bring people back to the club. We filled the party bus a few times, but more often, we returned to Sapphire with the same number of people we'd left with.

Two out of the nine times I went out on promo for Sapphire, a petite Latina accompanied me with larger-than-life-sized breasts who went by the name of Daisy Delfina. She may have been the first to spur my curiosity in the art of FinDomme or financial domination. Daisy had made herself a name in the sex industry, and I was eager to learn her ways.

Over those dinners, I asked her to teach me and listened closely to every word. Learning about her approach opened up a new world of possibilities. I'd already dabbled and played with the idea of taking on the role of a dominatrix, quickly finding I couldn't play the role if it meant degrading the sub. Verbal abuse always felt like a blow to my psyche. Daisy employed tactics that felt more endearing, which I translated as feminine empowerment. She'd been in the business for more than a decade and was still going strong. Her financial success was compelling. She was respectable and treated her clients with respect. Her approach was classy. Moving into this new climate called for an upgrade to my modus operandi. Daisy was the perfect role model.

I sent an email to my stripper coach, Jenna, after being hired at Sapphire:

How are you?! I met a friend of yours, Daisy Delfina! You do know her, yes? She mentioned you while we were getting acquainted and I was asking her for tips—VEGAS specific! I have only been here a week and started at Spearmint Rhino, then tried out Sapphire where I met Daisy.

I believe it was luck and my own positive expectation. As soon as I walked in, I had the owner's son grab me for promo! It was a lovely way to be welcomed to the club and to get familiar with Daisy. She really is a pro!

My how-to exotic dancer book is in my bag, and I've been referring back to our correspondence and, of course, the book. I'm leaving in a few days, and with all expenses, I'm only at 1k profit right now! WHEW! Vegas is rough! The secondhand smoke is really what's sucking the life! I'm just not getting those big spenders—I'm ready to get hypnosis training or NLP!

Spearmint Rhino (Tuesday)	$160 : X
Sapphire (Thursday)	$580
Sapphire (Friday)	$900
Sapphire (Saturday)	$600
Treasures	$380

I started feeling like there were too many girls with too much silicone at Sapphire and I might do better at a club where I really stand out?! It did seem a bit better, but the club itself was a bit of a downgrade.

I am so determined to make at least 5k before I depart. I have to break through! Sometimes, when I start feeling discouraged, I just start from the front of the room and talk to every guy (except the ones who clearly look like they're not worth talking to). One tip?!
Hope all is well and wonderful!
Xxxo

Unfortunately, all of those promo dinners did not support my financial endeavors. I was merely experiencing the perks of being a dancer in Vegas, which I later learned was a ploy for the manager's son to indulge in his desire to sleep with new dancers. Daisy offered her phone number and some guidance in optimizing my time in Vegas. I considered the lost time a win, as I'd met someone who had been consistently successful in the industry.

From Sapphire, I moved to Treasures, a sizable club off the beaten path. My experience at Treasures was more fruitful, but I also had more opportunities to utilize my unique skills as a Tantra practitioner. Each club attracts a particular type of clientele. For some reason, Treasures was where I would connect with many solo-traveling tech geeks and the like from Silicon Valley. Odd that I'd traveled hundreds of miles from home to find my neighbors. Treasures was also where I got acquainted with what it meant to work in Vegas.

The girls who lived and worked in Vegas lived this superlative exotic dancer lifestyle. They'd have the bouncers, door guys, club promoters, valet guys—basically anyone who would encounter potential clientele—working for them. One of the bouncers at Treasures instantly took a liking to me and offered to send me clients, and the valet attendant gave me his cell number before parking my car the first night. This was a new hustle for me. They'd help me make money because the more I made, the more I could tip them in return for their support. Still sharpening my sales skills at that time, it was rare that I'd close a deal. They'd often send me to high rollers who were perhaps looking for a good time in the club but mostly looking for a girl who would visit their hotel room after work. My unwillingness to do so was apparent right off the bat. They didn't waste any time asking for what they wanted.

If it weren't for my fear of becoming the victim of a horror story, I might have given these propositions more consideration. Still, Josh and I had agreed that, for him to feel comfortable with this work, I would not meet anyone outside of the club. With these opportunities off the table, I had to sharpen my skills in spotting the high rollers on my own. And not just the high rollers, but the high rollers willing to spend without any strings attached. Without the assistance of the hosts or the promise of fulfilling a sexual fantasy in private, my clientele was confined to a small niche. Who were the men who came to the club just to hand over a stack of bills to that chosen one?

Only a handful of times did I approach someone with the promise of sexual pleasure; in fact, I can only recall one time I approached a man and whispered, "come play with me," in his ear after first introducing myself with a handshake. He was undoubtedly disappointed I had meant only the typical VIP playtime. I had observed the girls in Vegas who would plop down on someone's lap, lean in close to place the perfect curvature of her breasts just below his chin, and stroke his hairline with long, sharp, acrylic nails while speaking softly in his ear. It was never my style. That sharp blow of rejection can't hit as strong if there is more distance between us. If I fully revealed myself and was dismissed, I'd often have to take a moment to rebuild myself before seeking the subsequent encounter.

My tactic has always been genuine. A girl-next-door appearance, moving in close without trying to intimidate, the intellectual allure to get them hooked, and uninhibited sensual exploration to keep them engaged. I try to find something about them that I can connect with as fast as possible, be it their love of travel, childhood stories, unlived sexual fantasies, or the simplicity of everyday life. Sometimes I'd skip over the seduction and let loose with unabashed humor.

Vegas became my university, my informal education. The moment I began, the heat was on. The clubs are cut-throat, and the girls can be ruthless. It wasn't unusual for a girl to slide in on the opposite side of someone I'd be in dialogue with and redirect his attention to her. I remember sitting next to a customer in the bottle service area. A girl came and sat on his lap, interrupting our conversation. He was so intoxicated I'm not sure he understood what had happened. Had confrontation been in my nature, I may have had a few words for her, but that's not my style. I never engaged in dramatic interactions or initiated altercations with the girls. Navigating this jungle of aggressive females became an art form. In essence, it's all an art, every part: accurately identifying a target clientele, captivating them within minutes, keeping them engaged as long as possible while allowing them to return one day, and all of this while maintaining peace with the competition. It is all an art.

Every few months, there would be a surprise. A new learning experience would emerge, like the night I truly became acquainted with the power of BDSM and, more specifically, "Findom." After meeting Daisy Delfina and having success webcam modeling as a dominatrix, I felt more comfortable playing this role. For a brief stint, this persona suited me well. I loved standing out because I was wearing thigh-high leather boots, a sleek black mini skirt, and black accessories, even though the infamous manager (John) of Spearmint Rhino always gave me shit about it. "You know, you'd look much better in a two-piece," he'd belt out as I hurried past the entertainer entrance, where he'd sit at the back of the club. I would look back to acknowledge him but act as if I was in a rush and keep walking. I'd bounced around a bit when I first started out in Vegas, from Sapphire to Treasures and, eventually, I made Rhino my only club.

In March 2012, I started dancing in Vegas. By late 2012, I'd learned that Rhino was the "best club" with the wealthiest clientele. My friend Destin had connected me with a couple who lived in Vegas, and they educated me as they'd lived there for years. It only took one night at Rhino to confirm that it truly was the best. The micro-celebrity strippers were all at Rhino, and the competition kept us all on our game.

After one month of being inactive in the system, we'd have to "re-audition" at Rhino. I had to do this countless times. Not once did I have any issue getting re-hired for the same shift. However, I watched a handful of girls walk back to the dressing room in tears after interfacing with John. Girls would wait to "audition," which meant walking to the back door away from John perched on his barstool next to the check-in podium. I remember one girl making her last two steps back toward John after the ignominious six-foot shuffle.

He said to her, "I thought I told you to start going to the gym?"

She replied, "I have been going! That was three months ago. I've been going every week."

He glared at her and replied, "Oh no, you haven't, sweetheart. You can come back and try again in a few weeks."

The girl turned red and said thank you as he handed back her ID and walked back into the dressing room in tears, which wasn't an uncommon interaction. John turned away overweight girls or those with noticeable stretch marks, cellulite, too many facial piercings, and other unattractive aesthetics. Little did I know it was all an act. John and I later became friends outside of the club, and I never feared his snarky commentary again (we'll save this story for a sequel)! It all made sense to me, and there is a fantasy that Rhino sells—the girls *do* have to look like they'd walked right off the set of a *Playboy* shoot (if they were on the floor before 3 A.M.).

Back to Dominatrix Vida. I'd been making my rounds in the 18,000-square-foot Rhino in Las Vegas on a Friday night. It was early, so the club wasn't packed yet or clouded with smoke. I had worked the night before and was a bit tired, not entirely on my game. I needed that surefire momentum of fifteen to thirty minutes in the VIP to get the ball rolling, and I was starting to get anxious, noticing the time passing. I had already assessed the patrons seated around the main stage, the three tables with bottle service opposite the "celebrity booths" maroon velvet curtains, and the solo creepers hiding in the corners. Just as I was about to give up and head into the dressing room for a ritual with my matcha latte, I noticed a dancer girlfriend of mine sitting with a heavyset gentleman wearing a black polo with a tiny logo on the right breast that read "Google." I flashed a smile as I walked past the two-person table, noticing they were facing my path to the dressing room and already had their attention on me. My black leather Tony's shoes were brand new, which meant my right pinky toe was numb, and I could feel the pain and tension tightening my lips, resulting in an inadvertent RBF (Resting Bitch Face). Perhaps this worked in my favor as I attempted to reveal my inner domme through outer appearance alone.

I made it five steps past the table before my friend called me back over. "Vida!" I turned as if surprised, noticing their eyes on me. She continued, "Someone would like to meet you." As she stood, she said, "I'll let you two take it from here." Before we could begin speaking, my mind was flooded with imaginings. *He wants to offer me an island for sex. He's going to ask me to come to his hotel room. He wants to be friends. We're going in VIP, and he's going to be raunchy and ask to put his fingers inside of me.*

I had no idea what was coming, but I could feel this interaction would be different than usual. He began with, "I noticed you earlier and knew I needed to meet you."

With a coy smile, I responded, "Did you?"

He continued, "Yes. I'd like to spend some time with you. Though I'd like to get to know a bit about you first."

My bullshit meter sounded like an ambulance had pulled up to our table. *Should I stay here? Does he want to have an hour-long conversation? Will he ramble forever and eventually say goodbye without any monetary exchange?* I took a deep breath, and my intuition took over. This man is The One. Every night there's just one—the one that makes the night. He's the one. So I sat. We chatted. He wanted to feel me out. After ten minutes, we headed to the thirty-minute booths.

We ordered our drinks, my usual Kir Royale and his vodka on the rocks. They were left untouched. I began as I always do, on his lap with my back to him, my hands sliding down the front of his shins to massage the anterior tibialis, that special spot that never gets attention—a new sensation for most guys and a way to build a sense of intrigue for me.

A high percentage of men who visit strip clubs are highly kinesthetic. They're seeking physical sensation until they realize I offer mental stimulation. He stopped me. "Have you ever dominated anyone?"

I smirked. "Yes, I have. Why do you ask?"

He explained he used to see a domme who would threaten to stop returning his calls if he didn't get into shape. From a humble, vulnerable place, he explained he was unhappy with how he'd gotten caught up with work, becoming so income-driven that he'd neglected his health practice and had become obese. He asked if I'd be working at Rhino on October 17 for us to rendezvous. He vowed to get in tip-top form by this date and wanted me to hold him to it.

I slid off his lap and tucked my fingers into his belt, pulling hard to release the bar buckle. I swiftly slid the belt from around his waist and, clasping each end in my hands with a firm grip, pressed the leather strap against his neck. "What is it that you're going to do?"

With an obedient expression, he whispered, "I'm going to have a six-pack by October seventeenth."

I crawled up on the booth, straddling him, and demanded, "Tell me again."

He never took my information, and I didn't offer it. The plan was to meet three months later in October. Though he tipped me generously, and I appreciated the opportunity to motivate someone to reclaim their health, I didn't make it back to Vegas. However, this interaction opened me up to a whole new world.

10

SEX WORK = LIGHT WORK

As the years went by, my mind developed new interests and a new focal point, which showed up more often. Not long after my experience with the sub who wanted to lose weight, I met a self-proclaimed "Shamanatrix," and that she was. Such a fitting title. We have to adopt these powerful labels from other cultures as they seem to be missing in the English language. Through unique circumstances, I ended up in this woman's home. She asked if I had ever been interested in becoming a dominatrix or tried it out. I was fascinated, though I worried getting myself into a routine of domination could bleed into my life, as stripping already had. Besides, Josh wasn't particularly thrilled with the idea. My deepest desire had become stepping out of the shadows. I did not want to live a double life anymore. If I didn't shed this layer of myself, I felt it would eventually drag me down. Becoming a professional dominatrix felt like another life hiding in the darkness. I chose not to visit her dungeon then, though I knew that eventually, I would. I *did* decide to befriend her, which led to a profound opening in my life. After years of inner-world exploration with plant medicines and psychedelics, Domina Colette, AKA the Shamanatrix, birthed Colette Pervette. Our mission was to bring light work into the shadows, fully aligned.

A few years later, while feeling the expansive, euphoric waves of MDMA coursing through my system, my eyelids fluttered, and chills ran down my spine as Colette's words traveled through the pinholes of the microphone. "I love you so much!" It was the third birthday party I'd attended to celebrate her birth in the San Francisco Bay Area. Her message was to sex workers. I closed my eyes, and a white screen appeared behind my eyelids. Black ink splashed onto the screen, and text appeared: "SEX WORKER." Then, a red "X" appeared "~~SEX~~ WORKER." The word "LIGHT" replaced "SEX," and the words "SEX WORKER" became "LIGHT WORKER." The resonance of Colette's speech was potent. It was confirmation. The plants, the psychedelics, the medicine work—it urges one to uplift all others in the field. Colette, a conscious, empathic being with altruistic intentions, offers her services as a domme with reverence. A true example of a conscious sex worker.

Around the same time I began working in Vegas, I got back into webcamming. I'd first created an account on the infamous "My Free Cams" back in New Jersey in 2010. I abandoned my account until I felt the financial pressure of living in Silicon Valley. The male half of my beloved Tantra teachers shared that their assistant had been making thousands of dollars as a webcam model. "She just logs on, and an hour later, she's made a grand!" Whether it was beginner's luck or I just believed I could because of my teacher's story, I made $800 in my first hour on cam. A man in his late fifties had been drinking and watching cam girls and found me. Being inexperienced, I dove into a philosophical conversation about life instead of launching into a striptease or masturbating. For some reason, he took me "private," paying somewhere from $2-3 per minute.

I was thrilled with this earning potential and kept coming back to webcamming. Quite a few viewers followed me off the sites, and I'd get paid directly for Skype shows, feet photos, and videos. I was never consistent enough to build a following. I also wasn't keen on public self-love performances. My tantra teacher had another suggestion. Why not teach Tantric practices? I gave it a go, and this shift enabled me to increase my earnings, as I had found a niche and was much more engaged myself, able to offer something unique and intriguing. A shortlist of repeat clientele began to build.

One particular man would receive a notification when I logged on and never missed the opportunity to enter my chat room. He'd spend about thirty minutes in a private chat with me, and I'd coach him on sublimation and circulating sexual energy. During one of my public performances, a man entered my chatroom and, after tipping a generous amount and showering me with compliments, asked if I'd be interested in joining a team to beta test a new cam site as the first live cam model. I accepted and met with the creators in person, an entire team in Calabasas, California. Because this site was new and small and I had full access to the team behind the scenes, my interactions with the viewers were incredibly unique. My name at the club, Vida, was the same name I used on the cam site, though I played with changing it around—Vida Tantrika, TantrikaVida, and a few others, to make it blatantly obvious I was involved in Tantric practices. After about a year, Josh joined me on cam for a one-hour special performance that we titled "Tantric Lovemaking."

It became a routine. After a long night of working in what felt like the trenches of Las Vegas, I'd arrive back in my hotel room and log on to the cam site. It began to feel like home. My viewers *knew* me because, despite the alias, I was still myself. I talked about psychedelics, psychedelic therapy, and holistic living; I cooked and ate organic high-vibe food on cam; and I often referenced Tantric practices. After some time, a group of regulars on the site collectively chose a name for themselves and deemed themselves knights of my kingdom; they became the moderators of the chatroom. Because it is impossible to separate parts of self from self, I also brought this mentality into the club. My persona, philosophy, and demeanor were that of a goddess, a queen, and most importantly, a teacher. The dynamic between me and paying customers rarely shifted. I intended to teach them something new and valuable (hence my article published on Medium.com and the following story, *The Pinnacle*).

I liked to stay alone when I worked in Vegas to stick to my particular routine and avoid indulging in the nightlife scene. On one trip to Vegas, I stayed in a renovated efficiency I found on Airbnb. On the second day of my trip, my girlfriend Katie flew in for a convention. It was the first time I had a close friend who wasn't working with me in the city. The temptation to skip work was strong. I'd take any excuse not to work. This is a journal entry from April 19, 2015, one of the last days I spent working in Vegas:

> . . . woke up sore and bothered that I'm in LV but slept better than I normally do here . . . I think. The neighbor's music is still loud as hell. He's screaming profanities. They're knocking on his door. This place is hood. I guess it's good to stick with what you know. I'm super depressed. I have to pull myself out of the slump. I'm not loving being here right now. I feel like such an idiot. I have a million resources and ways to make money, but I'm here, doing this. This makes me feel dumb. I called Josh, and I couldn't stop crying. I don't even know if he understands. Maybe this relationship isn't going to get me out of this cycle I'm in. I really want a change. I want a new life.

During this trip, I was microdosing with Ibogaine in supplement form. It turned out to be a terrible idea. Iboga is an aphrodisiac, and it works pretty well on me. With Iboga or Ibogaine in my system, arousal sparks and skyrockets within seconds. How I wasn't aware of this, I'll never know. I knew it helped keep me awake, enabling me to work from 10 P.M. to 8 A.M.

Interacting with celebrities had been fairly frequent in Vegas. This time was unique because I had no idea who this person was. Months before, I had left Rhino at 4 A.M., delirious, ready to be done. As I waited for the valet to pull up my car, Tom was outside with his brother, waiting for their car as well. Tom looked at me and said, "Why don't you smile? I'm sure you have a pretty smile."

Tightening my lips over my teeth, I replied, "I'm just tired." I had no interest in conversing with him. As the brothers sped off sixty seconds later, I glanced over at the bouncer who'd been watching our interaction and rolled my eyes.

He said, "Do you know who that is?"

"Should I?"

He pulled out his phone. "Let me show you." He pulled up a YouTube video of Beyoncé and pointed out the brothers. I shrugged my shoulders. I had never heard of them. Though intrigued, I was too tired to muster up an ounce of enthusiasm.

In April, he appeared again. This time he asked for a floor dance. Rarely did I accept offers for floor dances, but I was feeling hopeless and fatigued and wanted to make a last buck before leaving. My focus was less on the performance and more on how I could transition into that conversation I'd played out in my head after that first night I'd met him.

You're a great dancer, and I've wanted to reconnect with my training as a professional dancer for years now. Do you offer classes or lessons? I had the whole conversation planned out in my head. If I'm going to rub shoulders with people with incredible skills, why not connect with them? This wasn't the only quality I saw in him that I hoped to emulate. He was bilingual and made music. As a young girl, I'd always dreamed of being a professional dancer, performing on stage, microphone in hand.

When the song ended, concluding our single floor dance, I pulled out my phone to check the time. He asked to see it, slid it out of my hand before I could respond, dimmed the light on the screen, entered his name and number, and called himself so quickly, it was as if he'd done it a thousand times. His speed blew my mind. Unbeknownst to me, this guy and his brother frequented the Rhino and had been working on projects in Las Vegas for months. Hundreds of dancers at Rhino had interacted with them. The evening was crazy. That same evening, I spent a half-hour in VIP with another customer and witnessed demons crawling out of the paintings on the walls. I didn't feel high physically, but the visual hallucinations told me otherwise.

April 21, 2015: I couldn't work. I was freaking out. All day. Going nuts. What am I doing with my life, is my relationship worth more effort? Should I give up and live the life of a Vegas exotic dancer and hang out with the celebrities and millionaires who pursue me at the club? What a nightmare. I hate pondering these things. It makes me feel like my life doesn't have meaning. But then I wonder if this is the meaning. Thank God Katie is coming and I have someone to talk to. Perfect night. Kels and I went to a club, and to the Rhino with her friend Ahmed. It was really nice. It was nice to stay at Encore and to be treated to dinner. If Josh and I weren't together, I could live this life. Katie asked, why can't I live it now? I don't think I fully explained to her what "this life is." I think she just wanted me to enjoy myself, because it was clear that I wasn't. I wasn't doing anything wrong and I certainly wasn't doing anything with the guy . . . I guess she's right and I need to discuss this with Josh. It's just different so I get scared. Thus, I texted Tom Burns to hang out. With Katie. This way it wasn't like we were alone. It was strictly a friendly meeting. That felt good to me. Though nothing transpired with that. We stayed up till 4 and I was upset with myself for eating too many cashews before bed. Ahmed wants me to be his personal trainer for an iron man. Oh my God. I don't think I have the skills.

April 22, 2015

I have D [Katie's English bulldog] today. I'm glad. It's nice. I keep waking up and going back to sleep. It's like I'm never going to feel completely rested. Weirdest feeling ever. I brought D to Katie after my hair appt and went to work. Here I go writing about shit in my journal again for Josh to find. It's so challenging to wake up every morning in a state of panic, thinking that he's already going through my personal messages and intimate thoughts. The pot is brewing and he's going to explode in a fit of rage. Something has to give. This time I am going to tell him though [before he reads it], this isn't a secret. I wasn't looking to do something evil. I was genuinely feeling like dreams were coming true. Tom said he had called last night. I must have had my phone off already. I said we could hang out tonight. I was excited because I know Katie is so good at forming relationships with the opposite sex with no question of it becoming something else. This is a new thing to me because I feel very constricted by my relationship. I left work feeling like crap, not having made enough, but got a major ego boost from the manager who said, "You look great in a one piece, but it's eye popping when you're wearing a two-piece." He said, "Wear a two-piece and watch your money. See what happens with your money." I said okay and went to change. I didn't make much more and gave up around 1 A.M., which was the plan all along because I just wanted to go hang out with Kels and wasn't super attached to what would happen with Tom. He did text me around 2 . . . He came and met up with us, and we talked about what he was doing in Vegas, and had dinner. Then I drove him and Katie and her vending friend Hector back to their places, and he was last because he was the farthest. He told me that he was into me and I said, "I'm sorry I just want to be friends," and I think it pissed him off. Or maybe it didn't and I'm misinterpreting. This is why I am married. [Or should I say committed, as we were never legally married. Our spiritual wedding with the Indian saint "Ammachi" was official enough for us.] Guys are so confusing. I don't want to try to figure this dynamic out with anyone else. I feel so weird about this. I need to tell Josh, but I am not sure how to keep it from being some weird issue because it's totally not.

When we met up that night, Tom kissed me. It wasn't as if I'd refused—I kissed him back. This was something I'd never done before. I'd wanted to kiss perhaps one or two men I'd met at that club, but I never acted on it. This time I did. What changed? I was uncertain. Everything was moving so fast. The truth was that my relationship with Josh had been over for years. I was just too scared to leave. I fell into the belief that I would never find anyone else. The many times I heard from him that I was mentally unstable became a self-fulfilling prophecy. If I truly existed in a state of delusion, how would anyone else ever love me?

I'd already struggled with being unlovable. It wasn't a stretch to believe he was my one and only forevermore. My desire to connect with the infamous womanizer Tom was a deeper desire to sabotage a painful dynamic because I couldn't figure out how to walk away. My blueprint was laid for chaos, and I grasped it with everything I had.

> April 26, 2015
>
> Today was beautiful and fucking horrible. Tom sent me a text around 4 and said that he was in SF and I could come hang out. This is so fucked up. Josh is the one who saw it first. I had to explain. It was time. I did an okay job but then crashed and burned as he heard me say that I am interested in exploring a sexual dynamic with someone else. This is a nightmare.

Did I get starstruck? Tom was a famous dancer, musician, and model. Was the Ibogaine leading me in the right direction? Was I scared of completely changing my life and running away? Was this all to learn a lesson? Was I high and making poor decisions? Was it sabotage? At the time there were no clear answers. Why did I break my agreements with Josh and meet a customer outside the club? I knew I was desperate for change; I just didn't want to admit it.

In October 2015, I drank Ayahuasca for the first time, a psychoactive ceremonial "tea" intentionally used for spiritual awakening and as a sacrament. Messages of honor, respect, dignity, and integrity flooded my being. I had a vision of myself as a queen in a grand castle, wearing gaudy attire resembling a Mantua from the late 1600s. Racing toward the three-story gatehouse doors, I stood my ground and allowed no one to enter without my permission. The vision melted into a view from the inside. I saw my entire reproductive system as a sacred cave filled with crystals, semi-precious stones, and geometric patterns in every color visible to the human eye. A voice said, "You are sacred. Your temple is sacred. Honor your temple. Allow none to enter without permission, devotion, and reverence. They must earn the key to unlock this sacred temple. You are a high priestess."

The message was clear. Respect from others could only be felt through a reflection of deep respect for myself. Unsurprisingly, my interactions with the men I met in strip clubs became an entirely new exploration after experiencing the force of this medicine. That first experience with Ayahuasca solidified the practice I had developed while working in the club. I had already accepted and utilized the power of conscious touch and clear intention because of yoga, meditation, my studies of Eastern religions, explorations into the metaphysical, and early use of psychedelics, even without knowing it. When I was on point, I intended to see the boy inside of the men I would meet at the clubs and connect with these "wounded warriors" in a way that offered healing. The presence of any woman who is wholly embodied and in tune with her feminine power is healing in itself.

In my yoga studies, I learned the word "Namaste" and understood the translation as "the divine in me acknowledges the divine in you." I imagined I saw the divine in these men before me, and I would energetically send them love through my thoughts and connect with their hearts by consciously placing my left hand on their hearts during the private dance. I see this connection in my most elevated visions as my offering for a more loving existence. Imagine if we all saw the divine in one another . . . Also, imagine being surrounded by hundreds of individuals who do not share this vision. The day I found my tribe of goddesses who shared my vision, I was elated.

That first experience with Ayahuasca was not my last. The series of three ceremonies in three nights set the foundation for a lifetime of personal exploration with this powerful brew. As I cultivated my connection with this medicine, my path led me to another Amazonian medicine called Kambo. This substance is a secretion from the *Phyllomedusa bicolor*, or Waxy Monkey Tree Frog, that lives high in the canopy of the Amazon. Kambo is not psychoactive and is different from Ayahuasca. Still, my experiences with this medicine have supported me in healing and reconnecting to my sacred space, the sexual center of my being, in much the same way.

I initially sought out Kambo because I was experiencing the discomfort of parasites I had picked up during my travels. Josh and I had traveled to Bali, Thailand, Cambodia, and the Yucatán Peninsula of Southeastern Mexico. My body felt as if it was full of foreign invaders wreaking havoc on my digestive system. I researched and found that Kambo has been used to combat parasites. This is an ongoing mission for me. My passion for international travel is intertwined with my passion for health and longevity. Each adventure means further investigating how to prepare for and recuperate from these travels. It helped that my herbalist mother had educated me on parasites before I could even spell the word.

It took a few referrals and some diligent searching to find a Kambo practitioner in the San Francisco Bay Area, and it was worth the effort and the wait. I couldn't have asked for anyone better. Sebastian Hansen was a twenty-something modern hippie. He understood the plant kingdom, Indigenous Amazonian traditions, Indian traditions, ayurvedic medicine, and more. He was a wealth of knowledge and a kind, positive, lighthearted man. His reverence for Kambo and how he held this sacred medicine was immediately apparent in our first ceremony in early 2016. Josh was apprehensive before the ceremony. I, too, was nervous, though I did not doubt it was what I needed. Over the years, I have learned that these types of "medicines" call to us. This has been my experience. The medicine of Kambo was calling me. We arrived at a small home in Santa Cruz at 9 A.M. The three of us—Josh, Tony, and I—sat in a circle with several others.

After Sebastian opened the circle and prayed with mapacho (pure tobacco), we received the medicine. I began with three "points:" the top layer of my skin was burned with a small twig to create three blisters that would be removed to expose the dermis, serving as the "gate" where the medicine would be placed to enter the lymphatic system. Sebastian came to each of us with his candle, twig, and a wooden stick of dried Kambo medicine he had rehydrated with water to form the small, round balls of frog secretion. When he sat before me, he asked, "Are you ready for Kambo?" I nodded, and he placed the three points of Kambo on the gates he'd burned into my lower right leg. The tingling, burning sensation seemed to last a few seconds before I felt the heat rise and my heart race. The ringing in my ears drowned out all noise in the small room.

My stomach felt as if it was being squeezed in the palm of a giant's fist. I grabbed the bucket in front of me and vomited water, then more water, followed by more water, and then bitter-sweet yellow bile. I moaned in discomfort, trembling, shutting my eyes tight, cringing from the taste in my mouth. As I rocked back and forth, the room folded in around me. Sebastian sat across from me in the circle, singing a *Quechua Icaro* (songs sung in medicine ceremonies in South America). Our eyes met, and I whispered, "Can you remove the medicine?" Fainting was rare for me, but I knew I was close. He moved toward me, but I have no recollection of the points being removed. I lost consciousness but returned feeling completely blissful and at peace. Before Sebastian closed the circle, I felt a yearning to connect my bare feet to the earth. I was the first to leave the circle, standing outside with my bare feet on the grass and face turned to the sun. Colors were brighter, sounds were more pronounced, all senses were heightened, and my mind felt clear and spacious. At that moment, I knew this would be the beginning of a deep relationship with this medicine. The entire experience was profound. The pleasure I felt following the intense discomfort is indescribable, another understanding I've come to over the years of working with plant medicines. One of my teachers says these experiences "don't English well." The truth is they simply can't be described in words.

I sat in ceremony many times with Sebastian. During the fifth time, the extent of the healing power of Kambo was revealed to me. We began, as always, with an offering of Rapé (shamanic "snuff" of powdered herbs or "ash," often with a tobacco base) and the opening of the four directions. I had worked my way up to five points and felt this was sufficient for me, as my sensitivity level with all medicines is incredibly high. I feel it before I even arrive at the space.

I made it halfway through the ceremony this fifth time, then felt my uterus cramping. The sensations were strong, and Sebastian removed the medicine as soon as I verbalized what I was experiencing. Assuming I had to use the restroom, I got up but only made it to the bathroom door before I fell to my knees in pain. Josh came into the bathroom and tried to comfort me. I grabbed his arm and gripped it tightly as the waves of shooting pain moved through me. Laying on my side in the fetal position on the bathroom floor, I cried out to God and prayed. I had to crawl from the bathroom on my hands and knees to free up the toilet for the others in the circle. I laid on the floor for another hour, writhing in pain, moaning and muttering profanities. Sebastian offered a liquid antidote that only provided a moment of relief while my mind was distracted. Some other force urged me to stay with the pain and move through it. I clenched Josh's hand as I continued to cry and pray.

For years, I've preached about keeping the temple of the physical body pure, allowing in only what's unadulterated and close to the source. I've never been an advocate for pharmaceuticals. This pain and cramping had such a hold on me that I compromised all of my values and beliefs. I downed four Advil and was open to anything else that offered even the possibility of fast relief. Eventually, the pain subsided, and my body was flooded with endorphins. Perhaps the Advil kicked in, or maybe I'd simply passed through the eye of the storm. I felt as if I'd run a marathon.

I crawled onto the outside deck of the third-story room and collapsed on the balcony. That day, I relived my abortion. What I experienced was the most excruciating physical pain I'd ever endured. When I had the surgical abortion at twenty-two, it was as if I'd left my body. I disassociated to bear the pain. The entire process was surreal, from arriving at the clinic to exiting only a few hours later. Like a memory, it feels distant, almost like a dream. I had to question if it happened—until my fifth Kambo ceremony.

I was brought back to that tiny twin bed at American Women's Medical Center on North Western Avenue in Chicago. They had warned me before going into surgery, and I had to sign a document after refusing a general anesthetic. My thought was that the abortion itself was enough trauma for the day; I didn't also need to be jabbed in the arm with a needle. I couldn't bear being operated on while I was completely unconscious. I chose to remain fully present for the entire procedure. There was no option to opt out of a local anesthetic, though it seemed ineffective when I felt the doctor prodding my insides with what felt like a sharp metal rod. It felt like an eternity before the nurse assisted me back into the wheelchair after the surgery.

They rolled me out of the operating room into a room that reminded me of something from a film I'd seen about orphanages, with two long rows of twin-sized beds opposite one another on either side of the room. From the wheelchair, they helped me onto this tiny bed, where I rocked back and forth as I cried in pain. Before the surgery, I'd ingested a copious amount of MDMA, and I tuned into that euphoric, endorphin-induced feeling underneath the pain. As I accessed that euphoria, I slowed the rocking and focused on the female on the adjacent bed. I noticed she was also rocking herself as the tears rolled down her cheeks.

These details were clearly shown to me as I relived this abortion nine years later. I walked away from that Kambo ceremony with confusion. I remember wondering if death would follow this pain. My internal dialogue had been harsh and extreme. *I will surely die if I endure this excruciating pain a second longer. Something inside me is shutting down, or an organ has ruptured, and these are my last moments.* It wasn't clear that I was reliving the abortion until it happened again, both times also in ceremony with Kambo medicine.

The second time was during the first week of training with Karen, who founded the International Association of Kambo Practitioners. The second time was just as intense, if not more so, and not only was I completely exhausted after it ended, I found a pool of blood when I went to the bathroom. There was so much blood it had seeped through my yoga pants. My skin was yellow, and the whites of my eyes had a tinge of light green. Jaundice had surfaced. I'd noticed these symptoms in 2009 when I'd returned from India with Hepatitis A. I sat with Karen that evening and discussed what may have happened.

For me, Kambo has a way of clearing out old physical and mental traumas, stuck emotions, and negative patterns. I had been suffering from menstrual cramps for most of my adult life, cramps so severe I would have to cancel life for three days during my moon cycle to lay in bed and cry while downing handfuls of painkillers. I couldn't live like this. I couldn't preach about holistic living and depend on painkillers every month. I wasn't in alignment. I wasn't true to myself. I wasn't facing the truth. I had work to do, and Kambo wouldn't let me avoid it any longer.

I didn't complete the Kambo training. The morning I walked into the ceremony space for the warrior initiation (three lots of Kambo in three hours), I was consumed with fear. My journey to healing my womb space, and ultimately my connection to my feminine power, was underway. I wrote the entire journey in detail in a four-part series on my blog to give hope to all women suffering through their menstrual cycle every month. Perhaps Kambo isn't the answer for everyone, but it was for me, and I'm certain it may be the answer for someone else. This journey to reclaim my feminine power and connect with my womb continues. Already I am far from where I was before the first Ayahuasca ceremony and first meeting with Kambo medicine.

At this point, not only had I dove into healing with Kambo and Ayahuasca, I'd had an incredible multi-day journey with Ibogaine, 5-MeO-DMT, and experienced my old friends psilocybin, LSD, and MDMA in new, profound ways. The clarity and self-awareness that I'd cultivated with the support of these medicinal substances were making it more and more challenging to feel like I was just another "*zombie selling my time on this earth*" (thank you, David Goggins, for that gut-wrenching line). I recall this Jewish man standing next to the high table at the back of the club, swirling the ice in his glass cup of booze, flashing his rolex and sarcastic grin, asking me, "How long have you been doing this?" I replied without an ounce of shame, "Eight years." He replied, "You did it all wrong. This isn't a job. You do this for five years straight, and you go hard. You save all your money, make good investments, set yourself up for life, and get out of the game." At one point, I think I would have given him the finger or even a sweet smile and excused myself after that dagger. Though the countless hours I'd spend reflecting and doing deep personal work with psychedelics softened me. I was raw. I'd already looked into my eyes and said these same words to myself. I was playing small. That conversation left me feeling suicidal. I'd gotten what I needed. It was time to leave yesterday—last week, last year . . . I had to flip the script and come to the realization that this book needed to be birthed. I had to learn to alchemize these degrading encounters and feelings of defeat and rejection, into fuel.

The truth is that I have a unique opportunity to bring the teachings I've received to the sex industry through my work as an exotic dancer. The practice is a constant inquiry. How can I honor myself more? How can I be clearer with my desires? How can I be more confident in creating boundaries? How can I use my femininity to empower those around me? Working at strip clubs enabled me to create opportunities to better understand my patterns and habits, not only concerning myself but in the dynamic I co-create with others. I was to have many chances to ask these questions. While this journey back to myself was just beginning, I visited the exotic dancer Mecca yet again to discover something profound—mirrors of myself and my unfolding.

11
DAKINI DANCERS

Synchronicity played out as it always does. It was my last trip to Vegas for a long time and the best one out of nearly a hundred. Two dear sisters from other mothers, Kelsea Ernst and Ix-Chel Sandivel, had urged another Vegas dancer and me to meet, and we finally did after almost two years of passing one another like ships in the night. We were brought together, in the end, by the moon.

My heart felt heavy during this trip. I felt lonely and lost and yearned to connect with a community. A wave of relief came over me that eventually expanded into exuberance as I read an invitation to gather with women connected to a greater web of friends, from the San Francisco Bay area to Los Angeles. The text box notification on my phone from "Chelsey" had a particular heart character next to her name. Kelsea had shared her contact info with me years before, and I'd kept the heart. Chelsey Lehl has a gift for bringing women together to honor the feminine. She was organizing a "full moon ceremony" at Amy's house, where she'd lived during her time in Vegas. All of the women called to gather on that evening were gifted with their own unique acrobatic and artistic abilities and talents.

That night, I had planned to work at Spearmint Rhino, and I wasn't incredibly motivated. The night before had been extraordinarily unfruitful. Fortunately, my apprehension about working gave me more time with these women, allowing me to dive into a magical evening of play. Amy's home was the perfect vortex. I was in awe from the moment I

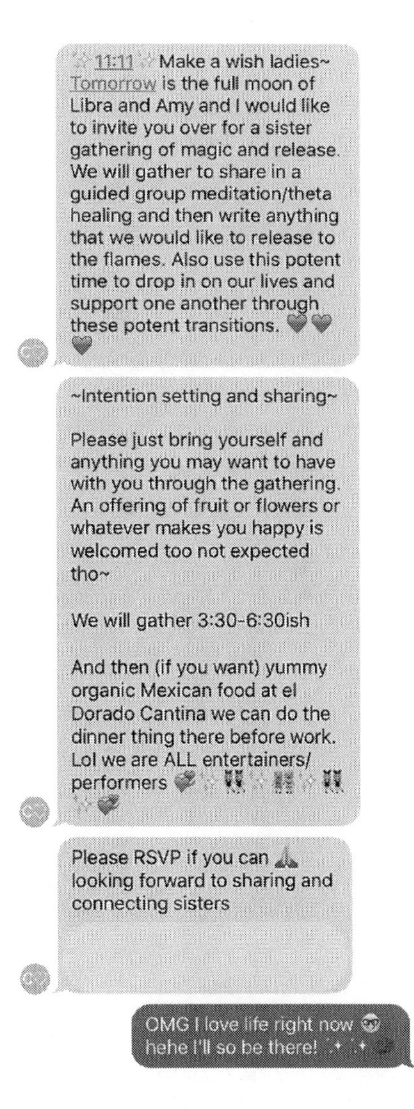

entered, seeing the twelve-foot pole in her living room next to the aerial silks and lyra hoop along with massive quartz, citrine, and amethyst crystals. Her home was a performer's playground. Across from the lyra hoop, a life-sized aqua blue mermaid tail hung on a wall. The decor made me feel like I was in a mystical, psychedelic yoga studio for circus performers, and the scent of palo santo lifted my spirit before I even removed my shoes at the door.

11:11 Make a wish ladies~ Tomorrow is the full moon of Libra and Amy and I would like to invite you over for a sister gathering of magic and release. We will gather to share in a guided group meditation/theta healing and then write anything that we would like to release to the flames. Also use this potent time to drop in on our lives and support one another through these potent transitions.
~Intention setting and sharing~
Please just bring yourself and anything you may want to have with you through the gathering. An offering of fruit or flowers or whatever makes you happy is welcomed too not expected tho~
We will gather 3:30-6:30ish
And then (if you want) yummy organic Mexican food at el Dorado Cantina we can do the dinner thing there before work. Lol we are ALL entertainers/ performers
Please RSVP if you can looking forward to sharing and connecting sisters
OMG I love life right now hehe I'll so be there!

Chelsey welcomed me and led me to the kitchen to offer a vibrant purple smoothie with a touch of this and a touch of that from each of the goddesses in the kitchen. I was one of the first to arrive, as always. The eight of us gathered in a circle about thirty minutes after I arrived. Chelsey opened the ceremony with a powerful meditation and theta activation. We each took a turn speaking and shared our intentions and what we brought into the ceremony that evening. There were tears, laughter, feelings of exhilaration, and most importantly, that profoundly intimate experience of togetherness in a somewhat isolating profession.

Waves of the sincerest gratitude moved through my being, and I shed tears of joy, which rarely happens. We drew cards, indulged in chocolate, and burned what we were ready to release, written on paper, in the fire of the candles around the altar. After we closed the full moon circle, the five of us that danced at Rhino headed to the organic Mexican restaurant attached to the other massive Vegas gentlemen's club, Sapphire. When we arrived, I was baffled that I'd worked at Sapphire for a month and never noticed there was an organic Mexican restaurant less than twenty feet from the main entrance to the club.

The girls were particular about what they ordered from the menu and how they nourished their temples. We all agreed on onion-free guacamole and sent back the first order, noticing our senses were overwhelmed with the salty flavor and spiciness (not to mention, strippers should never eat garlic or onions during a workweek). I was experiencing tremendous relief. I was in good company with powerful women, in tune with their bodies, operating on a parallel frequency. I'd found my people, and I couldn't have been happier. Toward the end of our meal, a mutual male friend joined the five of us as we headed back to Amy's mystical playground, where there was more chocolate. We found ourselves tangled in an intimate arrangement on one queen-sized bed. It was time for ancient wisdom-sharing. My eyes rolled back in my head while Chelsey stroked my hair, my head in her lap. We passed around the organic chocolate bars and listened intently as our male friend read from a book about ancient Mayan Tantric practices.

Midnight approached, and a few girls received requests from regulars to come into work. Our love bubble dispersed, and I reminded myself that all good things must come to an end. I felt as if I had received healing that night. I felt my soul being nurtured in a way it had never been. "Sister medicine" became a new phrase to me that night. I felt so deeply in love with these women, and I vowed to maintain these connections forever. Learning more about these women over the past few years has been yet another healing in itself.

Amy not only performs on the pole like a pro, but she was also trained in aerial silks, lyra, and could swim with that twenty-pound mermaid tail. She's a real-life mermaid! She's also an all-around renaissance woman. She leads workshops called "The Dance of the Divine Goddess," all about liberating women. She's studied and trained in Tantric Practices, Hatha yoga, and Ayurveda at the School of Sacred Arts in Bali, Indonesia. That evening when we first met, I discovered she was also a writer, and we vowed that evening to hold each other accountable to create and share our masterpieces with the world. Before she bought her home in Vegas, she'd traveled across the US in an RV, selling rugs and dancing at clubs. Her free spirit and devotion to her family and friends are heartening, and I'm grateful to have her in my life.

Kaya Rea, another goddess in this extraordinary circle, is a trained circus performer. I was in awe of her body when we first met. Kaya is a true nomad, always a few weeks from her next international adventure. She is currently building her empire around the principles of love, expansion, ancient Tantric practices, and plant medicines. When I called her to talk about this book, I wasn't surprised to find that we share many of the same aspirations. Her commitment, passion, and dedication to her vision of awakening have me in awe. I know that whenever I find myself experiencing the momentary shock of existential crisis, I can reach out to Kaya for words of wisdom. She's connected to her power in a way that urges others to do the work.

Chelsey, who organized that first gathering, has founded her own company to awaken the divinity in all women by connecting with their womb space through "yoni eggs." She has since become a dear friend (Ix-Chel and Kelsea, you were right), and her mission is to support the rise of the divine feminine through her company, Yoni Crystals. She has aligned with her calling to offer women ethically sourced, natural, organic gems and minerals of the highest quality for their healing and pleasure. Her mission statement: "To empower and enable women to tune in and listen to the subtle energies of their bodies and the crystals. We create new systems that are built around maintaining the health and happiness of individuals and our communities."

And just because it's so damn good and perfectly aligned with the depths of my own heart and soul, I'll also include from her website her explanation of her mission, "Why We Do What We Do:"

> To see what becomes of the world when women step into their power by choosing to learn, understand, know, love, trust, respect, honor, enjoy, and celebrate themselves through their divine feminine sexual vitality.
>
> It's really about the Yoni Temple. The creative womb space of all women who choose to do this healing, who choose their pleasure, who choose to take the crystals and program them with their heart-filled intentions and combine that with the life-giving force in the sacral sexual organs. What happens when those energies are combined?! Let's find out.
>
> This is a natural calling to help women to understand their sensual/sexual nature through the exploration of gems and minerals. We can't help but connect women to their authentic divine feminine expression. Furthermore, there are no sex toys on the mainstream market available to women that are all natural and holistic.

After getting to know Chelsey well, I learned she honors the men in her life the same way she honors women. Josh and I spent countless hours with her in one of the most transformative places on the planet—Burning Man. Because relations with others are often intimate and surreal in this setting, "getting to know" each other can happen at lightning speed. Josh revealed to me that he felt honored and appreciated by Chelsey. When he said this, I started tracking her. I noticed the way she interacted with everyone. This edification, adoration, and appreciation for others were natural for her. This was undoubtedly the same energy she brought to the club. It's no surprise she was in demand as an exotic dancer and compensated accordingly. She is real. What a gift she is. These women developed a deep connection with their divine femininity and, to me, are each fully embodied women walking through life in their power.

Ix-Chel Sandivel was the only goddess in the full moon circle that evening who I'd previously met. She was the first Vegas dancer I ever met when Josh and I had made that first trip to Vegas. The last few details we went through were getting my nails done and my indulgent blow-out for my hair. At the nail salon sat a slender Latin girl wearing a straw hat and drinking a smoothie in a recycled veganaise jar. Josh exclaimed, "Lana! Go talk to that girl. She's just like you. She's a hippie; look at her veganaise jar!" Something about her poise and presence was intimidating, and I shied away. When we got into the car, Josh double-checked: "Are you sure you don't want to talk to her? You might never see her again. I'm sure you want a friend here. What if she dances at your club?"

I said, okay, go in and ask for her number. He came back to the car with two of her business cards.

As he handed them to me, he said, "Now go in and give her yours!"

I rolled my eyes but ran in and immediately noticed she'd put a mask on to filter out the toxic smell of the nail salon (mind you, this was long before Covid). This all happened four years before the full moon ceremony. I met Ix-Chel as Claudia. I was fascinated by her unique online presence when I looked her up to learn more about this girl who felt like a sister. A blog post she had written about exotic dancing contributed to my opening as a light in this darkness. On May 10, 2012, she posted these words:

> I'm writing from the twenty-first floor of Veer Towers on the strip here in Las Vegas.
>
> I am self-initiating and dancing into the stripper world of Las Vegas as "iX-CheL Sandivel, The dakini who danced with fire." At the club I'm known as "Fuego," which translates to fire in Spanish. In many ways, I do feel like I'm dancing with fire, dancing between the fine lines of life, and bringing forth new elements in an already established toxic environment. I see myself as an undercover dakini, bringing light into the dark cigar and cigarette smoking club. Serving a missing energetic and Tantric transmission for the beings who are attracted to me and showing up in ways in which they cannot even possibly imagine, because Fuego is an authentic expression and appearance for my soul. I became a rare kind of a gem deal in a Las Vegas stripper club.

The entire post spoke to my heart and soul. As I read, the doorways of my mind opened. She concluded the post with:

> As of today, I still get emails and messages from men and women who value my work very deeply and profoundly. We are connected. I am in their heart and they are in

> mine. Together we are shifting and creating a world where sensuality, love, and all that is divine is celebrated, honored, and respected.
>
> I am so grateful for the empowerment and tools. I have walked away from being iX-CheL, the undercover dakini who danced with Fuego. I left with more than fire, wisdom, and most importantly, a deeper understanding of my gifts, the biggest gift of all.
>
> Stepping into the exotic stripper archetype is still teaching me the integration of healthy sexuality and spiritual lifestyle. This exquisite integration is the source of my creativity.

Ix-Chel had posted this soul-shaking manifesto months after I found that she was a competitive runner who had nationally ranked in the 10,000 meters and a former Nike elite runner for The Janes. She'd also performed as a dancer in music videos alongside Snoop Dogg, did a bit of acting and modeling, and created stunning art. Just like Amy, Kaya, and Chelsey, she is a woman of endless talent and skill. As the years went on, she stepped into the role of teacher and created a coaching business. She currently hosts retreats for men and women to come together and have the experience of embodying divinity through connection and sensual play.

These remarkable women supported me in maintaining the highest integrity while I worked in the sex industry. That first full moon gathering was yet another compelling sign. It was confirmed. A small community of women consciously brings Tantric spiritual practices into gentlemen's clubs. I found my tribe. I knew in my heart that, even if I never saw these women again, I was held and energetically supported by a global community of conscious women. We are each quietly going into the darkness and offering our light. This isn't to say there aren't many more women doing light work in the countless unmentioned dark corners of the world. Without question, every female sharing conscious intimacy with a man who yearns for this type of presence is a gift (and vice versa). The authentic presence of any woman can heal. I've heard it from dozens of men and felt it from hundreds. This work is sacred, and my time with these powerful women as my mirror confirmed it. The purpose and meaning in my life rapidly took shape after this Vegas trip.

12

PAID TRAINING GROUND

Cultivating and maintaining a stable relationship while working as an exotic dancer is difficult. Relationships require presence and attention; they must be nurtured, and everyone involved must be more or less on the same page. Being in an environment dedicated to temptation can be disastrous when an intimate relationship feels unstable and the mind is fragile. Navigating my internal storm of uncertainty and instability was a feat. Pulling through and coming back to baseline was a challenging learning experience. In the end, I left Vegas and switched to working at a tiny club in Silicon Valley. With my focus shifting to completing my bachelor's degree, putting more effort into my brand "The Sensual Foodist," and co-authoring a book about relationships, working at a local club was much more sustainable and respectful toward myself. The place had changed.

The manager who'd "fired" me years before was on his way out. I missed the energy and thrill of working in Vegas, especially physically connecting with the clientele. Cheer's is a "no-contact" club with no private rooms or closed spaces. The girls offer "air dances" in a shared space, visible from the main floor and stage area. The bouncers (and rule-following dancers) keep a close eye to ensure no physical contact. This dynamic left me with less to work with in terms of connecting with anyone who chose to spend time one-on-one with me. It did help me, however, to discover other means of cultivating that energetic link between myself and the customer. My voice and movement became the tools for building rapport. On a more metaphysical level, I had to step fully into my feminine power to cultivate that sense of interrelationship. A simple move that didn't raise any red flags at Cheer's was a brief hand-to-heart connection. In situations where I felt I needed physical touch to honor the soul of the man before me, I would use this touch. Though Cheer's is small, it's often fairly empty. I can do only so many moves in a tiny booth to perform a seductive striptease, and I only have so much time before I repeat the same routine and lose that titillating sense of variety and uncertainty.

After working at Cheer's for a year, the monotony started to wear on my psyche. I took a trip to Miami and tried out a few clubs. It happened to be the wrong season, which meant the clubs were pretty much empty. This left me feeling the uncomfortable pressure of an unbalanced trade of time for money. Then there was the culture of Miami. I went into the VIP with an intoxicated young man who told me I resembled his Latina ex-lover. He proceeded to slap my ass so hard the handprint was still there the next day. I immediately stopped dancing, grabbed his wrist, and said, "I don't like that. Do *not* do that again." He was so drunk he didn't take me seriously and said this was the same thing she (his ex) would do, except she would say it in Spanish. I threatened to walk out of the dance and keep the money if he didn't acknowledge my request. After making myself clear, I became softer and said, "I can teach you how to touch me and appreciate me if you want to learn. Not just me. Any woman. If they want to be slapped, then let them ask you. I do not want to experience any physical pain. I want slow, soft, sensual, and gentle." Despite his intoxication, he caught on and kept his hands to himself. He did grab my hips at some point toward the end, but the intensity and aggression had disappeared.

The Miami trip reinforced my desire to create something more uplifting in this industry. It's always the same everywhere: lots of alcohol and getting high, objectifying and disrespectful behavior, and loud, aggressive music. But Miami! Miami is a whole different animal. It's much like being in South America. The idea of a strip club is different in South America, and a lot of that mentality appears in southern Florida. That, in combination with the slow season, made it a bit of a nightmare. I could only push myself to work a few nights before I swore off Miami. A tiny brunette bottle-service girl with disproportionate "F cup" breasts at Rachel's Palm Beach tipped me off to Bourbon Street - World Famous Strip Club in Phoenix, Arizona. She had been nostalgic about a time when she worked there while living with a boyfriend. She urged me to visit and told me that she'd even put in a good word with the hiring manager. A month after I left Miami in late 2017, I gave Phoenix a shot.

Most cities have seasons. The bottle-service girl at Rachel's failed to mention that Phoenix, like Miami, was seasonal. Bourbon Street was full of breast implants. Then there was me. Then there was me walking out the door. The bottle-service girl was no help, and the manager told her there were too many girls. I think he meant to say there were too many boob jobs for me to fit in. I gave up after a few more disappointing experiences and headed to Sedona and the Grand Canyon to do some solo soul-searching. Seeing the surreal landscape and taking in the magnificent rock formations made me fall in love with Arizona. I committed to returning during high season and giving it another shot.

It took me nine months to make it back to Arizona, but it was worth it. This time I was accompanied by a top-earner at Cheer's, and we kept each other's spirits high. We caught the tail end of Spring Training in Arizona, and the strip clubs were packed. There was no shortage of upstanding gentlemen to choose from, and I experienced some of the highlights of my dancing career. It was a packed Saturday night, and I spent two hours in VIP with a young man deeply in love with France. For a moment, we were soulmates, fantasizing about a magical fairytale in France. We planned out our entire life: what we'd do each day, trips to the farmer's market to buy fresh baguettes, sharing Beaujolais wine under the Eiffel Tower on a Sunday night; it was as if we lived a lifetime together in just a few short hours. We parted ways as if we were in the last dramatic scene of a Woody Allen film.

Arizona was quaint, cigarette-free, easy to get around, and had just enough organic food to keep me fueled. The best part was Sedona. I said once that I would endure a subpar experience working in Scottsdale if the end goal was visiting Sedona again. Unfortunately, subpar became unacceptable on a third visit to Skin Cabaret in Scottsdale. The floor-dance prices went from an already low $20 per dance to $10. It was too late in my career to accept a pay cut, and settling for less wasn't an option. I'd already started at the bottom. The next best option was to give it my all at Cheer's. So I did.

My average increased. My regulars increased. My confidence increased. Consistency pays, although it pays much higher with an effective strategy. It's actually something that makes me cringe a bit. One thing I hear myself saying over and over, in my head and to others, is that I am an extremely inconsistent person. It's something I've explored in therapy. It's not in all areas of life. I wake up every morning, spray rose water on my eyes, oil-pull for twenty minutes with coconut oil, and stretch. I don't think I've missed a day in years. Despite the repetition of my "I can't handle consistency" story, I did pretty well for a while at Cheer's. I'm pretty sure I didn't miss more than one month my first year (I do have to travel monthly to maintain sanity). When I first came to the club, it was dead on some nights, yet girls still made money because they had these "regulars." I never saw myself as one of those girls. I didn't understand the concept. Why do the guys keep coming back? Isn't that like seeing the same movie over and over? Don't the guys realize nothing will ever change? The girl will never become their wife.

These girls worked every Tuesday, Wednesday, and Saturday (or some other three- to four-day arrangement), and somehow a guy would come in every Tuesday. Proximity is power, right? They'd see each other, and eventually, the customer became the girl's regular. I haven't actually gotten to where I can tell them I'm going to work every Friday or commit to once a month. It leaves me with a different, dedicated type of regular because they never know when I'm actually going to come in. They don't know if I'm going to disappear for a week or a month. Perhaps it makes me more intriguing. They're always checking the weekly schedule, hoping they'll see my name. I prefer to think of it this way because I don't see it changing. It frustrates me half the time, and the other half of the time, I feel free. Gone are the days when I couldn't be spontaneous because I was committed to being in one specific location every Tuesday.

Part of me hates it. Part of me wants to have a set, consistent schedule. It's more about the time of the day than the day of the week. I'd love to go to bed at eight, nine, or even ten every night and wake up eight hours later. It's a fantasy I've had for the past six or seven years as I've matured and felt the benefits of being in this rhythm. Those are two things that will never happen simultaneously. I will never live the life of an exotic dancer and have the luxury of going to bed before midnight. The only option is to create balance in my life in other ways and do the "deep work" to continually clear the energetic assault of working in the nightlife scene.

13
BALANCING ACT

I had less than twenty-six minutes to become fully present to hold space for deep transformational work. Josh and I had a Kambo ceremony scheduled, and six people would be arriving. Fortunately, fatigue generally leaves me when we open the Kambo circle, and I don't think about being tired or about my own needs. It's as if I can step into another version of myself. As always, the ceremony was smooth and uplifting, and we completed it in the usual three hours.

We went from the Kambo ceremony to Transform Fitness in downtown Mountain View, where we dove into an intense forty-five-minute, ass-kicking workout on a machine called the Megaformer. After class, I felt weak, almost as if I was going to faint, and had to lay down. Stress and anxiety set in. It's that familiar feeling of holding the weight of the world without any ground to stand on. In bed, Josh sat by my side and guided me to tune into my heart, release all thoughts, and feel into my body. After a few deep breaths, he asked me to respond to the question with the first answer that came to mind: Was I going to work tonight or not? I took a breath and replied, "Yes, I'm going." It felt good to be clear, though my resistance was still strong. My gut told me it was going to be a rough night. This wasn't the first time a mild anxiety attack crept in before heading to work. Being at a strip club requires a level of energy I don't always feel capable of putting out. When I feel drained, the thought of being in dancer mode brings on a flood of anxious emotion.

The guy who'd met me only a week before, who had told me he'd never been to Cheer's on a Sunday in an entire decade of visiting, showed up. I was in the back, getting ready as slowly as I had ever gotten ready. I was scrolling through Instagram, checking emails, applying makeup, eating food, arranging my things, talking to the other girls; basically, anything I could do to stall and avoid going out on the floor. One of the girls came back and said, "Vida, Ben is here."

I threw myself together and walked out in disbelief. "Hey, Mr. I-never-come-to-Cheer's-on-a-Sunday!" He said he had come solely to see me because he knew it would be another week before his next opportunity. I had told him to come to see me over email. We talked for a while before we went back to the private dance area, and I explained to him some of my philosophy and beliefs, attempting to paint a picture of my internal world for him.

This is a discussion I've had a few times while at work, and the general response is surprise or intrigue. I usually get, "What are you doing here?"

I appreciate the philosophy of "Jacq the Stripper," who I follow on social media. Do people walk up to a cashier at the checkout at the grocery store and ask them, "What are you doing here?" Jacq is a potent voice for all sex workers.

My friend Michael Ellsberg pointed out that one of her comics read, "You must have daughter issues," in response to a strip club customer telling one of the dancers, "You must have daddy issues." The awareness she brings to the world of sex work resonates with everyone I know in the industry. Mixing comedy with blatant truth is a respectable skill, in my opinion. Yes, I have daddy issues. He's struggled and suffered for his entire life, and I have not made peace with the fact that I cannot take away his pain. On the other hand, we all have something we're working on in this lifetime. Many men frequenting strip clubs are playing out not only "daughter issues" but a dysfunctional relationship with all women in their lives. Jacq has quit stripping, but her witty comics will live on forever.

To be frank, I wasn't telling Ben about my life for the shock value, even though I could have won a bet on his response. I was telling him because I was incredibly tired that all I could play out in my head was the truth, which was near and dear to my heart. This happens often. I'm exhausted because it's late, and I'm not on stimulants like so many others. I have little choice but to be honest because lies take more effort to create (and even more effort to remember). Not to mention that when I lie, I get confused. It's already enough work staying present sometimes. I've only ever lied about my home base or birth name for obvious reasons.

We had begun our conversation about what I'd done after waking and the process of the Kambo ceremony. I later realized this was way too personal. How many people are serving Kambo in Silicon Valley? I often give myself away with my honesty. It's a fault in terms of safety. I seem to attract the ones who want a real person. Big surprise. He slid into the conversation about how he was frustrated by my delayed email responses. I wanted to keep him as a regular, so I defended my delayed responses, telling him that things like the Kambo ceremony are incredibly time- and energy-consuming, and it's only one of many things I have going on in life.

He said I should check my email more often because maybe he'll be out some time and would buy me a gift. He killed his bribe when he pointed out my aversion to possessions: "You don't seem very materialistic, so it would be so hard. I can't get you something like a handbag or shoes. How would I know what to get because you don't like big corporations or name brands?"

This is one of my favorite subjects. I have felt strongly about it for over a decade. When I was thirteen, I was introduced to hemp fabric, and ever since, I have dreamed of owning an entire wardrobe of sustainable, organic fabrics from ethical companies. I love sharing this philosophy because it's difficult to debate. Once people consider the facts, they generally are inspired to seek out more conscious textiles. "Do you know how harmful it is for the planet and every living creature on it to continue supporting the use of synthetic agrichemicals on useless crops like cotton?"

Apparently, he wasn't interested in diving in to the subject with me. "I get it. So what would I buy someone who is passionate about synthetic agrichemicals?"

I explained, "This earth, our one and only true mother, provides us with everything we need to survive and thrive, and the only way we can continue to do so is by treading lightly." Then I offered a few suggestions: "I do love chocolate, but I'd prefer it to be raw and organic, from a conscious, environmentally aware company. If the packaging is paper, I'm into it." Ben smirked, and I playfully flipped my hair, poking fun at myself, to conclude my arrogant princess act.

We spent a few hours in the private dance area where I acted out my fifteen-year-old self (to shift up the energy a bit), the one who would do almost anything to get a laugh. I made my way out of the booth and threw my blanket on the floor. I carefully pulled the corners of the blanket to give myself ample space to display my flexibility through a few yoga poses. Ben protested and told me to get off the floor, slapping his hand against his forehead and rolling his eyes. I moved swiftly and kept rambling about how he would love it. I laid on my belly and rolled to my left side and then to my right, folding my arms underneath my torso. I laughed so much that I could barely catch my breath to get into the pose. I knew this wasn't the best idea, as I wasn't quite warmed up, but I was confident it would be a story for later and more compelling than the same dance I'd given him countless times. I lifted my feet and legs and curled them over until my toes touched my head while Ben shook his head and continuously muttered and laughed, "Oh my God."

I held the pose for less than five seconds before peeling myself off the floor and plopping back down on the booth next to Ben, giddy with laughter. Really, though, how many times can I shake my naked ass ten inches from his face before it loses its charm? I get frustrated with the mundane repetition and resort to any antics that come to my delirious mind at 1 A.M., as long as it's a regular in VIP. I get to be myself then. I get to act out all the bizarre scenes playing in my mind at those absurd hours. I've never been a night owl. I love the nightlife scene, but I've always loved sleeping at dusk and waking with the sun. It feels right, and the more I learn about health and wellbeing, the more I yearn to follow this rhythm. After 11 P.M., I start to get loopy, as my regulars can attest.

My favorite act always involves an invisible microphone. This began long before I started stripping. That night with Ben was yet another golden opportunity. I was fully nude by the time I whipped out my mic on our tenth or twelfth song in a row and lip-synced the entire song of

Aerosmith's "Crazy," complete with hand motions and hair flips. Ben was amused, without a doubt, but probably questioned why he was paying for this performance. After this grand finale, he decided it was past his bedtime and asked me to walk him out. We walked out of the two-song private dance area at the back of the club and circled the stage in the center of the room toward the door. We hugged goodbye, and then he asked when I'd be working again.

I offered my usual reply, "I'll text you. You know I'm never sure." He hugged me again and kissed me on the cheek before walking out. I rushed into the dressing room to grab one of my organic cotton cloth baby wipes to bring to the restroom with me and came out to find Ben back on the main floor waiting for me.

He dispelled my confused expression with, "I know it's going to be a while before I see you again, so we should do one more dance."

I laughed and replied, "Okay, but now I think you might be the crazy one!"

I feel privileged to know men appreciate a woman who is authentically herself. Ben enjoyed the quirky, weird me that doesn't hold back. I'm not always in the presence of people who honor this type of expression. Thanks to Ben, I made my average that night, yet I was so deeply torn about another night inside the walls of a gentlemen's club. As fun as some customers are and as stable as it feels to have a steady regular, there is always some risk in these interactions.

I met Raj in early February 2017. I got frustrated with him after only one dance. He asked for more eye contact. I despise eye contact when it's requested in the club. I feel like the person requesting is stepping into my personal space. I have no filter on my eyes. I am open. When someone looks into my eyes, they see all of me. I wasn't open to offering him that sort of intimacy. He wanted too much. He had claimed that he was giving me advice. He promised to see me again, and I figured I shouldn't complain if he were to become a regular, so I was cordial.

It took him less than a week to ask me to meet him outside the club consistently. I learned shortly after that he had never been to a club like Cheer's, which, in some ways, explained his lack of etiquette and naive propositions. He treated me like a girlfriend after a month. He would ask me to "miss him" via text and call once a week. His texts went from "Vida" to "baby," and every other message would be another request to meet in person for dinner, tea, drinks, any reason under the sun. A few months after I met Raj in April, I made it clear that meeting and creating a relationship outside the club was impossible.

He wouldn't take no for an answer.

For a time, things were seriously frustrating. He didn't understand that I wasn't open to any relationship, and I didn't know how to keep him as a regular. For a while, I gave up. He would see me, and I would approach everyone in the club except for him. He spent money on what seemed like every girl except me. Toward the end of one evening, I was in the two-song area with my customer, and Raj was in the back with another dancer named Dominique. This area was set up with four booths facing the other four, making eight booths in a tiny room. Each booth had its own table that fit flush with the half-moon-shaped leather cushions. When dancers performed, the customers were seated facing one another. Though the dancers were in motion most of the time in that area, they also ended up face to face for a portion of the performance. The walls were mirrored, and if one paid enough attention, it was hard to miss anything going on in the room. Raj sat in the corner booth, and Dominique finished her dance with him. I was seating my client when Dominique looked over at me and giggled, "He says you're stupid."

I responded without words, scorning him with my eyes and shaking my head. I'd managed to avoid him all night, barely acknowledging his presence until that moment. I was tired of his games. At the end of the night, he waited for me. The club was closed. He was the last one. I was in the back when three people came to tell me he was waiting, asking for me. The last person to alert me was the bouncer. I told him to convey that "I have explosive diarrhea." This was one of the few times I refused money from him. I didn't have the energy for his drunken stupor.

Of course, he later apologized for his behavior, and he continued seeing me often over the course of the year. We had real conversations. I told him about my desires in life with no filter. One night we spent over an hour talking about his ex-wife, whom, at the time, he had not yet divorced. I asked why he was still so committed to her, why he felt so guilty, why he felt responsible, and why he was torturing himself. We went deep. This wasn't a typical gentlemen's club conversation designed to pry more money out of the customer's wallet. This was a real, raw conversation.

He had a moment of awakening during that night and later confessed that he realized he wasn't worried about his ex-wife—he was worried about himself. He was worried about what would happen to him if she found herself in a predicament following their divorce. This was a frequent topic of conversation. His wife had schizophrenia, or he believed she had a severe mental disorder. Because I had similar interactions with my mother, we empathized with one another. We worked through the kinks of navigating these challenging relationships. Mostly I offered my advice on what to do next in his complex situation. All the while, we were in the private dance area, deep in conversation, while the girls next to me were sliding off their G-strings and swaying their hips. I was grateful for the refreshing interruption to the monotony when Raj visited.

A few months after that deep conversation about Raj's ex-wife, he came in with a new demeanor. He gleamed. He was dating again for the first time since they separated. He was a completely different person. Whether it was our midnight therapy sessions or the natural progression of his process, things had shifted drastically, and I was glad. Around August, however, things became increasingly uncomfortable with Raj. He had been asking for my "real name" for months, and I'd finally told him "Shay," and he did some searching online. He found me and my full name and sent me messages via text addressed to Lana instead of Vida. He commented on things I posted and sent a "friend request" on Facebook. He started following my public account on Instagram. He liked my videos on YouTube. Josh caught wind and asked me to block him from all channels. I did and let Raj know it wasn't a desirable direction for our relationship. He understood and took the news well. He became more aware of the dynamic of our relationship. He went to New York for a business trip and went to a gentlemen's club where he met a dancer. He took her out the next day, and they spent the day together, roaming the concrete jungle and flirting, even sharing a kiss or two. He recounted the story to me one night, and I warned him she was not looking to become his partner. She was working. He denied the possibility and was irritated I would suggest anything other than a magical romance. After his second trip to NYC, he visited me and admitted I was correct about his exotic dancer romance. She told him she wasn't willing to see him again because he hadn't paid her for the day they spent together. Another major realization: Exotic dancers are not candidates for future lovers. Of course, Raj and I had a different relationship from what he'd experienced with the girl in New York. I was raw, real, and honest. Always. He knew what I wanted. He also knew me—the real me.

I was completely myself with Raj. I let loose when he came in. On slow nights, when he and I would have the entire private area to ourselves, I'd do cartwheels and dance on every booth in the private area, moving from one to the next with twirls, backbends, and high karate kicks. I'd lip-sync every song that played, complete with hand motions, hair flips, hip gyrations, and boobie shakes. Our time together was either talking or acting out my twelve-year-old self. I was always grateful to see him because there weren't any surprises. I could be me, and I let him be him.

Over a year later, in August 2018, Raj stopped coming to see me. He had found a girlfriend on a dating app. He still texted here and there to see if there was a pulse. He asked if we could transition, one last time, into me becoming his health coach. I accepted but did not follow up. I actually wanted to coach Raj. He was receptive and would probably have been a great student. However, he could have also been a terrible student with no intention of learning, seeking only to get closer to me in an unwelcome way. I didn't want to invite him in and give him hope that we could spend time together.

The boundaries can get blurred. I was molested as a child and sexually violated; my walls had been torn down, and I didn't learn to rebuild them until I started dancing. It wasn't something that happened overnight. With Raj, for example, I started dancing an extra foot or two away from him so he couldn't sneak in a kiss on the cheek or anywhere else. That was a clear boundary for me. I didn't want to feel like I had to allow this for him to keep coming back.

Oddly enough, I couldn't seem to draw these lines with everyone. There were late nights in Vegas when I would feel a hand slip under my bottoms and would catch it later than I wished. This is a journal entry from May 20, 2015:

> Last night was insane. The last guy just slid his hand down in between my legs and rubbed my clit, and I was so tired I didn't relocate his hand for five seconds longer than I'd wanted to. I wonder if that's what happens with girls . . . they stop caring. I almost didn't care. Then I thought of how disgusting his hands were, and that they shouldn't be that close to my fucking stuff! This was a really weird experience. I am usually quick. It's over. Whatever. I left with $860 thanks to his nasty ass. He said I made his night. Ew. That's it. Ew. That's not cool. You need to ask. You don't have permission to touch my sacred space, or anywhere else for that matter, just because you gave me money. Money is the appreciation for my time. Your words and intention are the only keys that may grant access to my temple.

I allowed some people to caress and massage me simply because I enjoy touching and being touched. If there's no question of whether or not someone will touch me in a desirable way, I let my guard down. There's something energetic at play. Physical touch is on that surface level. Raj got in too deep. It felt like infatuation. When I allow touch, it should just feel fleshy, human, raw. Touch is natural and normal. It's not about how it's done or what is said. It's about energy.

Raj came in one last time in early 2019 and stood by the door. I'd just walked out of the private dance area and plopped down on the cozy cheetah-print sofa chair in the corner of the club, directly across from the door. I looked down at my phone and pretended not to notice him. I figured he'd come to visit another girl since I hadn't seen him in so long. A bouncer came over and notified me that he'd already asked for me and had been waiting. I looked up and stood. He walked toward me and we embraced. He'd just come to say hi and congratulate me on completing my book. His energy was different. He said he was in the middle of the divorce and was happier than ever, with a new lover in his life. I felt happy—it was a happy ending. Watching and supporting transformation became my new high. How can I be a catalyst for pleasure, growth, and expansion in these men's lives?

What I really, deeply enjoy is "being first." Being the first female to invite a male into this new experience of the feminine as an awakened seductress. According to Raj, I was the first, but there's something different about a man setting foot in a gentlemen's club for the first time. I could only endure and tolerate these dramatic scenarios because I was fueled by the opportunity to set the trajectory for a younger client's future dynamic with the opposite sex. I journaled about one of these particular experiences after one of my last experiences at Cheer's:

> In just one week, Josh and I will embark on a long-awaited journey to Europe to celebrate the tenth anniversary of the day we first met. I am giving my best effort to work as much as possible without burning myself out. I went in tonight because one of the older girls got married today, and most of Cheer's real hustlers were at the wedding. Half of the usual number of girls are on the floor tonight, and it's a Friday. Of course, this absence extends to the clientele. One or two regulars were also MIA because they knew their favorite girl wouldn't be in tonight. This doesn't account for the scarcity of people walking through the door, however. It's dead again, not a big surprise.
>
> It's bizarre to most, but I actually prefer it this way. When there are fewer people, I can strategically approach every single person. If they say no the first time, in most cases, I can approach them a second and sometimes even a third time. There have been a few rare cases where I'd drop in on them all night—a wink here, a hello there. I might make contact with someone ten times before they make a decision. Tonight, the third time's the charm, though a few don't budge until the fifth or sixth time. Eventually, they accepted my offer to spend some time in the private dance area.
>
> Toward the end of the night, two twenty-somethings were stationed at the end of the bar, right underneath a blaring speaker adjacent to the fireplace. They weren't communicating with one another. They simply stood and stared at the stage with straight faces. I intuited a hard sale from a distance, so I approached with determination and a waking dream of the Amalfi Coast in Italy. As I neared, my stomach churned. They reeked of stale cigarette smoke. In all honesty, I prefer it over most body odors and most definitely over pungent halitosis, so I began to pray they were only plagued with one of the three aforementioned assaulting odors. One of them had long, wavy, dark hair matted under a backward cap. The other one was a lanky blonde in a black tee exposing his full sleeves of black ink.
>
> This is part of the job. How do I approach these two? They're young and perhaps easily persuaded, though often the younger ones are unsure of themselves and hide behind a shield of cockiness. I doubt I could carry on a conversation with them, so I went in quick. "Hey!" I locked eyes with the blonde. I noticed my attraction to his face and felt my own expression soften. "Wanna come with me?"
>
> I felt his humility and kindness through one simple sentence: "Can't say no to you!"

I interlocked fingers with him and led him to the one-song private dance area, figuring that he'd have enough money for at least one dance. I unlatched my hand as we entered the room and turned to meet his eyes again to direct him to one of the two corner booths—the only two with a mirrored wall to serve as an additional prop for the brief performance.

I asked his age as he sat and began counting out his $45 for the single dance. He asked why. "Because you look very young, and I'm just curious."

He grinned and said, "I'm twenty-one." I smiled.

"You're a baby! So young!"

He wasn't smiling anymore. "I don't feel so young."

I straightened my spine, lifting my heart. "Why not?"

He alluded to a harsh reality. I felt it before he spoke. He had certainly been through some shit. There's some truth to the story of the young soul in a challenging existence using cigarettes and other drugs as a distraction. It felt as if he was ready to break down. He was unhappy yet kind-hearted and sweet. If no one had informed this young man of his birthright to be happy, I intended to convey this important message.

I put my hand on his heart as I repeated silently through my eyes and movements, "you are loved." I placed my palms on his shoulders and pressed back and down to open his heart and release the tension he was holding. At the end of the dance, he expressed his gratitude for his very first experience in a gentlemen's club and his first "dance." I felt a momentary rush of joy, knowing I had initiated him. I see these initiations as rather fortuitous. Perhaps this young man will not allow women in strip clubs to treat him with anything less than the utmost respect and kindness. Maybe he will develop an attraction to a powerful archetype with the intention of raising his spirit and drawing out his most desirable attributes.

This is my intention. I love to be the "first dance," the first introduction to this environment. I hope this will pave the way for more uplifting experiences, free of the stereotypical aggression and demeaning, emasculating words and actions. That isn't the world I want to live in. A man abused and taken advantage of isn't going to have a positive relationship with a woman. This no-longer-a-virgin thanked me three times over and promised to return to show his appreciation for my performance. It was enough for me when he confided that he'd "never been to a place like this," and though he had no reference point, he "didn't expect to find someone 'nice.'" What an opportunity; to set the tone for all that comes after in the underground realm. An opportunity to initiate men.

14

THE STRIPPER'S ESCAPE

For almost the entire month of February and half of March of 2018, I was so ill I couldn't leave the house, much less go to work. I'd never been so sick—even contracting Hepatitis A in India or the first round of Covid-19 wasn't as prolonged and intense. This wasn't a viral or bacterial illness; this was emotional sickness. This was the result of a major upheaval. I had gone through an insane time, and my immune system was compromised.

My thirteen-year-old sister had been going through a major struggle managing the instability of her home life and the challenge of being a millennial. A broken home caused the usual problems one sees in school and social life, and she began cutting herself. For a short stint in middle and high school, I explored what it meant to feel by inflicting pain. I wasn't in my sister's head, but I could empathize. Her father had separated from my mother and been villainized. Not to say that he didn't have his many shortcomings, but he was made out to be the Devil himself. My sister, young and impressionable, became insecure, confused, and depressed.

Our mother wasn't doing well. She felt disconnected from her business and considered closing her doors, which meant money wasn't coming in. My mother had been diagnosed with bipolar disorder many years ago, likely due to PTSD from her numerous traumatic experiences as a child. My mother is extremely sensitive and empathic, so things that cut her cut deeply. She couldn't seek out the tools to heal before the scars became major blocks in her ability to self-regulate. The same happened to my father. They were both abused as children, and it's played out in their adult lives. It's not a big surprise that my little sister couldn't bear the weight of living alone with my mother and witnessing her pain. It was a vicious cycle, and they seemed to spiral together. I feared I would lose them both much sooner than expected. My sister ended up in a mental hospital for a week and was put on a cocktail of pharmaceutical medications. Big pharma is the bane of my existence. I had watched the small, orange bottles of pills and the system that created them take Mikey's life, my grandmother who raised me, and others who were dear to my heart. It felt like my worst nightmare. My young, sweet, pure sister was being poisoned. My baby. My two sisters mean the world to me, and I feel their pain and struggle as if they are my own (not claiming that this is a benefit to any one of us).

I have always felt somewhat responsible for my younger sisters. My mother has always said to me, "Call your sisters. They need you. Be there for them. Teach them. Stay close." It's always felt like so much pressure, yet it's always been innate. I've always felt more responsibility for them than a sibling dynamic. I allowed the situation to affect me in a way that was crippling. Historically, my energetic boundaries have been weak with my family. Their pain has the power to shatter my world.

While my sister was in the depth of this experience, I had trouble sleeping, eating, and anything other than contacting everyone I knew that might be able to intervene. For over a week, I woke up every morning and contacted therapists who worked with children in Madison to see if any of them could take on a new client immediately. I looked for programs to support both my sister and mother. I called old friends from high school and reached out to my California community to see if anyone had connections in Wisconsin. I called my sister's father daily, begging him to help me seek solutions. I sought out medical advice to get her off the medications. I read online medical journals and countless articles about the medications she'd been prescribed. I educated myself on self-harm and suicide prevention.

I couldn't believe how challenging it was to find help. This situation shed light on the failure of western "culture." Why are dysfunctional families and broken homes so prevalent? What happened to villages raising children and community outreach? Doing it independently has always been bullshit to me. I need (and want) everyone in the massive network of friends I've cultivated. I need my community. I need support and resources. We all need each other. I am grateful for the countless resources I have and have celebrated this accomplishment in my life. I've woven a web of incredible humans in my life. However, we can't change anyone's life without cooperation from all parties involved. I needed to get face to face with my sister to direct her toward the light.

After a few weeks of waking up shaking with anxiety, my nervous system on overdrive, I decided to take my sister myself. My mother had been asking if I could take custody of her since the last time my sister had visited months ago. In our tiny shoebox of an apartment with our high school teen full of angst, living in the most expensive place in the country, even with our travels all over the globe and my financially unstable lifestyle, we considered it. I had wanted nothing more than to rescue my sister and couldn't think of a better way to shift the situation. It was heavy. I prayed for a miracle. The thought of taking on the role of parenting my thirteen-year-old sister was trying, but I had moments of determination when I convinced myself it was right. I'd mulled it over with my whole network and asked for advice from everyone in my life with a sound mindset. I had a medicine journey where I came out full of conviction, vowing to take my sister and be the best role model I could be, transforming my life to support her. I had visions of taking her to dance classes, practicing Spanish, tucking her in at night, packing her lunches for school. I visualized her entire high school experience and her graduation day, where she was happy, healthy, and confident. It felt like the right thing, so I told my sister and mother it was an option. They both pushed for it—hard—and when it didn't immediately happen, things bubbled into chaos in Wisconsin.

Things escalated until my sister dropped out of eighth grade. I agreed to have her stay for winter break as a trial run. Even though she hadn't been going to school, I booked her trip within the dates of her Christmas break, hoping things would fall back into place because Josh hadn't agreed to her moving in with us. My mother threatened not to send her if I didn't agree to have her move in, but I didn't want to risk things going haywire.

When my sister arrived, she seemed overjoyed. I drove to San Francisco Airport and parked so I could go in and meet her at the gate. When we hugged, it felt like a thousand pounds of immobilizing fear dissolved instantly. She was safe. I had her, and I wasn't going to let her out of my sight until I was confident she wouldn't be harmed by herself or anyone else.

Until mid-January, I did everything to support my sister to heal every day. I paid close attention to everything she ate and drank and got her outside, moving her body, and getting sunshine every day. I kept her around my positive friends and did my best to make space so she'd be comfortable enough to speak to me about what was going on inside her head. Even though I was doing everything possible to remedy the situation, I didn't know what would happen when she left. There was still so much unknown. I was still anxious. Josh and I struggled. One morning, while he listened to me going through my hundredth time processing the situation, he said, "I am not doing this anymore. I am just going to leave while you get this figured out. I don't want to be here anymore." I crumbled. I wasn't ready to take my sister at the expense of my marriage.

We decided she had to leave. Josh had said over and over that he couldn't give me advice or assess the situation until my sister was in front of him for a few weeks. When that moment came, he said we couldn't keep her. She would have to move in with her father. He seemed to be in a stable relationship with a woman who lived with her two children in a sizable home. He said he was able to accommodate my sister. I flew back to Wisconsin with her, planning to stay a week to help her move into her father's new home and enroll in a new school. It hurt that I couldn't say yes and take her myself. I felt like a failure. I wasn't stable enough. It would be such an easy fix if the money were there. All of the things in the world that could be solved with money . . . I hated myself.

My mother protested and told me that if my sister ended up living with her father, she would take further legal action. She'd already been in court with my sister's father countless times over the past few years, and nothing would stop her from making another move. I slept on the couch of my sister's father's home, me on one side of the L-shaped couch and my sister on the other, and waited until we could get her enrolled in school and moved into her new bedroom.

My heart sank when we arrived at our mother's home to collect my sister's belongings. It felt dark and cold. I heard my mother crying, screaming. The house was a disaster. There were candy wrappers everywhere, a clear indication my mother was drained and she was reaching for anything to give her a boost to get through the day. Sugar is a powerful, addictive drug. A psychic channel I'd consulted while visiting Tulum, Mexico, told me that my mother was addicted to stimulants, causing her depressive and erratic thoughts. I thought to myself, yes! This is what happens to all human beings on stimulants. No surprise there. The erratic thoughts weren't just thoughts—they became an outer manifestation, and her house was the proof. It was a low point. We all have them, but this one was hard for me to swallow. I couldn't help but see the greater picture. This isn't just the reality in my home. This is happening on a global level. Individuals are experiencing mental instability due to trauma and the collective shit understanding of how toxic our lives are.

As we were about to leave, my sister had second thoughts. Feeling guilty, she told me that our mom had no help or support and that she needed to be with her because she was the only person she had. More than anything, she wanted our mother to be happy, and she believed it wouldn't be possible if she moved in with her father, away from our mother. I knew the opposite. If she didn't move out of her mother's home, she would continue to suffer and feel more and more ambivalent toward the world. I had moved out of my mother's home and into my father's place at this same point in life, in the winter of eighth grade, in the same city, at the same school, when my father moved back to Wisconsin after being incarcerated in Washington. History does, in fact, repeat itself. Once again, where is the support within our system? What happened to community? Where are the resources for people who really need it? Better yet, where do we cut the root and kill this trend of children becoming traumatized, dysfunctional adults?

In the end, my sister moved in with her father, and I flew home with my fingers crossed and my heart broken. It wasn't what I wanted, but I trusted she'd be okay. I had no other choice but to trust, and I couldn't bear the thought of my baby sister or mother potentially going into a deeper, darker place. I had to tell myself this wasn't the case. I left Wisconsin just before my birthday on January 13. I didn't return to Cheer's for another few weeks, and when I did, I only got a night or two in before I fell ill. It felt as if I was holding onto a rope, hanging on the edge of a cliff for months until, one day, I finally let go.

When I let go, my system snapped. My symptoms worsened daily. For the first time in years, I visited a medical doctor for a diagnosis. She labeled it a sinus infection. That sinus infection became so intense that I had suicidal thoughts. I made it through the month and came out the other side after five visits to the doctor, three acupuncture sessions, three visits to an ENT, twelve hours with a doctor of Chinese medicine, hundreds of dollars of natural remedies, and over seventy-five hours in front of my computer watching videos on curing sinus infections with natural remedies. It was a wild ride. Being emphatic, sensitive, and lacking boundaries has some major drawbacks.

When I finally made it back to Cheer's, I found out a few people had been wondering where I was after a month and a half of being absent with no social media posts of the usual exotic travels. One of my regulars, who chooses to stay private outside the club, claimed that he had no way of contacting me, even though I'd given him my card numerous times. One night he finally confessed he hadn't written to me because his wife checked his email. "She checks everything," he said. He continued to explain himself. "I only come here when she goes out of town." I checked myself before the expression on my face revealed to him the disgust I felt at the thought of having to hide desires in marriage. He sat in the middle of the booth with his hands at his sides, palms down as if bracing himself.

I repositioned him for the fifth time, grabbing his forearms and sliding his palms further away from his body, so he had no choice but to let his shoulders relax. I shook my head, making eye contact. "You're always so tense! Relax a little! Let your shoulders down."

He surrendered while arguing with his usual wide smile, "I'm just sitting here."

I continued to dance. Mid-twerk, he asked if I'd given anyone poison recently. I went into the full cliff's-notes version of my month of illness and the whole ordeal with my sister and family. I apologized after speaking for five minutes without pause.

"No, no! This is part of why I come here. I love hearing about all of it. You girls are interesting. You're the most interesting," he replied. I'd forgotten. This was all entertainment for him. He'd made a point of mentioning this every time he visited. *Lucky you,* I thought. *You don't have to experience my reality. It's just amusement for you.*

The first time we'd met, I'd been apprehensive to approach him because he was the regular of another girl, Snowy, who is rather possessive of her regulars and will put up a fight if any of the girls so much as glance in their direction. Despite my hesitation that night, I acknowledged him calling me over. "Hi! Do you need something? I can get Snowy for you! You came to see her, right?"

He seemed caught off guard, "Yes, I did. I also came to see Tiffany."

I turned my head, questioning him with my facial expression.

He said, "I'd actually like to ask you—"

I cut him off and said, "I can't give you a dance. Snowy will be upset. She's also my friend, so I'd rather not."

His lips tightened as I spoke. He was silent for a moment, and then his tone changed. "I didn't come here just to see her, and she'll be fine if you give me a dance."

I objected again. "She won't be fine. I'll do it only if you tell her. Tell her that you called me over, and I did not approach you and that you asked for a dance," and I walked away.

He was clearly agitated that I wouldn't spend time with him. Five minutes later, when I walked into the private dance area with another customer, he was in the back with Tiffany, not Snowy. I looked over at them and could tell they'd been talking about me. He was still bothered.

Almost an hour later, Tiffany came into the dressing room, took her seat in the corner, and sipped her energy drink, eyeing me. "You know, that guy is super mad you won't give him a dance."

I responded, "I know, but he's Snowy's regular, and I know she won't be happy."

Tiffany rolled her eyes and flashed her mischievous grin. "You know he doesn't only come to see her."

Fine. At least I'd made it known I wanted to respect that he was "her" regular. I walked back out and grabbed him.

He asked, "What? Did she say it was okay?"

I stopped walking toward the private area and looked back at him. "You didn't tell her? I told you to tell her. You're the naughty one here. You called me over."

He said, "Oh, stop!" Five seconds later, Snowy slid into the booth next to us and began glaring at him.

I said, "See? What the fuck."

He said, "Oh, don't worry. I'll take care of her later. She won't care after I pay her."

I knew he was probably right, so I avoided her until I saw them together again. I was relieved when the night had ended and no drama had arisen between us. The truth is that it's business, and we're all there to make money. If I'm leaving money on the table in this business, I'm shooting myself in the foot. There's no point being a dancer with one foot.

This guy had a specific type, and four of us fit it. We didn't have the same exact figure, but we were all curvy in the right places, with long dark hair and natural breasts. He seemed to converse with each of us more than simply enjoying our performance for him. Because I knew I'd be seeing a lot of him, I didn't hold back, even in the first private dance. I was completely transparent. Psychedelics, Kambo, conspiracy theories, my alternative lifestyle . . . I told him everything. He scoffed at all of my witchy medicine and alternative healing stories, and that's how I quickly learned about his profession as a heart surgeon. He always had that cheeky, cynical undertone in his reply. He was an East Coaster, after all.

By this time, I had been seeing him for over a year, so I asked why he chose to spend time with all four of us. He replied with something I found strange: "I like to spread the wealth."

This didn't make sense because the few girls he would spend time with were the top earners at the club, including me. The first time we met, he overpaid. He always seemed to overpay. I heard him say, quite a few times, that he didn't know what the rates were. Something about it felt wrong, and I told him how much everyone else was paying. He handed me $340, and I told him he could spend half an hour with me for $360. I'm quite certain the other girls would put less money in the machine, do less time, and take more from him instead of asking him for the extra $20. I had a moment of regret and felt like kicking myself, but he clearly didn't care. He wasn't price-sensitive. He'd handed me hundreds before as a tip.

The dances with him were rarely unpleasant. There was a good amount of talking and no creepy blowing, heavy breathing, or raunchy commentary. He was Mister Cool, Calm, and Collected. However, I got ruffled when he started nonchalantly talking about something while I was bent over naked in front of his face. Like, jeez, is it really that bad? You obviously aren't enjoying this. I eventually learned he didn't have any real desire to have a vagina two inches from his face. He spoke when he was disinterested. It wasn't uncommon.

He was nothing like that other guy, Ken, who came in and expected me to work like a robot. As soon as the money was in the machine and the green light switched on, I was supposed to stay in character like I was on Broadway. I could only talk when the light turned red, or he'd let me know he wasn't getting what he thought he paid for. I didn't like him, but I was grateful he was so damn consistent, and I laughed hard every time we were together. The heart surgeon was much more easy-going. I could stop, sit, and talk. He didn't even pay attention to the light, and when he noticed it may have turned red, he'd hand over my money swiftly. Ken, the robot-lover regular, clenched the money like it was his last dollar until I pried it out of his hand. It wasn't about the money; he just wanted to squeeze every last second out of his private time. This is where I could empathize with Snowy's temperamental behavior. She trained the heart surgeon, and he was rather desirable for dancer clientele. Not like Ken.

One night, I recall walking into the dressing room to recount the private show I'd just given Ken. He had been coming to Cheer's for over ten years. It was baffling to me. How could he possibly still be amused and aroused by the same experience? He was a self-professed alcoholic, and perhaps that's the trick. Maybe he doesn't recall the details. Ken would come in and see the same three girls every other week. Always on the same day because he'd had the same job, with the same schedule, all that time. I would go mad with Ken's life. I never knew whether to take him seriously or not. All I knew was that he wanted me to perform for him as soon as the light turned green.

During a particular dance with Ken, I fed the $10 bill into the machine and slid off the ledge of the leather booth, like a cat tracking its prey. Nine times out of ten, I start private sessions the same way: standing on the table, facing away from the client. Inside of each half-moon, navy-blue leather booth is a half-table about a foot and a half high that tucks in and, quite literally, locks the customer's feet and shins inside of the tiny space. Ken wasn't a big guy, so I could slide the table close, which was to my advantage, being only five feet tall. "White Iverson" by Post Malone was blaring. If a dancer likes the music playing, the dance is always better. Nicki and Beyoncé were onto something because I was "Feeling Myself." My attraction to Ken was non-existent and didn't excite me, so a good song benefitted us both. His intoxication was repulsive, though I appreciated his sense of humor and the consistent income. Mostly, he was another regular I could be weird with.

Post Malone gave me a beat to rock my hips to, nice and slow, exactly how I like it. I aim for slow, sensual, and erotic, and I rarely leave a handprint, though I spank my bottom occasionally. I was already fully nude because we were on our third two-song set. I hovered over Ken, rocking my hips slowly back and forth while sucking on my fingers, looking down at him. I'm never wet, like some girls who get aroused doing this work. I think it does the opposite for me, so finger sucking is a necessary seduction tactic.

Ken's mini-fro was just short enough that it didn't quite reach the inside of my thighs, though I was swaying close enough to make a momentary connection for extra stimulation. He was already doing his heavy breathing. He did this sucking thing through his nose. I heard a story in which he successfully snorted a close-hovering nipple into his nostril, and it seemed like he was going for his second shot that night. Don't ask how it's possible. I wasn't there. His nose was always a little moist, like a dog's. I assume it's what happens when you have a quart of alcohol running through your system. I reached my fingers down, sliding them over either side of my clit. I looked away as he looked up. It's a problem I have. I can't maintain eye contact with anyone I'm not attracted to when I'm intimate with myself. It instantly kills my mood when I feel them entering my energetic space. My saliva dried on my fingers, so I pushed my open palms against the mirror behind Ken's head as I squatted over him, making sure to leave some distance as we were, in fact, a no-contact club (which I think is bullshit). At least 98% of the clientele who visited Cheer's prayed for physical contact. They wouldn't come back if they weren't hopeful or successful in fulfilling this desire.

I never intentionally touched any body part of Ken besides his shins, shoulders, and afro. Some customers will get fingertips on the back of the neck or my foot on their thigh if I need help propping myself up. I tried to avoid touching Ken. He'd seen a few girls at other clubs with full contact, like the Spearmint Rhino in Las Vegas, and didn't seem attuned to any of the girl's boundaries. Or was this only my experience with him? I laid with my back on the booth next to him and put my legs up to expose my hands, caressing my thighs and labia. After ten seconds, I slid onto my side to exit the position, and Ken grabbed my thigh. I yelped in pain. He jumped a little and apologized. I stopped the dance. "Ken! I'm going to have a bruise! Naughty!" He stopped his heavy breathing and hip writhing. I slapped my own ass hard, which always made him jump (another reason I never believed in his jumpiness), and continued the dance at a distance.

That was our last set. Ken never did more than three or four two-song sets. I went in the back to get a baby wipe and drink water. I saw one of the girls in the back who'd been working at Cheer's for eight years and counting. She knew Ken well. I knew she'd be empathetic, so I said, "My leg hurts! I think Ken just bruised my leg!"

She had been sitting in the back for over an hour on her phone, looking at memes on social media, and she was ready for a change of scenery. "What?! Is he still out there? I'm going to tell him that he can't fucking do that. Someone didn't train him well. He's too fucking handsy."

Luckily, he'd left because I had no intention of playing out that drama with her. Her comment was a great reminder, though. There are customers who are trained well and those who are not. Snowy, for example, trained her regulars well, and it was clear other girls coveted them, conceivably unaware of her impeccable coaching. Who'd trained Ken? I became one of the girls who re-trained him after that night. When we met the following month again, I made sure to tell him I'd bruised from his spastic outburst, and my husband was perturbed. That was the last time he used his hands. Ken actually didn't mean any harm. In all honesty, I was grateful for Ken. I laughed, usually hard, when he came in, and our emails were gold.

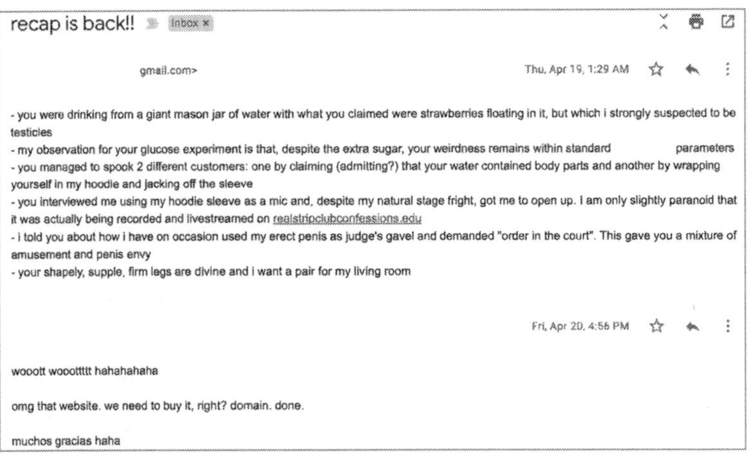

recap is back!! Inbox ×

gmail.com> Thu, Apr 19, 1:29 AM

- you were drinking from a giant mason jar of water with what you claimed were strawberries floating in it, but which i strongly suspected to be testicles
- my observation for your glucose experiment is that, despite the extra sugar, your weirdness remains within standard parameters
- you managed to spook 2 different customers: one by claiming (admitting?) that your water contained body parts and another by wrapping yourself in my hoodie and jacking off the sleeve
- you interviewed me using my hoodie sleeve as a mic and, despite my natural stage fright, got me to open up. I am only slightly paranoid that it was actually being recorded and livestreamed on realstripclubconfessions.edu
- i told you about how i have on occasion used my erect penis as judge's gavel and demanded "order in the court". This gave you a mixture of amusement and penis envy
- your shapely, supple, firm legs are divine and i want a pair for my living room

Fri, Apr 20, 4:56 PM

wooott woootttt hahahahaha

omg that website. we need to buy it, right? domain. done.

muchos gracias haha

- I dig your glam ear plugs, making self care sexy is an underrated part of the style
- we played booth musical chairs
- if the green light goes off, but the red light doesn't go on, you have to continue half dancing
- you somehow accurately pinned me as having a sensitive gag reflex after I sort of deep throated my pinky
- there's a rhino in SJ now. I imagine we will rendezvous there in the not so distant future

- you were intrigued by the notion of oiled women in bikinis using power tools. Well have I got a music video for you! https://www.youtube.com/watch?v=V5bYDhZBFLA . See also the Bloodhound Gang for a more comedic take: https://www.youtube.com/watch?v=JZpxaiNV_sM

- you improvised an amazing one woman music video of "Crazy". I particularly liked the driving and the exploding head. You are now the primary association I have with this song. This is no small feat, considering the original music video, which I saw on MTV when I was indefatigably horny in 7th grade, involves Alicia Silverstone and Liv Tyler skippy dipping and pole dancing

- After the final dance, you emphatically demanded something of me along the lines of "Pat the pitter!" (or was it "Pit the patter"?). I was so nonplussed by this that I stated the quote of the night (month?): "Am I having a stroke or are you just being weird?" A question I could only pose to you

PS you danced to a remix of "Careless Whisper". I like this song and have a habit of playing air saxophone when I hear the opening solo in the original. I'm too self-conscious to do this when I'm not alone, but you since you're special and your "Crazy" rendition inspired me, I made the attached video. Hope you enjoy it!

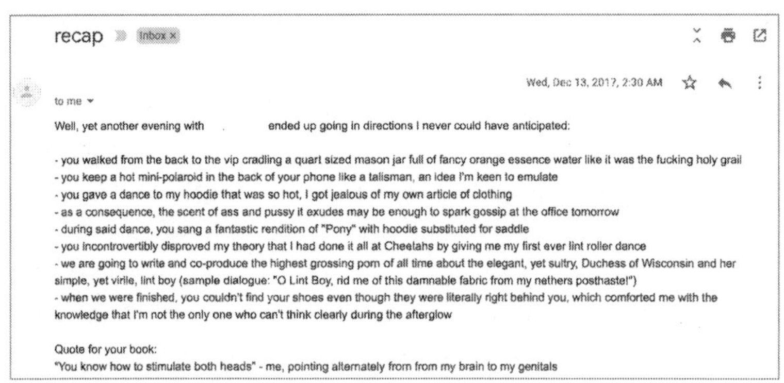

recap Inbox ×

Wed, Dec 13, 2017, 2:30 AM

to me

Well, yet another evening with ended up going in directions I never could have anticipated:

- you walked from the back to the vip cradling a quart sized mason jar full of fancy orange essence water like it was the fucking holy grail
- you keep a hot mini-polaroid in the back of your phone like a talisman, an idea I'm keen to emulate
- you gave a dance to my hoodie that was so hot, I got jealous of my own article of clothing
- as a consequence, the scent of ass and pussy it exudes may be enough to spark gossip at the office tomorrow
- during said dance, you sang a fantastic rendition of "Pony" with hoodie substituted for saddle
- you incontrovertibly disproved my theory that I had done it all at Cheetahs by giving me my first ever lint roller dance
- we are going to write and co-produce the highest grossing porn of all time about the elegant, yet sultry, Duchess of Wisconsin and her simple, yet virile, lint boy (sample dialogue: "O Lint Boy, rid me of this damnable fabric from my nethers posthaste!")
- when we were finished, you couldn't find your shoes even though they were literally right behind you, which comforted me with the knowledge that I'm not the only one who can't think clearly during the afterglow

Quote for your book:
"You know how to stimulate both heads" - me, pointing alternately from from my brain to my genitals

He was consistent. He was always happy and in a good mood. I couldn't hold a grudge. I had simply ignited his sexual fire, and how can one truly comprehend appropriate behavior if it's never been taught? Does anyone really teach us how to channel this powerful energy? It's certainly not taught in a formal education setting. It's certainly not in most parenting books.

So how do we learn how to allow sexual energy to move through us and release in a way that honors everyone involved? It's a crucial skill to learn, teaching people how to treat you and demanding respect with presence alone. Dancers are in a unique position to teach these things. Lexi, one of the twelve women I'd met in Vegas who, over the course of four years, brought their Tantric studies and deep introspection through psychedelics, yoga practices, and personal development work into the club, shared a story with me over the phone.

On Saturday nights in Vegas during high season, more than six hundred dancers clock in, and hundreds, if not thousands, of patrons enter Spearmint Rhino Gentlemen's Club in Las Vegas. Lexi has been pulling in over ten thousand dollars per month for more than fourteen years at the Rhino. On one particular Saturday evening, she found herself in the celebrity booth with a man who'd downed one (or five) too many Vodka Tonics. Stumbling into the private booth, he kissed her cheek and slapped her ass. He aggressively grabbed her hips and pulled her onto his lap, slurring desires. She grabbed his wrists and pinned him to the booth behind the closed curtain, demanding he behave like a gentleman.

They danced the power struggle to exhaustion, and after repeatedly attempting to tame his belligerence to no avail, the dakini emerged; the conscious sex worker. Lexi knew she couldn't fight fire with fire, especially while this man was in an altered state. She sat beside him and caressed and massaged his arm and shoulders until his head fell into her lap, then she guided him through breath work while stroking his hair. Before the end of their hour in VIP, he'd fallen asleep. Her intention was to calm him. She stayed grounded in her power, taming the man's alcohol-induced, brute nature. When the VIP host came to notify them of the time and roused the patron, the aggression had dissolved, and he thanked Lexi and respectfully tipped her before departing the VIP booth.

* * *

Everyone knows that at some point, tension will arise in a group of women "working" in a tiny little box together day in and day out. There's no surprise or great mystery in revealing that I witnessed (though was rarely directly involved in) some pretty volatile situations. The saga with Lexi or Snowy's regulars were everyday scenarios. I journaled about the tension at Cheer's the following day after a night of chaos, attempting to process the drama that I thought I'd left in my teenage years:

> Last night I was sitting with Snowy, the girl that everybody seemed to dislike when I began working at Cheer's. I've seen why and I am not confused by the general consensus. I've heard her complain about the other girls and say things about them to the clientele that I wouldn't want to hear about myself. Today, I feel the urge to talk to her. Don't I have to tell her? I see how she's making life more difficult for herself. I had to reflect on my impulse. If she doesn't see it, is my perception going to offer her clarity? No guarantee there. And the truth of the matter? She's a good person. They all are. We all are. We all have our issues, human kinks to work, though. More importantly, the drama goes in waves. Perhaps it's the moon cycle?
>
> My sexy Latina crush is supposedly giving Snowy dirty looks, and the week before, she'd verbally assaulted her on the main floor. It wasn't a new story. My crush confronted Snowy about what she had said to the clientele about her. Something about having a boyfriend visiting the club who would get upset. It'd be an interesting game if it were true, and it likely was. The club is small, and that scarcity mentality can get dark and heavy fast.
>
> Snowy and I dove into our holistic living conversation to pass the time since the club was empty. These are the nights when the heat gets turned up. We went in the back to get dressed and check out, and Latina crush wasted less than a second before she hurled profanity from across the room, going on about how she was no longer taking her (Snowy's) shit and she'd had enough.
>
> Snowy repeated over and over, "I'm not going to talk to you about this back here; we can take this somewhere else; we don't need to talk about it here." She'd repeated herself five times before finally leaving the dressing room as Latina crush continued to rant about her to everyone else, though no one seemed keen to join the scene.
>
> I walked away while she was still going and went to tip out with the doorman in the booth. Snowy was in the back of the club, crying in the manager's office, so I gave her a hug and asked if she wanted her bag from the dressing room, but she only wanted her shoes. I went in to grab them, hoping no one would notice so I could remain neutral. No part of me wanted to engage in the drama. I simply had empathy for the situation. It felt like one of the many times I ended up in the principal's office in high school.
>
> Snowy moved to a relatively hidden booth in the lap dance area to wait for my crush to leave. While we waited, I offered her my arsenal of essential oils and

mood-lifting tinctures from my oversized purse. She was shaking from the adrenaline, and I didn't have it in me at 3 A.M. to start leading her through a process, so I squeezed a few dropperfuls of my "liquid sunshine herbal extract" into her mouth. She cringed and shook her head and said "thanks" with a disgusted look on her face. I said it should be quick. Five minutes later, I could see her breathing more deeply.

Soon she perked up and exclaimed, "Wow! That really works!"

I said, "I know; how do you think I manage working here?" We both smiled, and I hugged her again before handing the bouncer my Victoria's Secret bag to walk me out to the car. Another dancer had offered the bag up for free in the dressing room a year back, and I'd had first dibs since I was sitting next to her. I was elated to have avoided bringing one of my own bags into the building, knowing it would be forever tainted with the nauseating mélange of cheap perfumes.

On the drive home, I pondered . . . Why the drama? I wondered if it was just the heat of the moment and the slow night that sparked the flame. I sent a text message to Latina crush, hoping to diffuse the situation. I figured a voice of reason couldn't hurt. I had pure intentions. I wanted the situation to dissolve. I genuinely enjoyed both of these women and appreciated seeing them at work. My words came through in a delirious state, but I figured it barely mattered what I said because I knew my intention was clean and clear.

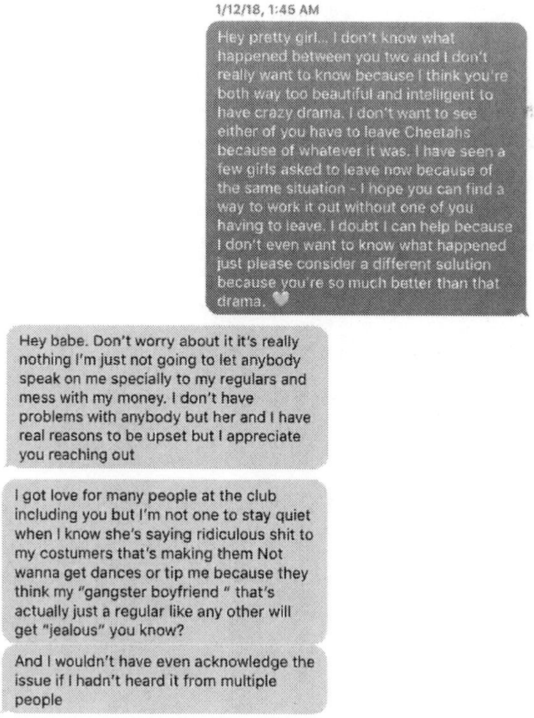

1/12/18, 1:45 AM

Hey pretty girl... I don't know what happened between you two and I don't really want to know because I think you're both way too beautiful and intelligent to have crazy drama. I don't want to see either of you have to leave Cheetahs because of whatever it was. I have seen a few girls asked to leave now because of the same situation - I hope you can find a way to work it out without one of you having to leave. I doubt I can help because I don't even want to know what happened just please consider a different solution because you're so much better than that drama. ♥

Hey babe. Don't worry about it it's really nothing I'm just not going to let anybody speak on me specially to my regulars and mess with my money. I don't have problems with anybody but her and I have real reasons to be upset but I appreciate you reaching out

I got love for many people at the club including you but I'm not one to stay quiet when I know she's saying ridiculous shit to my costumers that's making them Not wanna get dances or tip me because they think my "gangster boyfriend " that's actually just a regular like any other will get "jealous" you know?

And I wouldn't have even acknowledge the issue if I hadn't heard it from multiple people

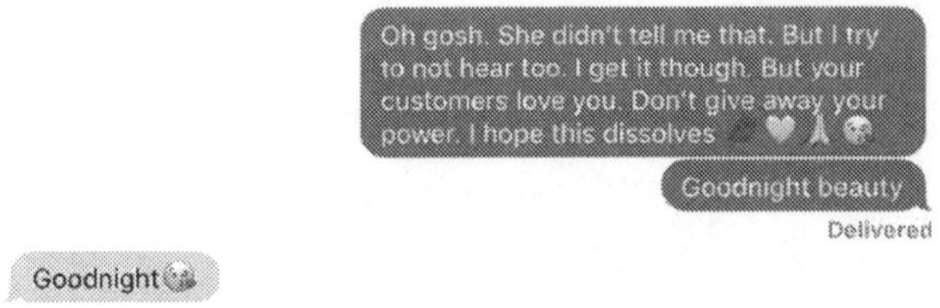

Oh gosh. She didn't tell me that. But I try to not hear too. I get it though. But your customers love you. Don't give away your power. I hope this dissolves

Goodnight beauty

Delivered

Goodnight

The truth was that it was likely true. Snowy did have a lot to say about the other girls. A lot of things she said were harsh and derogatory. I'd heard it with my own ears. I can only lead by example. I vowed never to participate when she rants at me and to remember that drama with other girls is not only unnecessary but harmful to everyone in the establishment.

I'm not totally immune. I had a moment of tension with another girl once. I'd said, a bit too loudly for the dressing room, that one of the clubs in Miami that I'd worked at was "hood." Somehow the whole situation spiraled into another dancer deciding I was racist, going so far as to decide that she was offended. The whole thing resulted in her closest friend ceaselessly harassing me for over a month. Ironically, I wasn't the first one to receive this treatment from her. She invaded my thoughts daily, and I even woke from a few nightmares in conflict with her. My level of sensitivity had skyrocketed in the years working at Cheer's while engaging with plant medicines and psychedelics. When I got fed up with battling the emotions, I called up the owner of the club and said, "If she doesn't disappear, I will." He said he'd watch her and see if he could legitimately let her go, but he couldn't fire an independent contractor without seeing an issue himself. However, he was eager to appease as complaints were coming from the club's highest earners.

Two weeks later, she came to work so drunk and belligerent that she yelled at a customer, walked away, stumbled, and fell flat on her face. That was her last night. I returned from traveling three weeks after the scene to find a much more tranquil club.

MJ, one of my favorite dancers, sent me a text the night before I returned from the hiatus and said, "Vida! Did you know that Ms. Sassy Pants was fired?"

I was so relieved I could have cried. The girls are brutal, and I believe in the vibrations of our actions. Treat people like shit, and you get shit on. Though I felt hurt and attacked by this girl, I also realized that only hurt people hurt people. God only knows what kind of pain she was experiencing in her life that led her to project on me. I also agree with the teachings that say we're all mirrors. I have something to learn about myself from all of these girls.

15

TINA'S STORY

Before I share Tina's story, I have to first explain my relationship with her and how it evolved. I wasn't the eldest at the club, but I interacted with many of the girls in a nurturing, motherly way. At some point, I'd talked with almost every girl about how to address an ailment or a heavy personal situation. I'd take any opportunity to support and uplift the girls. I knew that a better environment for one of us meant it was better for all of us. I "adopted" Tina as "stripper daughter," as she'd often call me her stripper mom when I'd offer her support.

When Tina was hired at Cheer's, I was wary of her. Her innocent voice was a red flag for me. She seemed naive. My lifestyle forces me to maintain a circle of street-smart individuals to feel comfortable and safe. I had no desire to communicate with Tina. When another girl asked if Tina could join a Kambo ceremony with her, I was apprehensive. First, I said no, but then I gave her a chance when she approached me on her own. I knew the best way to feel her out was to go on a journey in the Redwoods, so we did.

I was wrong about Tina.

My first impression of her sweet innocence was accurate, but she was also witty, quick, and extremely intelligent. I had nothing to worry about. She could keep up. We became closer after that journey into the woods. Later on, I left for work in such a hurry that I didn't bring food, so I went next door. I was on the phone with Josh, waiting for my boba tea and praying it wasn't laced with poison, when Tina walked through the door behind me. She beamed and squealed in her high-pitched voice, "Vida!" I relayed the scene to Josh and disconnected to call him back on FaceTime. I asked Tina to wait and say hi. Josh immediately invited her to a birthday celebration. She said she'd have to call out and miss her shift to join us.

As we walked back to Cheer's with our boba, I urged her to skip work to share this experience with us. She accepted, and we arranged for her to carpool the following day. When introducing herself to people at the birthday gathering that night, she, giggling, labeled me her "spiritual guide." She loved to joke but actually truly felt this way and continued to reach out for support over the subsequent years. It was an honor, and I did my best.

Not long after, Josh and I went on our ten-year anniversary adventure to Italy and France and celebrated like royalty. I disengaged with the club and all of the girls for a while to fully escape and enjoy every moment of our adventure. I didn't have a plan to return to Cheer's after the trip, but it wasn't long before I felt the financial need. After two nights back at work, the manager entered the dressing room and announced that Tina was in the hospital with a potentially fatal infection. She'd left Cheer's in the middle of her shift just a few days before, complaining of a severe headache. That night she dialed 9-1-1. She'd visited Mexico earlier that month, just before raging for a week with five other Cheer's girls at Lightning in a Bottle, a festival in Central California. Tina was new to the party scene and still fairly new to life as a stripper. Just as summer hit, she'd met an underground provider in a hotel room for butt injections. She was diving headfirst into a new lifestyle with wild abandon.

Cheer's is like a big family, as I've mentioned before. Our sister was going through a challenging time. To support Tina's healing, I thought it would be a powerful gift to see everyone's face from the club, verbalizing their admiration for her. I sent out this text in hopes of getting at least a few responses:

> *I am sending a text to girls at the club that I think would be interested in being a part of a small project. As you may know, Tina was in the hospital not too long ago and is now home healing. She had a rough time, but it may have been rougher in the past few weeks*

> *dealing with the repercussion of her family (who she's very close with) finding out that she works at Cheer's. If you feel inclined, I am creating a video for her to hopefully speed up (or boost) the recovery process. I know that we would all hope that for our trials and tribulations in the future, that we have the same support! If you feel inspired to share, I'm looking for a one to three minute or less video of yourself telling a story about her or just simply speaking about aspects of her that you appreciate. This could be specifically about her presence at Cheer's, or elsewhere. Whatever feels right! Please send me the video by August 12, and let me know if it's okay to be a part of a group thread of girls who will be contributing to this project <3*

One Cheer's girl, who goes by the name Katya, quickly sent me a video. Six other dancers, including the manager at the time, assured me I'd be receiving videos from them as well. I put up signs in the dressing room and sent text reminders. After a few weeks, I let go. There was a massive lesson for me in this experience to take the initiative when I want something. I could have asked each girl to join me outside to capture these short videos.

What was much more important than this major undertaking of compiling a montage of Cheer's girls that never actually happened was what *really* happened. Almost ten girls, three bouncers, and the club manager had visited her during her multi-week stay at Stanford Hospital, during which she underwent three major surgeries. There may be issues and tension from time to time, but when things get serious, the girls are there for one another. What a blessing to have found Cheer's. I've worked in some clubs where I've had to watch my back. Here, most girls had my back. This was also a blessing for Tina, who maintained her sense of humor and wit throughout the entire ordeal and through weeks of rollercoaster emotions that came after. Her positive attitude was an inspiration to all of us.

To top off this traumatic experience, Tina's family had found out the secret she'd kept about her career as a dancer.

Tina's story lit me on fire. It hurt to know that while she was fighting hard to keep her spirit alive, her family—the most important people in her life—were tearing her down. When she and I went on our first journey together, she spoke openly about her relationship with her family and how deeply she cared for and loved her father. Now she was crushed.

6/24/18, 9:40 PM

Hey [redacted] I really need your advice :/

Ever since I was hospitalized my family found out where I work and they weren't too pleased with it. I explained to them the no contact rule and I never did extras but they're super conservative & religious and sorts gave me an ultimatum that if I continue to work there after I recover they will completely cut me off. They also said that the only reason mike visited me every day at the hospital was bc when I called 911 I was at his house so I'm his responsibility. They also said that my younger sisters look down on me even though I know they still love me. Idk how to win them over. My dad still talks to me and I'm closest to him but I know they're convincing him to give me an ultimatum so I would listen to them. I told them dancing is not my end goal and that it actually saved my life from all the connections I made there but they are not convinced. Idk what to do or say or think. But it is putting a strain on me emotionally and mentally.

Before I send my lengthy response... can I ask you what your heart says is the best decision for you?

iMessage
Today 3:24 PM

I was wondering if we can meet up in person cause there's just a lot more and I think it's better for me to vent and get my point across and easier and you are like my spiritual guru lol I love you and I'm sorry I don't wanna stress you out but I know you're busy. Every morning I still have to take my antibiotics and there's 3 syringes I flush in my system and I have my own IV pole at home which only takes an hour and my left side is weaker than my right but I took your advice and drank probiotics to replenish my good bacteria. Even though physically I'm almost getting better emotionally it's tough and I think my family is slowing down my recovery process for thinking I sold my soul to the devil

My advice is to not stop dancing for your family.

You also do not need to change their opinion. That is not your job. You *can* be and example. You can continue to dance with integrity and intention as you have. There is a lot of stigma in the adult/entertainment/sex industry. By choosing to stay, you are taking g a stand to untangle that stigma. You are an "ethical stripper." By taking on this role, you are supporting a conscious shift with this old stigma. ✨✨✨✨✨✨✨✨✨✨✨ Never make decisions out of fear. Fear that you won't be loved or accepted... you may end up resenting them if you quit for them. You teach people how to treat you in life by the way that you respond to them. They live in a reality that you do not need to accept. Or you can. It's up to you. All choices are yours. You've already chosen to dance. You are a sovereign being and you can choose anything you want in life. Every choice has a consequence. Evaluate the consequences of your choices without fear. Discomfort is where we grow. You've been through a lot just recently and it seems the universe is continuing to offer you teachings-to learn, grow, expand. Let this bring you up. Rise! Your family will learn that disowning you will only hurt them. Or they won't... and they may suffer.

I am driving to LA tomorrow morning for a few days. Would you like to stop by tonight?!

Wow that made me feel 10xs better !!!!!! I think that about sums up what I needed to do. When I'm better enough to drive I'll come see you when you get back! My nurse said I can start driving as soon as the hole in my neck closes!! It's closing 90% so I'm excited so I can give you more insight. I love you so much thank you for being there for me. I think my main concern now is my 3 younger sisters from my dads side and I'm worried what they think of me cause I know my family is probably spreading misinformation but they know how I treat them and that I have a good heart so I'm not too worried. I love you

Info not insight lol

Have fun in LA!!

She was also confused. Did she have to choose between her main source of income and her biological family?

I could fully relate. My father had once referenced that Chris Rock quote: "You know you done fucked up if your daughter's a stripper." It has rung in my head for over a decade. I've never talked to my father about dancing. My mother, on the other hand, I've brought to my stomping grounds in South Jersey.

I recall bringing my father to one of my favorite places on the planet—Esalen Institute in Big Sur, California. We were headed to the hot spring baths, and my father peered down the hill and noticed the bodies bathing in the hot springs were nude. He exclaimed, "Hey, fuck that! I'm not going down there! Those people are naked!" It was a reminder that my father is not comfortable with nudity or sexuality and the sensual nature of humans. I have no desire to speak with him about stripping. The discomfort would simply be unbearable.

Just before releasing this book, my father messaged me out of the blue. We'd been having issues where he'd verbally abuse me because he felt I "didn't care that he was dying." Basically, he wanted me to spend every waking moment with him for a one- or two-month stretch. The caveat is that he's been "dying for over five years." It's been an eternal guilt trip. Being with him means destroying my mental health as he's the most negative person I know. So, the messages flooded in and shook me to the core:

It's not funny it's reality if you have tics then you have to deal with that. You always have an answer maybe now an then you should have empathy. I don't think your capable of that. Your a Kundert through an through. If it's not fun it's not for you. Sorry your so shallow Lana. Your answer is always think positive. I'm dying and you don't care it's not fun. You will run to your mother's side but you won't even pick up the phone for me. I hope some day you will take a deep look into yourself. You do nothing to help mankind but tell women how to fuck. That's stupid just keep being stupid that's the Kundert way. I looked you up on google I'm embarrassed. Saba's family is right your life is about your pussy. Everyone knows how to fuck your not teaching anyone anything. 8 billion people on this rock we know how to fuck. Quit using people ya lazy bitch. Go ahead hate me my parents did. Someone needs to tell ya Lana your an idiot. Can't give your dad a minute why because your an asshole. I feel sorry for Saba. You use people that's disgusting. Well your your mother. Sorry I'm dying just have to be honest. Don't ever tell the world I know you. Your nasty. I'm at a point in my life I need to be honest. Your so shallow what is your biggest concern your cunt. Well

I'm sad I'm mad you don't need to be concerned. Bye

Your a horrible daughter

Your Pusey is everything

It's sick to google you

Your dad is dying but your pussy is more important

Your a sick human. Don't ever connect with me

You never care unless it's your mother. That's weird
You will visit anyone but me fuck off girl.
Your nasty Lana how you could hate me don't know don't care
Did everything i could do to be a good dad wasn't enough for Lana
I need help but who cares not Lana
Why wouldn't care about your character, your a lazy user.

How many girls have to hide their profession from their family or friends for fear of being judged? Or any number of other reasons? Future employment options are frequently a concern. This is another stand I'm ready to take. How many of us can release shame, fear, and judgment? Sex workers are providing a service. Just like the people who come each week to collect our garbage. Just like the attorney we call for legal matters. There have been women (and men) in these roles for centuries; prostitution may very well be one of the oldest professions on the planet! We know this, so why the stigma? Is it any more wrong or right than a cashier at the local grocer or the CEO of Exxon? Who gets to decide what's right or wrong? We all came into existence after our parents had sex. It's a completely natural part of human existence. Yes, it's challenging to see it as a benefit to society when a man spends his life savings on one night in a strip club. However, this isn't the only scenario that plays out on average nights at any gentlemen's club.

Take Tina, for example, with her sweet innocence. She takes the hand of her willing individual and leads him to a booth to sit comfortably and enjoy his connection with this divine embodiment of God in human form. Not only is he granted viewing pleasure, but he's also offered this connection with a feminine essence that could possibly uplift his spirit for days, weeks, months, or years (likely forever)! The authentic presence of a powerful female is, without question, a gift. She isn't aggressively ripping his last penny from his fingers. She's inviting him to have an exhilarating experience. Yes, sometimes these patrons aim for a goal or target that's impossible to hit, yet this learning process is an inevitable aspect of life!

I've seen men walk out of a private show with Tina with ear-to-ear smiles and melted hearts. They're not tormented or frustrated. It's quite the opposite. And in the Disney/stripper land of Cheer's, it's good vibes that customers leave with and nothing more. There's no alcohol or physical contact or rooms with closed doors. When they leave with smiles, there's no confusion. That fulfillment didn't come from a climax or intoxication. Tina is a priestess, a dakini, a healer, like many women in the industry. She's offering a well-received gift. The fact that her family will likely never come to realize this truth is tragic, from my perspective.

Most dancers are riding a mental without any pressure or judgment from the world around them. I certainly have experienced a hellish emotional rollercoaster of my own. A journal entry from late 2018 might offer a glimpse of my internal dialogue toward the end of my stripping career:

August 2, 2018

In just a few short months, it will have been ten years since the very first day that I took the stage as an "exotic dancer." Lately, I've been incredibly frustrated. Why am I still doing this? Why haven't I moved on to bigger and better things? Especially since entering the world of plant medicines. The more psychedelics I ingested, the more I wanted to burn my bag of exotic dancer clothes, never to introduce myself as Vida again.

It seems the biggest lesson that I need to learn is that of internal validation. What I receive the most is external validation about how attractive I am, how hard I've worked on keeping my body in shape, and, on a more personal level, how worldly and intelligent or how witty and funny I am. That's all wonderful. But how is it truly making the world a better place? That's really what I want to hear: that I'm making the world a better place. More than just hearing it, I want to be able to say it to myself.

This is where the internal validation comes in. The only way that I can sleep at night, or continue to do this any longer, is if I somehow find the belief within myself that I am truly creating a better world. Not even better, actually; just being a contributor, someone in service. I fall in and out. It goes in waves. I do believe that every time I am kind, gentle, or intimate with someone who is so deeply craving this sort of attention and affection, giving from my highest, I will inspire them to do the same—an energetic loop. If I can authentically share this creative life force with someone, perhaps then they can authentically share with someone else. Perhaps they haven't made love to their partner in days, or weeks, or months, and maybe I can support them in igniting the feeling that urges them to go home and make passionate love to their partner with absolute presence.

That said, I often fantasize about it being my last night. I've done the good deed, over and over. I've served my time. Some nights I really go there. I tell myself that I won't ever set foot in another strip club. Countless visions I'd had during psychedelic journeys would flash through my mind every time I was rejected by a customer. My inner critic was growing louder and louder. You are old! You have been doing this for too long! You have wasted your life! You are stuck, and you will have to do this for the rest of your life! This critic always reared its ugly head when I went home with less money than expected or when I acknowledged the physical pain and exhaustion.

Vegas had a whole new way to trigger the noise of my critic: a comparison. I looked at all of the celebrities and self-made millionaires, billionaires, celebrity cam models, and exotic dancers that graced the Rhino, and I couldn't help but compare myself. Why wasn't I where I wanted to be? Why didn't I have millions? Fame? Where did I go wrong? The move from Jersey to California was tough. We didn't have a clear path. In Jersey, I identified as a yoga teacher, dance instructor, jewelry designer, and blogger. Who the hell was I in California? An exotic dancer. It was the only thing I was actively doing. I hated myself when I took a good hard look at my reality. One night the certainty of it being my last night hit me like a slap in the face. I really am in the wrong profession, and I really need to quit, like, yesterday. I just can't always be thinking, "How can I get as much as I can from this person?"

If I can keep my eyes pried open past 2 A.M., there's always money to be made on the weekends. There are the guys who come in after bar time, and then those who wait until the last minute—the ones who need to be under pressure to make a decision. One Sunday at 2:30 A.M., a man at Cheer's approached me from behind to ask if I was busy. I was going for someone else who seemed like the more desirable company because I can only stretch myself so far at the end of the night, but I rarely refuse someone who approaches me first. The sale is already made! My physical advertisement worked, and they wanted to pay me. Companies spend thousands or millions on this kind of marketing. I also have a small-talk phobia. It's a feat to approach anyone in the club while fearing that they may want to talk about the weather, what I went to school for, where I'm from, where I live; it all makes me nauseous.

I scanned this man and noticed a thick gold chain and a big brand name slapped right across the front of his oversized sweater. Bad news. Dammit. This style is generally linked to a culture-A mentality, lacking respect for girls in my industry. In this business, there has to be some stereotyping. After approaching a thousand men all wearing the same outfit, opinions are inevitably formed. The guy that's dressed well has more money. The young guys haven't yet made their millions. The guys in suits are either scammers who want too much, or they'll pay well to get exactly what they want.

Most of the girls who have worked in Las Vegas for years are familiar with brands of shoes, watches, and any other expensive accessories. It only took me a few moments to realize that this one didn't fit. He was young and kind-hearted. He was also very high. I gave him a dance, and he asked over and over what I was doing after work. I told him over and over that I was going straight to bed. When the dance ended, he asked my age, and I didn't hesitate. I usually ask what they think before I reveal my age. This is a simple way to stretch out the conversation and shorten the time performing. If they want to ask questions, clearly, they don't mind me taking the time to answer. Of course, there's always Ken, who definitively states that he doesn't want any talking to interrupt his expensive performance. Since this kid had waited until the end, I answered fast, gave him a hug, and walked away.

He approached again after the last performance while I was waiting to approach someone sitting by the stage. "I need another dance."

I replied, "Well, this time, you should probably start with two because you won't be able to come back for more this time." He agreed, we went in the back, and again he asked my age. I said, "Didn't we already go over this?"

He paused and shook his head, "Right, right. Sorry, I thought that you were the same age as me—-twenty. You're thirty-two, right?"

I said, "Oh good, you remembered!"

He apologized again. I kept dancing and then sat down on the table in front of him on my gray, sequin blanket.

I knew that he was high, but I started by asking, "Did you drink tonight?"

I wasn't surprised by his reply. "Yeah, but I also took a Xanax." I cringed. He said, "What, is that bad?"

"Yes, of course. When you mix Xanax and alcohol, you can't remember anything the next day. It's a bad combination." Memories flashed through my mind of the one time I made that mistake and had a horrific experience.

He continued, "Well, I also smoked some weed." I shook my head, trying to make eye contact, but his eyes were wandering and glazed over. "Yeah, I've actually been having trouble with that lately, like remembering what happened. In the last few hours, I don't remember what happened."

I said, "You can't take Xanax anymore. Go ahead and smoke weed if you feel like it's alleviating something uncomfortable for you as a first option. Xanax is never going to help you." I knew he wasn't prescribed it.

Sometimes some random person's simple piece of advice can stick forever, especially if you're looking at them with desire. I can remember plenty of attractive members of the opposite sex offering me advice in my early twenties. If I saw them as someone I'd want to be in a relationship with, I almost always listened. We all know that sex and sexual attraction is a powerful motivator. Whether or not this young man listened to my words, at least I planted a seed. At least a voice of reason might ring in his head the next time he reaches for a drink to wash down his Xanax.

Yes, dancers sometimes (or maybe often?) give unsolicited advice. More than half of the time, people come back and thank us. I'm mostly a therapist and sometimes an exotic dancer. People divulge all of their deepest, darkest secrets to dancers because we are anonymous, and they may never meet us again. I see this as a powerful position. I also believe in Karma. This was yet another opportunity to create the world I wanted to see around me. I have no desire to live in a world where pharmaceuticals are so accessible to youth. Maybe that was my one shot to deter this one single soul from a challenging path. Then again, maybe on his path, he is meant to explore his shadow.

Many people who walk through the door of the club are on a path, exploring their shadow, including staff and dancers. I've watched a number of girls become so incredibly inebriated after a night of work that they can't even leave the club to go home. They can't leave, they can't work, they're basically doing a whole lot of nothing while exploring the deepest, darkest shadow of themselves. They make this a weekly practice. Had this young man asked for time in private with one of these girls, perhaps she would have popped another Xanax with him right then and there. I've turned around in VIP to a guy taking key bumps of cocaine during our VIP session. I had to walk away mid-dance as his arm extended toward my face, attempting to lure me into his 5 A.M. coke binge.

These are the moments when I am grateful that I had my fill in high school. I experienced every narcotic I could as fast as I could in my youth and lost all desire once I saw enough friends lose everything. The man on a coke binge that I left in the VIP booth might have gotten the message, just like the kid on Xanax. Whether or not they hear it, my intention is always to stand for what I believe in. I don't support a toxic lifestyle.

I'm grateful that I've never had to get drunk or high to work in a strip club. I drank in Vegas for the first year or so because I didn't have the confidence to speak with conviction or take the aggressive approach I witnessed with most girls. As I built my confidence and discovered my niche, I was sure to let customers know I don't drink and can't be persuaded to. It's no surprise that this decision shaped my (rather small) target audience. I'd tell them, "My body is a temple, and I don't poison my temple." It's an asset and, of course, the only place I have to live. I also feel like absolute shit when I drink. You won't see that fun, loose girl you think you're going to get.

All dancers know that if they drink or even pretend they're drinking or act drunk, many customers will spend more money, thinking that they will get closer to sexual favors as the inhibitions fade. I vote for more sober dancers. Drunk is sloppy. It's gross. Let's kill the trend. It's lame. This shift is possible. Men can learn that an intoxicated woman is not attractive or enticing. I'm not voting for men to come into clubs intoxicated and be taken advantage of either. Vegas is where I learned to really take a stand for what I believe in, despite the norm, and go against the grain—no more pretending that I enjoyed emasculating men and only looking out for myself.

It's the second night of my new exciting performance, which seems to be helping me maintain my sanity, quenching my thirst for variety. Once in a while, I bring something new to the stage to keep it fresh for no one but myself. I make my way up the three stairs onto the stage, slowly, with poise, grace, and mystery. Before I hit the last stair, I toss down my tiny leather handbag, bursting at the seams with my essentials: one orange-scented Merry Hempsters lip balm, lavender-scented hand sanitizer by Dr. Bronners, my organic Uncle Harry's Natural Products breath freshener, homeopathic eye drops, and some cash (a few Benjamins, but mostly Jacksons). In the middle compartment was a stack of business cards with my name, email, and phone number (Vida, Google voice, and Gmail). For a moment, I firmly grip the wood colonial ball post tops on either side of the stair banister, allowing my five-inch black stilettos to float onto the stage as I suspend myself in the air. This time I don't begin by making contact with the first static pole on the stage. Instead, I direct my gaze across the stage and make my way to the second pole, drawn by the boisterous voices of three middle-aged men.

A performer loves an audience wild with anticipation. "Wow. Check out this one!" Because the money is in the hands of the patrons around the stage, I like to stay low and close. I dive into my usual floorwork routine. Splits, arched back, hip drops from plank (push-up position), leaning in for a gentle brush up against the neck, cheek, or ear. My second song is "Closer," by Nine Inch Nails. Midway through the song, as the energy plateaus, I slide my middle finger into one of the holes right in the center of my fishnet stockings, between my legs, and pull until I hear the threads popping. I continue to pull until I rip a hole in the stockings, exposing every inch of skin between my legs, along with my right butt cheek. The crowd falls silent, and I roll onto my back and make eye contact between my outstretched legs. I'm dripping with sweat. When I hear the last few chords of "Closer," I begin brushing the dollar bills toward the center of the stage into a pile, while the bouncer hands me a red plastic basket to collect my tips.

I slide the basket over to the noisy bunch and introduce myself to each of them with a handshake. The tall blonde, appearing to be in his late thirties to early forties, tells me that he'd love a dance. As always, I say that I'll return to him in five after I visit the dressing room to put my panties back on and drop off my basket of ones. After our dance, he confesses that he's insanely attracted to his ex-wife's sister and wants to have sex with her. The not-so-surprising kicker is that I look like her. He completes his story and asks, "Do you think that's bad?"

I grin and say, "You're human! There's nothing wrong with being attracted to someone. Did you act on it?"

He says that he has not. I'm curious to know if his wife became his ex-wife because of this forbidden attraction. Apparently, it was not the cause of the divorce, but he is still dreaming about his one-time sister-in-law, who took such good care of her body. I hope to release him of that shame he's been carrying, or at least inspire him to let go of it. The world can do without more shame and guilt.

I ride the rollercoaster and hit the high highs when a client leaves with a glow—that feeling of connection—and affirms that they feel fulfilled or when I feel sparks of inspiration.

16

INSIGHT FROM LIVING BY THE NIGHT

Formal education rarely trumps experience. What I learned in more than eleven years of stripping didn't only come through experience but also a willingness to study myself. I learned the sanskrit word *svadhyaya* at a very young age (thank you, Uncle Jeff), and it's never left me (that yoga fanatic is still at the core of my being). This word means self-study, and for as long as I can remember, I've been on a quest to understand the unique geometry of my own mind at a deeper level.

I took advantage of the opportunity to be whoever I wanted to be, with every new face. The men who walked into the many clubs I graced across the country knew nothing about me, and I had free rein to guide our experience together and create any version of reality. I tried out different personas and telling the story of my life from different angles. I never lied, because it was always too challenging to remember the lies, and I've always found joy in genuinely connecting with the men I met in gentlemen's clubs. Sometimes, I'd tell them I had a crazy childhood with mentally ill parents and it was rough. I'd flip the story and tell the next guy that I'd been raised by an herbalist and destined to live a holistic lifestyle and become a medicine woman. I'd pay close attention to reactions and responses based on the stories I told and the way I chose to build rapport with each man. I played the role of a friend, a coach, a mentor, and a guide for many men and many dancers. I had girls calling me their stripper mom and regulars coming to see me for marriage advice and spiritual guidance. I also had girls come and sit on someone's lap while I was talking to them as she shooed me away. There were men that would tell me I didn't have big enough breasts and they couldn't care less what else I had to offer. It wasn't all sunshine and rainbows. BUT! Every single moment was an opportunity to learn. I kept a journal from 2012-2021. I never missed a day. I've written nearly ten eighty-thousand-word books in the past decade of my life, including many of the insights and realizations that came while wearing 6-inch stilettos and French lace panties.

1. BARING THE BOOTY

Every club has its slower nights. Cheer's in Sunnyvale not only has slow nights, but it also has painfully slow nights. Completely dead, even on a regular basis. Perhaps it's not the prime location for a no-contact gentlemen's club? Every once in a blue moon, every hustler contracted by the club is on the night shift together. This is generally an unenjoyable experience. Then there are those rare nights where the dynamic seems like perfection. There isn't any tension between the girls, and everyone seems to be operating on the same frequency. These are the magical nights when I wish Cheer's a television show.

We all seemed in rare form on a particular Thursday night in March 2018. We closed early, as we often did when it was that slow. We were in the dressing room, getting dressed and emptying our plastic baskets of our very few one-dollar bills we'd made onstage, counting our money to tip out staff. It was about 1 A.M., and it felt like there was some bizarre astrological configuration or something unseen that had us moving in slow motion. Perhaps it was that none of us had moved for the entire night except to give dances or perform on stage? The girls seemed ravenously hungry (i.e., over-tired and bored), so we lingered for an extra half an hour after closing. Four or five of us offered bites of our uneaten snacks and dinners for the night. Forks and spoons were passed around the dressing room.

Along with the club exodus comes the ridiculous banter. The banter tonight was especially entertaining. Someone started the conversation about bleaching buttholes and laser hair removal. Of course, we couldn't just converse about these things; we had to check each other's behinds to see about hair or unsightly anal discoloration or darkness. It's not long in a small club before everyone has seen each other's everything, and rarely does that make us uncomfortable. Not to mention, in a fully nude club, after countless private dances for customers where we bare all, eventually, it's only natural to let go of any discomfort with being seen naked.

From my perspective, we live in human bodies on this planet, and there is no reason to feel shame or discomfort. This is huge. Fortunately, I have always been comfortable in my skin. I remember myself as a ten-year-old, stripping down and standing in my window completely naked while the neighborhood kids watched in disbelief. I can't remember my thoughts at the time, but I know I was comfortable fully nude, and I wanted everyone to know it. This never changed.

Even when I was depressed for a short stint in 2009 and gained thirty pounds, I was still willing to shamelessly bare all at the local gentlemen's club. Being uncomfortable naked seems to be a symptom of our broken system. We are sold lies that say we need things because something is wrong with us. Human bodies grow hair, for example. We are told we need to purchase and own the latest and greatest razors and hair removal products or purchase expensive treatments because hair is unsightly and will make us less attractive or desirable.

This plays on the deepest fear of most humans. Being unloved or unwanted means death to an infant. As an adult, the fatal aspect on an individual level is, to some degree, removed, but our species is innately driven to procreate. How can we procreate if we're so disgusting that the opposite sex has no desire to mate with us? To capitalize on this fear is deep and dark. Think of all of the things marketed to us. We are perpetually bombarded with product advertisements for a myriad of things to make us better or fix the terrible unattractiveness of our natural physical body. I am referring specifically to the culture (or lack thereof) that I grew up in. America—a materialistic, consumer-driven nation where everyone is at risk of aging and becoming more repulsive each and every day! Maybe once we are fully aware of what's happening on the subconscious level, we can choose to shift the focus away from all the external noise.

Dancers are not exempt from scrutiny. Most are still, like many of us, their own worst critics. However, there exists the option to *choose*. Buy into whatever belief system works for you. If it doesn't work, toss that shit out and keep trying on new ones until there is a belief system that feels good. I've chosen to take in the plethora of compliments directed at me each time I work. Yes, I've gotten a few harsh judgments and some I haven't yet forgotten, but the things that stick are the compliments. Being told every night that I'm beautiful, hot, sexy, stunning, gorgeous, perfect, you name it—these are the messages I choose to believe, because why the hell not? No reason to let it go to my head, but why not love my temple?

My body is my only place to live, and I have taken care of it with this important fact in mind. Yes, technological advances allow us to beat up our bodies and repair them in ways that have not been available before, but there's nothing like being healthy and in great physical shape because of discipline and devotion to health. I've spent countless hours educating myself about health and wellness, and I honor myself for my dedication. Most of the girls at Cheer's and many other strip clubs do the same, and for that, there is reason to be proud. Perhaps I could have disconnected from my high level of comfort being nude had I not become an exotic dancer—I'll only ever know what did, in fact, happen—but dancing has helped me maintain the confidence of being comfortable while fully naked and seen.

2. NEVER MISS AN OPPORTUNITY TO USE THE POWER FOR GOOD.

It was my first night back at the club after a European romance trip with Josh. I sent Raj, one of my regulars, a text through my Vida-only line and didn't wait for his reply. I wasn't sure if I'd see him, but at least I'd made an effort. I was on the other side of the room when he walked in. We met eyes, and I walked toward him, but I didn't maintain eye contact as I moved his way. I moved casually at my usual pace. Though I knew it would make his day if I sprinted over to him and maintained eye contact while doing so, like long-lost lovers reuniting after years apart, I couldn't bring myself to do it. This is exactly why I have this "worst exotic dancer ever" label. So many of the girls are incredible actresses. I don't have it in me. Perhaps if it was truly take two and the cameras were rolling, I could get into character. This wasn't the case, and I didn't want to give him the wrong impression. I was not in love.

This is where ethics come in. This is where that "terrible exotic dancer and me" gets played out fully. I can't lie. Not only am I not in love, but there is also absolutely no physical attraction, and there's no way I can pretend. I *hugged him* and told him it was nice to see him because it was. It was always nice to see someone that knew me enough that I could be myself with them and didn't have to do small talk. We had gotten to the point where he no longer asked me to dance or perform. He would hand me the money, I would sit down, and we would talk. I paid attention. I cared. He felt heard. I didn't remove any clothes, and at that point, I doubted that he expected me to. At least he didn't ask. My dances for him were subpar anyway because I could feel him getting more excited than I was willing to entertain. Besides that, his body odor was so overwhelming that getting close was offensive. I had to turn down the volume on my sensuality when I danced for him. It seemed that he truly believed there was some sort of attraction to him when I gave my best performance. This is, in fact, the goal. I want my clients to feel loved, wanted, and enticed to spend more time with me. I guess this is a success, but again, my comfort is my first priority.

I pulled away, and I think he realized there was no chance of moving our relationship outside the club. The first question he asked was, "Are you glad to be back?" He followed that question with, "It must be so horrible to be here."

I laughed. He knew me well. I decided not to get too dark or raw right off the bat. "It's not really that bad." I *can lie* if I realize my truth at the moment is the most depressing thing I can say. It was horrible to be back. It was horrible to feel as if I was exactly where I was supposed to be, doing exactly what I was supposed to be doing, completely in bliss, and then return to a place where I questioned my identity and my sanity. I knew I wouldn't have to dive too deep into my tunnel of darkness because what he really wanted to hear about was France. He had lived in Paris years ago. We'd talked about it many times. We'd even had an entire night where I attempted to only converse in French. It was a dream to be paid to enjoy myself and speak French. It was one of the nights that kept me coming back. He'd seemed happy that night. He was heartbroken I didn't make it to the Fifth Arrondissement of Paris.

He had asked me to take photos for him. He asked which was my favorite place, if I wanted to go back, if I spoke French with anyone, if the conversations went well. He wanted me to recount every detail. Once he'd asked everything he could, he said goodbye. He simply wanted to live vicariously through me, attempting to reconnect with this long-lost part of himself. He was stuck in the US, waiting for citizenship. If he left the country, it was unlikely he would receive permission to re-enter. It could be years until he had the opportunity. I never understood it. I've never liked any place enough to sacrifice my desire to travel. Land of the free, right? Wrong. We're not free in America.

3. LEARNING ABOUT BOUNDARIES.

Stripping taught me to claim my feminine sexual power and acknowledge my self-worth. If I'm worthy, I am allowed to ask for what I want and say no to what I don't—at any moment. Not learning this would be detrimental to my income potential as a dancer, so I had to learn and integrate it as fast as possible. Not only did this learning process affect my income potential, but there was a direct correlation to burnout. If a dancer is constantly taken advantage of and working without boundaries, never exercising her right to say no, it's likely she won't be in the game long. It's exhausting to feel like you've been violated regularly. It wears on the soul.

Touching isn't the only place where boundaries are necessary. Customers often arrive at the club with a deep desire to confide in someone and end up crossing boundaries of time and mental intimacy, overburdening the dancer with the details of their life that aren't for us to hold. The space lends itself to this. People feel completely open because they know exotic dancers know nothing about their personal or private life. Everything is anonymous. Of course, things were a bit different with Raj since my identity was revealed, but he also knew he could tell me anything because I'd never share his secrets with anyone close to him. Ninety-nine percent of the time, real names are not exchanged, and no connection to life outside the club is made. Clients can share their deepest, darkest secrets and pull every skeleton out of the closet.

Often customers arrive intoxicated and sometimes feel this somehow grants them a pass. They can act out. They can tell elaborate, mildly fictitious stories or go deep into their shadow. They can come in one night and act like a fool, then arrive the next night with flowers like a chivalrous prince. He'll say he didn't remember anything from the night before, all of the crazy confessions and declarations. Many dancers, myself included, continue to accept them and their generous donations.

This reminds me of Sam. Sam would come in drunk and not even remember. Once in a blue moon, he'd forget who I was. He would rant about his crazy exotic dancer girlfriend, Tina. I would tell him the same thing every time—"You're too good for her. You don't deserve it." I recommended therapists, medicine work, retreats. He was a bit of a masochist—another man carrying the trauma of the relationship with his ex-wife.

When Sam began visiting Cheer's, he had just gone through a painful divorce. His wife was having an affair with his best friend. He didn't speak about her much. He wasn't looking for advice, support, or anyone to confide in. He would come in joyous and seemed optimistic about his new single lifestyle.

Tina was a young dancer with a nasty habit. She lived with complete disregard for her mind and body, and her drug addiction threw her off course. She labeled herself bipolar, but the stories Sam would recount, week after week, sounded more severe. Her psychotic episodes erupted daily. Sam lived a life of complete chaos. She'd started an illegal marijuana operation in his home, even though he paid her to live with him. She would get upset with him and threaten to call the police. He became paranoid that she was bringing other men into his bed when he was at work and installed cameras to spy on her. She found out about them and left him but still expected her monthly allowance. She'd leave him abusive voicemails and texts that he'd read and play at Cheer's. He'd take her on exotic trips, and she'd disappear with other men and blame him for her behavior. She was unstable, unquestionably a threat to herself and anyone on her path. I listened to Sam's stories night after night, telling him he needed to get away from Tina, fast, before things got too real. He'd tell me he was in love with Tina, unable to distance himself from her even though he knew he was crazy for his devotion to her.

One night Sam came in completely intoxicated. He just couldn't get his shit together. This psychologically unstable female had a tight hold on him, and he had no intention of getting out of the mess he'd co-created. During a private show with Sam, some girls, of course, are completely unaffected and would pretend to listen to his stories night after night. I couldn't bear it after a year. I listened with compassion for the first twenty encounters, then sent him therapists and different resources I'd mentioned at the club. He took the initiative to call one of the therapists I referred him to, but he told me she wasn't right for him.

People can't be helped if they're not ready and not asking for it. Sam wasn't looking for help. He seemed to enjoy this whole saga that was playing out. I maintained the boundary with Sam by changing the subject. Either I'd feel distraught listening to his stories, or I'd put up a wall and turn it off. I chose the latter after realizing these stories weren't coming to an end any time soon. Sam was a reminder to carry with me the truth of one of my favorite quotes from Plato: "Be kind, for everyone you meet is fighting a hard battle." Same just wanted to be the hero and help the girl. He was a good man with a kind heart; however, he created a problem in his life and needed to learn the lesson by solving it himself.

4. MUSIC PROFOUNDLY AFFECTS US.

Let's acknowledge that I'm biased, but I believe dancers have superpowers. They can shift the energy in the room (whether they want you laughing, crying, or aroused), can captivate a massive crowd, and make choices that will affect tens, hundreds, or even a thousand patrons. Musical selection feels like a superpower to me.

We all have a favorite DJ to experience live, right? At Cheer's, we had the opportunity to read the room and choose our music before we went on stage. Most girls would play what lit them up, working with DJ Sal, and others would vibe check the club before choosing. The ability of dancers to choose their own music is power. We are all influenced and conditioned, in a sense, by the music we hear. What are the lyrics of the songs that you have heard? How many songs can you remember the lyrics to? Hundreds? A thousand? Songs train our brains. They can lead our lives by becoming wired in the subconscious.

I love to reference Dr. Emoto's experiments exposing water to different words, pictures, and music, then freezing the water and viewing it under a microscope. He concluded that positive, uplifting music, words, and vibrations created beauty. The negative words and music resulted in distorted structures in the frozen water crystals, and the positive, uplifting vibrations resulted in beautiful patterns. Our bodies are over 60% water. Just imagine what effect the vibrations around us have. Like any research, these claims are not accepted by all, but there are other studies where plants, like water, responded positively to uplifting music.

We respond to stimuli without question. If the stimulus is unintentional, violent, and aggressive, we reflect that back. If the stimulus is loving, kind, and uplifting, we respond in kind. How often is it that you see someone respond to love with hate? It's certainly more common to see love reflected as it is given. If the lyrics of a song are, "these hoes ain't loyal . . ." that's fine if you want to bring more unloyal hoes into your world. One of my favorite songs to dance to is by Frank Sinatra, with the lyrics, "Fly me to the moon, let me play among the stars." I find it much more uplifting than most of the top-forty hip-hop commonplace in most strip clubs.

Familiar songs get customers in a more receptive state to build rapport, but introducing something they've never heard that they just might enjoy feels much more compelling. My vote is for more conscious music being played in strip clubs. We can talk about unloyal hoes in an environment where it's not programming the subconscious. Albeit Chris Brown's lyrics, we all know that there are women who aren't loyal, but let's not call them hoes on top of it. That seems like we're making matters worse by labeling those who already have low morale stemming from trauma or unconscious programming. Dancing is taxing enough, mentally. We can do without *these hoes ain't loyal* type-lyrics, regardless of who or what he was speaking to.

5. LAUGHTER IS THE BEST KIND OF MEDICINE.

Most of the dancers I've met share a similar sense of humor. It's generally a bit crude and often offensive to people outside the industry. Then there's me, with my completely oddball sense of humor. I'm always looking for something to "tickle my funny bone." Laughter at the club is a must. A night without laughter at the club is a terrible night. Fortunately, it's a rare occurrence.

One night was good not only because the girls were giddy and in good spirits; it was good because it was just *good.* It was a weekend, and the girls were making money. Of course, there were still girls who always seemed to sit in the dressing room, gracing the floor for a brief moment every hour. It was the opposite for me. I was in my brief moment of gracing the dressing room to freshen up and drink water.

My spot for the night was next to the only door in or out, opposite the counter space where most of the older girls who have made Cheer's their home club for three to fourteen years sit. One girl in particular, whose slapstick humor always caught me off guard, had planted herself in the dressing room and hadn't moved in over an hour.

Sammy was slumped in her chair with her back against the wall—her usual position. Tabitha walked from the opposite corner, speaking to everyone within earshot as she paused just inside the doorway separating the two sides of the dressing room. "Look at my bangs! I just don't know how I'm supposed to work like this. My forehead is *so* big! They look like—"

"Like you have a facial deformation?" Sammy finished, glancing in Tabitha's direction. With Tabitha's bangs tucked to the side, I noticed that she had a rather large forehead. Sammy began belting out "deformed face girrrrrrrllll!" in her deep, sultry voice while looking at her phone, no longer paying any attention to Tabitha.

Monique seemed unaffected by the new jingle being sung one foot to her right and continued talking about her cute dog photos. I was hyperventilating listening to Sammy singing. I had to exit the dressing room swiftly as I was clearly alone in this fit of laughter.

Five minutes later, I returned to find Sparkle displaying her personal porn to six girls. Her new fuck buddy had sent a video of himself moaning and stroking his massive "wand of light." The girls cooed at the size of his erect penis and shared their sexual fantasies, stories of dick pics, and late-night sexting. I had to rip myself away when DJ Mikey called out, "VIDA! You're next. VIDA! Coming up next for you, guys."

I finished with no success selling dances and bee-lined to the dressing room to put my lingerie back on. Sammy was in the same spot I'd last seen her. She asked, "What's it like out there?"

The girls knew what I meant when I said "Indian. It's Indian out there and one weird white guy, and he looks . . ." I stumbled on my words.

Monique screeched, "THAT GUY WITH THE WEIRD SIDEBURNS?!"

I was already in a fit of laughter again. "YES! Him!"

She stood to continue the guy-with-weird-sideburns commentary. "How does he wake up in the morning, look in the mirror, and say, 'Yeah. This is all right. I'll just go out like this today.'" Tears streamed down my face. We were all displaying our late-night, overtired, punch-drunk demeanor—more of the nights that keep me coming back. A Cheer's TV show would go down in history. When the girls get going, it's all worth it.

Most girls say it's the money. Or the pole. It's certainly not because we love all the attention from the men. For me, it's really the girls—the camaraderie. Cheer's Gentlemen's Club is an anomaly in the heart of Silicon Valley, California. The girls are like a big (dysfunctional) family. Of course, there are a few black sheep, just like any family, but overall, the girls really are one big, strange family.

Once, Serene commented on my drop-crotch onesie. Then Mazie, Sugar, Max, and finally Cinnamon all joined in. Serene ranted about how good my ass looked in the outfit, even though it had no form. I told them it was my favorite outfit after work because I could air out my vagina and not wear any underwear (which is only partially true—the shower is much more crucial than air). Then, for some reason, one of the girls decided to start singing "Hakuna Matata."

Within moments, the lyrics changed to "airing out the vagina." Then five girls belted out the Cheer's rendition of "Hakuna Vagina" in unison.

"Vagina! Air out the va-a-agina! It means an aired-out Va-GINA! For the rest of your days. It's a problem free-philosophy . . . Aired out VA-gina!"

With the exception of that one black sheep, everyone in the dressing room joined in. At these times, we were high on money and lack of sleep, fantasizing about driving away from the club and crawling into bed.

Sugar sat on the counter with her back leaning on the mirror. "I'm just itching my crotch."

Cinnamon responded, "Oh Sugar, you're not getting paid anymore; you don't have to be sexy!"

Sugar maintained her nonchalant demeanor and topped herself: "I just don't know how to hold in farts!"

The banter shifted to how they would hold in farts during dances and how one of the most attractive girls to ever work at Cheer's (the spitting image of Megan Fox) would walk up to a group of guys. If they rejected her, she would fart and whisper, "YOU STINK," before walking away. Somehow this story struck a chord, and I found myself, once again, in a fit of laughter. We seemed to share a childlike sense of humor, where bodily functions served as appropriate punchlines. I'd dance for another ten years to relish the humor that comes just after the club closes on a busy night.

6. THERE ARE ALWAYS OPPORTUNITIES TO BE A ROLE MODEL.

It was one of those nights I couldn't care less if I was asked to leave and never return. My personal life had worn me down to the point where the only priority was maintaining sanity. I was two hours late and missed my stage set twice, which never went over well with the DJ or management. My friend and fellow dancer MJ had sent a text asking if I was coming in. I replied that I was and asked why. She was sweet and empathetic. When I arrived, she noticed I had been crying and asked if I needed a hug. It was a long, warm hug, and I sighed with relief. This was the first time that I'd worked on my birthday in my entire dancing career. It wasn't the official day, but the night carried into January 13.

The planets must have aligned. It was the busiest night I'd worked in months. Getting customers into the private dance area was effortless, and each patron was surprisingly kind and well-composed. A few of them asked if I was twenty-one. On my thirty-second birthday, this was music to my ears. I felt grateful to be seen as full of youth, mentally thanking myself for all my efforts to treat my body and mind well. This was one of those magical nights that kept us coming back, night after night. I left with nearly $1,300, which I couldn't complain about, especially having arrived hours late. Leaving January 13 with $1,300 seemed divinely synchronistic. Maybe working on my birthday wasn't the worst idea in ten years of stripping.

During our early morning dressing room antics, MJ, pausing from counting her ones out of a red plastic basket, glanced over at me from across the room and said, "You're like the mother I needed when I was younger."

I laughed, continuing to count my basket of ones. MJ was a comedian. She had that off-the-wall sense of humor. She'd catch us off guard with some bizarre yet witty comment, and we couldn't help but laugh.

Pixie overheard MJ and followed her comment with, "You're like the dirty babysitter I always wanted." Past 2 A.M., our banter was always a mix of aggressive flirting and crude innuendo, unless it was delirious nonsense.

I had just tipped out the bouncers and DJ and was on my way to the dressing room to grab my obnoxiously oversized bag of exotic dancer apparel when MJ moved in swiftly and gave me another hug while saying, in her ever-innocent tone, that she really meant it. She went on to say that she felt God had brought me into her life because she really needed me, and I had helped her so much. I knew there was a punchline coming or something I wouldn't expect. She topped it off with, "God must have brought me to you as well because, of course, I'm a good person to be around!" She laughed at her joke, as she usually does, and then said she hates being conceited.

Pixie and I had just finished telling her she needs to stop saying terrible things about herself because she's lovable, and everyone agreed. When girls are down, most of us will lend an ear or extend our arms for hugs. Thank goodness for my small-town club full of conscious California girls who have a lot of love to give.

17
THE NIGHT I MERGED

For days and weeks and months and years, I prayed that one day I would be able to release my alter ego and integrate all of my selves into one complete, whole self. Thus, I'll never forget the day I *merged.* I'd begged Josh to take a trip to Jersey with me for three years. Nostalgia is a magnetic force. Years of laughter and smiles and the adventures created by careless young minds yearn to be remembered. We booked a one-way flight, planning to support Josh's mom in packing up "the safe house" to begin the next chapter of her life. Penthouse hotel suite hopping and clubbing was a momentary thrill for us, and we had our run during this late October visit. My one request for the trip was to visit Bare Exposure Gentlemen's Club, to revisit the part of my life that felt so new and carefree. We did just that on a Sunday at 3 A.M.

Entering the club as this version of myself seven years later, I experienced a whimsical joy. Have you ever watched a child run onto a playground? Bare was my adult playground—this venue, which once felt so grand, shrunk before my eyes after only a few minutes inside, though it will forever be the home of my favorite stage. All dancers who travel have a favorite club, and some have a specific stage. They aren't necessarily in the same place.

Bare's stage two is less than twenty feet from the DJ booth, past the main stage. Years ago, this felt like such a trek through the crowd of intoxicated patrons. On this stage, I once floated over the sea of men waving their fans of dollar bills, begging me to descend. This exact location is where I first tapped into my feminine power and the impact I possessed as a performer. This is where I fine-tuned my skill of captivating a crowd with sensuality and eroticism. When I feel down or hopeless in daily life, I yearn to be on this stage, exuding that potent feminine medicine, that *shakti*. Of the thirty-something stages I've graced across the US, this is my all-time favorite, all because of memory. The stage is barely a stage. It's quite pathetic in terms of size and location.

To my surprise, a familiar voice announced the next rotation of dancers while I waited at the front booth to pay and check my cell phone. "The same DJ?! What's his name? I'm drawing a blank!" I directed my line of questions at the four club staff within earshot.

The bouncer checking IDs replied in a bored tone, "Ya, Lloyd. It's the same DJ."

I entered the DJ booth, and Lloyd's jaw dropped. "You?! What are you doing here? I thought you'd left this planet or exploded into some sensual cosmic existence in another dimension!" He was right, and I'd planned to leave the planet. What he didn't know was that I had left, only to return. We picked up right where we'd left off, and I called in Josh to introduce Lloyd, the DJ, to this faceless partner that had always been.

Josh caught me off guard by starting with a provocative request: "Can she get on stage?"

Lloyd shrugged his shoulders and said, "Why not?"

I refused while leaning in with anticipation. "I don't want to step on anyone's toes."

Lloyd reminded me that customers are pulled up onto the main stage often.

"Can I go on stage two?" I asked, giving in with a smirk.

"Of course, you can go up after this song."

I rushed down the three stairs leading to the main floor from the DJ booth, off to the right of the main stage.

Lloyd announced, "Special guest LANA, comin' up on stage two."

In my sherpa-lined motorcycle boots, asymmetrical knee-length black skirt, and wrap-around crop top, I grabbed the pole from floor level and climbed onto the stage. It was slightly more challenging to climb with the boots on, but I made my way to the top and looked down to make eye contact with Josh. As I whirled around the pole, I slipped the straps of my top down and hiked my skirt up to reveal my white lace Cosabella boyshorts. I had Josh stand next to the stage so I could do my signature move, wrapping my thighs around his neck and draping my legs over his shoulders to tap my yoni against his face. The girl who was called up after me came up around the side and watched. I leaned in to better hear her.

"You're really good!" She was a short, round girl with a big smile. I thanked her and shared that I hadn't been on stage two in years, but I had loved working at Bare, and my signature move always got me dances and time in the champagne room. She said she didn't care to get on stage and I could have the next song. A customer approached just as I stepped down, tucking my breasts back into my top. I figured it wasn't worth a dollar to get back onstage since I couldn't offer a dance. I ran back to the DJ booth and said goodbye to Lloyd before bouncing out of the club, exhilarated.

Josh started the car and said, "You just merged." His words caught me off guard, and I asked him to repeat himself. "You merged. He announced you as Lana." I was so taken by the moment, I hadn't considered the implication. For years and years, I've prayed for that moment, and it had just unfolded. I had prayed to merge. To be Vida, but also Lana. I'd prayed to just be myself, without separation, without the need to use an alias.

Now I had.

* * *

This book began with a declaration and a dream. I dream of a reality where there is an option. Conscious strip clubs. Temples of healing. Settings that are warm and inviting, where men and women can enter to be loved and embraced. Instead of a man entering a club and feeling attacked, viewed as a dollar sign, he's seen as a mirror and a seeker. This mirror is the mirror of every living being. He's a reflection. She sees in him the pure qualities she has acknowledged in herself. We are just looking back at ourselves through one another. This man is deserving of love, empathy, and compassion. What is he seeking? We can listen with open hearts and find out. He's likely seeking connection and to be seen for the divine being he is. My tantra teacher, Freddy Zental, reminds us that we're all Gods and Goddesses. We may not realize our divinity throughout life, but it is there, seen or unseen by the self. What better time than now to step into power?

The term *dakini* originated in ancient India and refers to the priestesses who helped transport dead souls to the sky. The energy of the dakini helps unlock creative forces and realize full potential. In my understanding, a dakini is a woman who supports the warrior returning from battle. This wounded warrior has been to battle for some time and has lost touch with the feminine energy. His time with a dakini supports the process of remembering how to touch, hold, and be with a woman once again. Whether or not this is an accurate depiction, this is the archetype that has resonated with me because, in all honesty, how do we know which story in history is completely accurate? To me, this rings true: We all can use the support of a sensual, kind, compassionate soul to reflect our connection to these qualities.

And thus, *the vision*: A man completes his mission for the day around four in the afternoon. He has a light dinner and heads over to a conscious strip club nestled in the redwoods of Northern California. It's a venue with the look and feel of a home, with multiple rooms and structures spread over a five-acre property. The valet service parks his vehicle, and upon entering the temple, a goddess greets him two steps inside with a warm, gentle embrace. She's wearing a long, white dress and almost no makeup. She's a natural beauty and interacts with him tenderly as if he were a lover. She takes his name, adds it to a list of the thirty attendees for the evening, and leads him into a palace-like space, illuminated by candles and soft lighting. He hears harmonious, soothing, expansive music. He walks past life-sized deities carved from stone, holding all corners of the interior perimeter as the woman from the entrance leads from his side. He passes through doorways adorned by arches with hand-carved Balinese woodwork and rose quartz crystals four or more feet high. Before entering, his shoes were left at the door, and sheepskin rugs caress his feet as he walks and sees the lounging areas, draped with natural fibers of silk and Egyptian cotton.

The goddess by his side opens the door to a dressing room for him to change out of his work costume into breathable attire. He leaves his belongings in a safe place and once again meets the goddess. She leads him to a room with a large circular sofa, where five other women sit with men who entered before him. She leaves him to fetch a warm elixir of cacao and herbs to ease his mind and body. They sit together and casually discuss why he's come and what he'd like to experience. After about thirty minutes, they've been acquainted and move to a more private space, where thick, sheer curtains separate them from the six others in the room.

She guides him to lie down and massages his entire body, intentionally guiding him into an altered state. After some time, she feels his body soften and leads him through a breath practice. The interaction is casual and light. They laugh and move slowly with ease. She reminds him that this is his time to ask and receive, so he requests four additional women join them in the space to honor him. The women enter and circle around him. He shares his desires and vulnerable stories of pain and triumph. The women listen intently. As he concludes, the space is opened for the women to reflect. They each share what they see as his strengths and what they admire about him. His expression softens more with every word. The tension he brought into the temple melts, and his breath deepens as the session ends.

He leaves his energetic exchange in the form of currency in a small wooden box for the woman who accompanied him for the evening and something in a separate box for the other four women. A minimum exchange has been agreed upon through an online form or guidelines presented at the entrance.

On the other side of the curtain is a man who's come to cultivate his masculinity to attract the woman he will choose as his partner. The goddess with him is guiding him through hands-on tantric practices. Intimacy is an offering in the conscious strip club, though sex is not guaranteed, and all interactions are sacred. All intimacy is valued as initiation and lessons for continued personal practice. The club is a place to learn, expand, grow, heal, and connect more deeply with oneself.

Each month, the temple offers a weeklong stay. During this stay, there will be work on the organic garden on the land and communion with nature. The organic garden nourishes the goddesses of the temple and the participants of the weeklong stay. Tantric practices, ceremony, breathwork, and medicine work with sacred visionary plants are offered for seven to twenty-one days.

My good friend Naval once referenced something to the extent of, "if any man on the planet could have sex with a gorgeous woman any time he wanted, then there wouldn't be any war." Often, his words send me into a contemplative state, and this was one of those moments. This one struck a chord, as I will never understand what a man feels in his desire to be intimate with a woman, at least not in this lifetime. Apparently, there is quite a bit of evidence to support such a claim. I believe the most authentic way to address this is to simply ask. How do you feel when you are making love? How do you feel after you've made love? Individuals who visit the temple and cannot offer an energetic exchange in the form of currency can give their time in the garden, caring for the land, maintenance, or renovations. No one will be turned away. Each individual will be offered an intimate healing experience. Intimacy does not equal sex. The goddesses of the temple are supported not only by each other but by the land and can call the premises home if they so choose. The name of the temple is the Dakini Dome. The home to honor and uplift all that is sacred.

EPILOGUE

I launched the book campaign for this book with a crowdfunding literary agency in February 2019. I put the cart before the horse as I do with many things because I'm a "do-er." I'm not always so strategic. Somehow, without any planning, the campaign was rather successful. I hit the goal. I didn't go above and beyond, but I hit the goal. It was stressful to go through this process without a plan, yet I felt supported by my community, friends, and family that it all worked out in the end. However, it caused strain on my marriage.

I won't go into details, but I will say we attempted conscious uncoupling. We had an MDMA ceremony together in late July after I moved out after our eleventh anniversary in May. We went deep. We talked about everything and recorded the entire thing so we could go back and transcribe it to understand ourselves and each other. He told me I had no rights to the company we'd built that night, even though I responded personally to hundreds of long, intimate, and heartfelt emails that came in over the first few years. I spent countless hours on admin work, played a major role in creative direction, including the logo, and was the catalyst for the podcast. There are a thousand more reasons why my being removed from the site as the cofounder felt like unethical bullshit.

Despite this absolute nonsense, I can still say that the short and sweet of it is that I learned so much from this man and grew during our relationship. I am grateful despite the inevitable pain and suffering. I cannot and will not live in regret or resentment. To be honest, I am congratulating myself for finally walking away from a painful and dysfunctional relationship. I still question if it was all a karmic bond with his son. I was invested in his future. Trauma bonding, perhaps. I knew what it felt like to come from a broken home with unstable parents. I believe we did our best—his son is an incredibly intelligent young man with unlimited potential. I know he has suffered from my mistakes in attempting to play the role of stepmother, but I also know I deeply cared while I was present. I feel honored to have played a role in the life of such an upstanding individual. Josh and I made many, many mistakes, but we also did something right because I'm proud of who this little boy has grown up to be.

We officially cut the cord during Burning Man. My dear sister Rebecca Jean Alonzi became my rock during the separation and orchestrated my entire Burning Man 2019 setup less than two weeks in advance (if you've been, you know it's a feat to land in an amazing camp with a meal plan and RV last minute). There's more to this that I found out later, but this story isn't about how friends showed up during my divorce. I didn't think I'd make it to The Burn without Josh. He made everything happen for the five years we attended. It overwhelmed me. Fellow burners, I confess. I was a self-proclaimed sparkle pony. Deepest apologies. It was all worth claiming this title.

Everything changed in August 2019. I felt like a fucking superhero. I got my ass to The Burn. I drove in alone. I drove out alone. I packed all my shit. I found my camp. I did the damn thing. It was so fucking empowering. And yet, I felt like shit as I drove onto the playa all alone to locate my bike (thank you, Matt Black), bins brought in by friends, and then arriving at a stranger's RV at Camp Mystic. I bawled my eyes out every day. Tearing myself away from someone I was glued to for ten years felt like death. Mind you, we spent less than two full weeks apart during the entire duration of our relationship. Yes, codependency is real.

Spending my entire solo Burn in tears felt pathetic. This was my moment to finally fucking shine for myself. It was time to show up for myself, and I was determined to do so. I arrived Tuesday night. Two days late. Josh and I had to pack up our house in Calabasas and separate our belongings from the previous decade into neighboring storage units. I began The Burn on Wednesday morning.

In the breakfast line at Camp Mystic, Rebecca Jean blurted out, "Isn't Lana's outfit hot?"

An exotic shirtless man in board shorts replied, "Yes, it is."

I said nothing and felt like hiding under the table like a two-year-old. In recounting this story to friends over the next twelve hours, this man's nickname became "Peach." The goddess I shared the RV with came up with this name after referring to him as a soft, juicy piece of fruit (which we're all dreaming of in the last days of The Burn).

Peach appeared behind me as my soul sister Chelsey Lehl and I exited the "foam dome." We'd just lathered up in lavender soap and lubricated our fresh naked bodies among hundreds of other squeaky-clean Burners swaying their hips to intoxicating music. I lost my breath when I spotted him and grabbed Chelsey to whisper in her ear, "Oh my God. That's the guy!"

She looked around, "What guy?"

I squeezed her arm, "Behind you. The guy from my camp. The acrobat aerialist guy from Costa Rica." I turned around and took a deep breath before speaking to him. "You should take a walk with me."

He didn't flinch. "Walk with you where?"

My anxiety dissolved. His energy was so calm and grounded. "To my RV."

Chelsey approached, "Come with us!" I was anxious and excited again and couldn't even look at him.

"Where are we going?" he asked.

Chelsey turned to him as he followed us. "The healing sanctuary."

I was healed, all right. The cord was cut. This was when my eleven-year marriage officially ended and the Costa Rica chapter began. Peach followed us that day into the healing sanctuary at Heart Tribe, later on that "walk" to my RV, and then I followed him all the way to southern Costa Rica. Little did I know the world would stop spinning during my second visit in February 2020, when the border closed and I decided to stay.

Best decision of my life.

Living in the jungle during 2020 healed me. Sleeping under the stars under nothing but a mesh bug net healed me. Completely removing myself from a painful, toxic environment healed me. After being in a volatile relationship, my nervous system was shot. I was taxed. A year in nature allowed me to recalibrate. Peach sat with me for countless hours and edited this book because he's an absolute genius with words. He's a genius in many other ways, and I am infinitely grateful for every moment I've spent with him (even the painful moment we split, and he had his ex move into his home—that we lived in together—immediately after). Honestly, I couldn't have ended the relationship without this rude awakening. Thank you, Peach, for setting me free. Life just gets better and better every day. The stepping stone was everything it needed to be.

In January 2020, just before I (intentionally) got stuck in the jungle, I met one of Peach's three sisters—Melissa. I fell in love with her as fast as I fell in love with Peach and introduced her to the Spearmint Rhino in Las Vegas, just after a major transition in her life. She'd just completed a deep immersion in the Tantric arts in Bali. Our month-long experience together in Vegas was profound. It was bonding and exhilarating. I loved it. Never in ten years had I worked with another dancer so closely. It was healing to have her by my side as I stepped back into this dark underworld.

I also started working at a sensual massage temple in Los Angeles and dipped my toe into dominatrix work with my domme mom and sister wifey Domina Colette. I dove back into sex work full force. I have countless new stories not in this book. I have grand intentions of writing yet another book, because every moment, I continue to evolve and grow. This shit keeps getting better and better, but let's talk about the shit that still lingers.

Countless friends, mentors, therapists, and coaches have questioned the emotional mask I used to wear. What was I hiding? Was I numb? Quite the opposite. I. Felt. Everything. It's a blessing and a curse to feel deeply. I reach higher highs, but that comes with lower lows.

I saw the film *Twelve Years a Slave* in the theater over a decade ago with my father. As I watched the leather whip lash through the smooth dark flesh of "Mindy," the main character, I felt my chest tighten, my eyes well up with tears that moistened my cheeks and chest within seconds, as I trembled and shuddered. I could barely breathe. The first brutal lashing was more than enough. I had to keep my eyes closed for most of the film. I had nightmares for months and couldn't sleep well for over a week. It wasn't that I didn't know this had happened in history—I just didn't feel it so deeply until I took it in with my eyes. This is my usual experience observing brutality on screen. Scientific studies have revealed that the body experiences everything the eyes see. As I learn more about myself and how I navigate the world of emotions, I make different decisions. I no longer watch these types of films. I have sat before a million more bloody scenes, yet none were "based on true stories." Knowing that this was real had me experiencing it as if it were the present moment.

Violence and brutality don't only happen in films in my life. I woke up to a blood-curdling scream at 3 A.M. in a state of panic so crippling I almost had to crawl to the front door.

"LANA! Lana! Help me!"

My knees felt weak as soon as I stood from the flood of adrenaline. I watched two of McFarland, Wisconsin's police officers aggressively kick my mother's ribcage while a third held her face down with his foot in our gravel driveway.

It was almost impossible for her to look up to see me standing five feet in front of her, but she knew I'd approached and screamed louder through her tears and rage. "LANA! Help me! They're breaking my wrists! Please help me!"

I attempted to come closer and was met with, "Ma'am, if you come any closer, we'll have to restrain you." I stood before the scene in shock again, trembling and shuddering in tears, feeling completely powerless as they beat my mother because she tried to run into her home and avoid being arrested for driving home from a local pub intoxicated. Less than five minutes after I'd approached the scene, three police vehicles were illuminating the street with their red and blue flashing lights and an ambulance carrying away my mother in handcuffs. I had to leave for work four hours later, and my one-year-old sister's mother was in a jail cell and her father was hunting elk in Montana. There weren't any family members to come to the rescue. I spent the following days a nervous wreck.

I was twenty-one years old the night I internalized my mother's cry for help. For over fourteen years, I've heard her screaming in nightmares, both sleeping and awake. Fortunately, I completely missed the police brutality my father experienced. However, I've heard the stories over and over, during the first eighteen years of life that he was mercilessly beaten and abused by his own mother and father. Every single detail. He has recounted his trauma, over and over, as I mentioned at the beginning of this book. I spent my adult life attempting to escape my upbringing—my family, my birth city, my home, my roots. My entire life has been spent searching. I've desperately yearned for the highest high—removed from the paralyzing lows (as my trauma response isn't to fight, flight, or freeze. It's called "fawn."). My unconscious response is to please, appease, or pacify the threat. Not to say that I don't take flight or run as well.

I'm often physically traveling with wings, wheels, or waves, or I'm internally traveling through alternate dimensions and astral planes. Sex is an escape. Pleasure is an escape. When I escape, I visit that place of peace, where my past does not determine my future. I can look at it from an observer's perspective. When I settle into a peaceful existence, if only for a moment, each time, it becomes wired into my system stronger. To sum it up, this is a part of my healing process.

I had grand intentions to complete this book years ago, and my many excuses include the pandemic of 2020 and ending an eleven-year marriage. This story has become one of my practices. As I write and shape and reshape the story, I learn more about myself and how to heal. What a gift that I still have the opportunity to add this very important chapter of where I am now.

As I mentioned, I went back to Vegas after Josh and I separated. I began working as a dakini, offering sensual, tantric massage. I fell in love and spent just shy of a year living in the jungle of Costa Rica. Most importantly, I took the first step toward truly acknowledging and honoring the countless years I've spent working with men in such an intimate capacity. We all remember that line, "If you build it, they will come," right? From the 1989 film *Field of Dreams,* starring Kevin Costner? Whether you've seen it or not, you get the point. It implies that we must make the space in life for the things we dream about, we desire, to show up. To take that first step. My *first step* was believing that there was value in my thirteen years dancing in and out of the sex industry, that I hold wisdom, and ultimately, that something to share and teach. I created my first digital product just before I ended up in the jungle for a year (the Tantric Lap Dance online mini-course wouldn't have happened without you, Margaret Beim. Thank you for being such an encouraging sister).

And because 2020 left us all with no other option than to transition our work to screens, I channeled my skills into a mentorship program with a friend I deeply admire and respect—Nadine Lee. The five-week online course, "Masculine Eros," that I co-facilitated with Nadine, was transformative. The decade I spent in the club, assisting couples' tantric workshops, on the phone with my clients as a recovery coach, countless hours in my own coaching and therapy sessions, yoga teacher training, Zendo training as a trip sitter—all came into play over the course of five weeks with these twenty-eight men.

The creative juices in 2020 were strong. I had no deeper desire than to create and execute. I met so many powerful women in Costa Rica. We recorded hours of deeply personal conversations from a magical location in Santa Teresa—big thanks to Stephanie Berk for appearing in my life and co-creating what became the "Pleasure Palace" with Fern and Su and all of the powerful women who came through. What an incredible chapter.

I started a podcast with a woman I adore, Annalisa Raghunandan. The "Divorce Unfiltered" podcast was an epic Covid project that has been a major source of joy in my life. I started an OnlyFans account and realized that there are countless channels to share the Tantric Arts. My Patreon account was created in 2020. I started leading virtual women's circles thanks to Samsara De Leon. This continued to unfold into "The Sensual Collective," a women-only collective committed to creating spaces for women to connect to their sensuality and embody their queenhood, which I co-founded with Samsara and Damian Madray.

I'm writing this paragraph on October 20, 2021. Tonight, I'll be co-hosting a virtual women's full moon circle as the cofounder of the Sensual Collective. Just over a week ago I received an email with an attachment—a contract from a publisher. I'm in Vegas on the fifteenth floor of a casino hotel with a girlfriend whom I admire. She's squinting right now, leaning in toward her computer screen, legs crossed, eyes laser-focused, fingers tapping away on the keyboard. She's in creation mode. Her identity will remain a secret in this book, but I can tell you she's doing big things in the world.

I'm visiting my old stomping ground—Las Vegas. Headed into the good ol' Spearmint Rhino Gentlemen's Club. This quick trip won't end with a flight home to SFO. This is a new chapter, and although it looks familiar, there's a whole different feel. Saba, my lover, is driving us home to Manhattan Beach after this quick hustle. I've told Saba that I was done last time I was here, a few months ago. Apparently, I wasn't quite ready yet, because here I am. I'm not upset—I'm excited. Being here with my girlfriend has been magical. The synchronicities and the abundance of moments that have felt divinely aligned are confirmation that this can't be wrong.

I have a love/hate relationship with stripping. I will always love being on stage; performing and being "in the zone" is an insatiable craving. Men walking away from me with smiles on their faces, feeling uplifted, won't ever feel wrong. Our time together improved their lives, and if only for a moment, I'll admit it's still enough. Why do I still hate it? Being up all night and having my ass slapped so hard it bruises, along with the crippling physical pain from more than six hours in seven-inch stilettos. This isn't my dream. I'm not working on bigger hopes, dreams, and aspirations in this 12,400-square-foot building. But I love it more than I hate it. There's no question why I am still here. Yet, this is still a new chapter.

Life is different. My focus has shifted. Saba and I have cofounded a management consulting firm to support the psychedelic industry. Thank you, 5-methoxy-N, N-dimethyltryptamine (AKA 5-MeO-DMT), for the little reframe in revealing to Saba that his path in the corporate world was soul-sucking. One dose of the God molecule, served by a stellar human in Topanga, California, and here we are: MJ Biz Con, launching *Entheo Ventures*. New endeavors, a new relationship, and as always, new realizations about my path toward a sounder mind and heart.

Podcasts somehow make me feel at ease while stuck in traffic, so I tuned into an unfinished episode already cued up after my booty facial on my first day in Sin City. Yep. Booty facial. Episode #533 of *The Tim Ferriss Show* with Paul Conti, MD, is titled: *How Trauma Works and How to Heal from It.* It hit me as I heard the line, "So this idea that trauma changes how we think about ourselves, and then we're trying to recognize that it's like looking at the mirror and saying, 'Is that me?' But you don't really remember what you looked like yesterday." Fuck. *Does it ever end?* I thought to myself. It's so true. Paul's words hit home and the tears flowed.

Often, I've forgotten seemingly crucial events and pieces of information. There are huge gaps throughout my childhood and, quite honestly, to this day. I wasn't working on healing my trauma when I met my former husband at twenty-two. I didn't yet have the understanding of how to begin that process. Instead, this relationship dynamic seemed to play into my trauma in various ways. I'd get triggered and disassociate to the point I couldn't remember exactly what I said the following day.

I'd wonder years into the relationship, "Who was that girl that did and said those things?" Better yet, who was the girl that was blind to the manipulation, control, gaslighting, and violence? I was presented a thousand opportunities to wake up and walk away. The term "red flag" wasn't in my vocabulary. Who was the girl who said, "it's okay you logged into my social media accounts or my phone and read my personal messages, my journal. It's fine." The second, the third, the fourth time, the fifth . . . I said it was okay by not walking away. I asked for it by not walking away. It often felt like we tortured each other.

So much has changed. I can't really remember the way I felt or why I operated the way I did in my twenties. When I look at photos, I can rarely recall what I thought or how I felt. Before we separated, Josh and I had a few calls with a "love coach" named Annie Lalla. She said, "It's as if you've completely adopted his frame of reference." Josh had been lied to and abandoned early on. In his eyes, I became another liar that would abandon him, and I believed it. The reality that I'd adopted was that no one would put up with my shit. He'd say things so often when we'd argue that would cut so deep that I'd started hearing them in my head in my voice. I'd truly adopted the cruel words and struggled to leave the relationship, believing I'd be lonely forever.

More importantly, this is how I remember what was said. She conveyed that I'd given up my power, my autonomy—my agency. A complete lack of safety, rooted in my childhood trauma, was controlling my life. I wrote this book from that place. I lived in fear for a long time, and I wrote this book in fear. I feared I wouldn't be loved and wouldn't be safe if I was honest. The truth is that the sex industry was my training ground. It was often a place where I felt powerful and solid, where I had merit and purpose. It was also a place that kept my trauma alive. My "people pleasing," lack of boundaries, lack of self-worth, because I fell into a pattern in how I interacted with clientele.

This isn't a self-help book. This is my story, so I won't pretend I'm an expert and can explain the psychological effects of trauma. What I can say is that I have experienced trauma. There's no question there. Most of this story has been a snapshot of a disassociated individual. Most of this story took place during an eleven-year "marriage." I can't tell my former partner's story; however, I can tell you what I experienced while he was in the picture. I had unprocessed trauma. I likely needed a competent therapist. Perhaps I needed a whole team of therapists and tools to unravel the knots of the past. These professionals and tools came into my life over time, but this marriage began while I was in an incredibly unstable place. He became a mirror.

This book has become a cathartic, therapeutic experience, and even though it's been a long time coming, I am grateful this book wasn't published before I could add this chapter of unfolding truth. I no longer recognize the girl that began writing this story in 2015, and I'm grateful for that. For me, growth and evolution are the reasons I've chosen to live this one precious life.

ACKNOWLEDGMENTS

This magnificently beautiful and bizarre planet we inhabit is a better place with all the humans dedicated to bringing light into all the dark places. Thank you, first and foremost, to all the sex workers; my stripper sisters who are out there doing the work and maintaining integrity. Thank you to the dakini goddesses who were mentioned in the book: Amy, Chelsey Lehl, Kaya Reagan, and iX-Chel Sandivel. Thank you for continually inspiring me and being integral pieces of this divine web. All of the women who made Cheer's a complete and utter anomaly: Veronica, Chandra, Taylor, Raine, Honey, Medusa Mayhem, Pixie, Teagan, Serenity, Nessa, Lily, Kyra, Hannah, Katya, Dominique, Kadence, Mia, Princess, Misty, Samantha, Evian, River, Lucky, and the many others who I shared intimate moments with in that lively dressing room tucked into the heart of Silicon Valley. All of the sisters in my life who have encouraged me and supported me in being my authentic self: My tantrika wifey Nadine Lee, Kristen Michaela, Mari Mu, Julia Grace Vishnepolsky, Margaret Beim, Chantell Tautua, Kelsea Ernst, Jillian Love, Libby Miga, Valérie Disle Morgan, Adriana Martell, Alexsandra "Divine Kika" Marianetti, Vanessa Moazezi, Patricia Lanier, Melissa Rose, Krystle Cho (extra thank you for your support with the book cover!), Melissa Chapman, Naomi McDonald, Nancy Yeh, Nicole Rando, Michaela Gonzalez, Daliah Barkan, Savana Rollins, Giovanna Garcia, Serra Smick, Patra Arnold, Anneliese Vandenberg, Amanda Carlson, Malen Hounshell, Jade Bondoc, Domo, Sophia Rollando, Mercedes G. Delgado, Cristina Pilo . . . I truly want to mention every supportive woman in my life. All of my girlfriends in high school who supported the exhibitionist in me. The list is truly endless!

Not only all of my sisters, but the brothers in my life: Hernan Botbol, Kyle Coursey, Jean-Luc Piriou, Steve Alexander Dumain, Ian-Michael Hebert, Naval Ravikant, Jerry Lin, Ari Barkan, Kai Harper, David Dacus, Niraj Mehta, Dan Rein, Anthony Bublitz, Andrew Dannaoui, Reza Moazezi, Alan Jones, Lee Schwalb, Preston Temple, Gopi Kallayil, Allan Badiner, Martin Polanco, Joel Vazquez, Eric Omoro, Mike "Ohrangu" Tang, Jason Rubinson, Lee Klinger, Jonathon Conant, Anthony Giacobbe, Ray Lanier, Gardner Cole (for literally planting my broken root), and Wesley Goo for jumping in making that last preorder before I passed 500 for the book campaign! There are way too many amazing men in my life to list them all.

Johnny Del, without you my life would be drastically different. I love you deeply, may you rest in peace until your beautiful soul reincarnates. Psalm Isadora, you are a legend, your vibration is still rippling throughout this planet. Christopher Smith, you came in with your tech savvy skills in that final hour and saved the day, love you and your genius lyrical skill. My beloved Tantra teachers: Freddy Weaver, my dear friend, brother, teacher. Your brilliant mind never ceases to amaze. Your encouragement has been everything. Dr. Elsbeth Meuth, I humbly bow to your strength and discipline, poise and grace. Destin Gerek, I can't say enough. You and Elie Prana are an example for the world. Thank you for being a true voice of change, and your dedication to the path of the Evolved Masculine. You are a true pioneer. I am so grateful to have your support. Thank you to everyone in my tribe, and community that live unconventional lives with purpose and meaning, you're an inspiration to me, to do the same.

While I was in the process of writing this book and building the plane of the book campaign as I flew the damn thang, Rebecca Jean Alonzi swooped in like superwoman and made connections that were beyond magical. Michael Ellsberg, I am so grateful for your time, support, and guidance. Let's not forget the entire hour you spent on Zoom with me, dissecting this memoir. You are one of the most integral pieces of this book being published, and I can't thank you enough. Rachel Lena Esterline, you are yet another angel that landed at just the perfect time; your documentary is going to forever change the world for the better. Thank you, David Miller, for making the connection and for risking your life to capture a photo of me in the middle of the road with my stack of $2 bills (and Rebecca Jean, for capturing that behind the scenes). Jacqueline Frances, AKA Jaq the Stripper, thank you for supporting the book campaign and speaking up for sex workers around the world!

Lauren Elms, thank you for being so on point and open to supporting this book coming to life. Jesse Chapman for countless hours of editing. Thank you for igniting my sapiosexual flame with your genius mind.

Thank you to all of the men (and women) I had the honor of meeting inside the walls of the one and only Cheer's Gentlemen's Club in Sunnyvale; who accepted all my hair flipping, lip syncing, and endless hand sanitizer applications. Jason, Karl, Anu, Brandon, Chris T . . . and so many more. You know who you are. Thank you for offering your hard-earned money in exchange for my shenanigans. The staff at Cheer's: the bouncers, the DJ's; Sal and Mikey, the manager Sheryl Estrada, the owner Bob, who treated me like family. You will forever be in my heart. Elise Gee, the Tuesday night we did the photo shoot was epic. Thank you for your time and genuine enthusiasm in entertaining my silly ideas. Cheer's is truly the Disney Land among strip clubs. A big thank you to Bare Exposure in Atlantic City and DJ Lloyd Brown who kept it cosmic while we rapped in the DJ booth and helped me keep it real. Doug Boynton, my fav Spearmint Rhino DJ in Vegas, the cumulative hours of philosophical conversation were a savior. Thank you to all of the incredible musicians and DJs whose music sends chills up my spine and allows me the opportunity to move my body to those ear-gasmic rhythms. Thank you to Eric Wexel and the tech-y boys who entrusted me with their new site and allowed me the honor of being the first model on Cam City.

Club Brickle in Sun Prairie, Wisconsin, the first time these feet ever graced a stage with a pole. All of the men I met in Vegas, Miami, Arizona, and beyond, thank you for being receptive to the hippie stripper who wanted to "just breathe" with you in the champagne room. Your rave reviews were worth the risk and daring to be different.

All of the people along the way that I shared my vision with and received encouragement from: KC Baker, Tim Chang, Dr. Matt Cook, Kelley Mountain, Alita Arose, Aimee Isabel Lora, Aladdin Kazran, Evan and Sasha Bailyn, Marc Scherer, Gil Penchina, Neil Strauss, Puma St. Angel, Morgan Langan, Tina Anton, Dimitri Mugianis, Marla Schmidt.

Christine M Cordova and Stephen Flynn, The Red Temple will go down in history. Thank you for making it happen.

John and Adrienne Litchenberg, a true example of a successful couple working in the adult industry. Thank you for opening your home to me in Vegas. Stephanie Shelburne, your temple was a haven during my many trips to the city of Sin. Elizabeth Bast, you are a true dakini. Thank you for your support. Uyen Adelyn Ly, I can't wait to continue on this path with you. I am honored to share a parallel vision of what the future holds.

A deep thank you to my uncle Jeff Kundert for stepping in as a mentor on a conscious path and inspiring me to explore meditation, Eastern Philosophy, spirituality and directing me on this quest to personal development. Kris Krajco, I'm so grateful that you're a part of our family. My father, David Baumgartner, for letting go of your fears and bars of your mind while still in a jail cell and committing to being my father. All the mornings you read to me from the Urantia book while I experienced teenage angst paid off! I love you, and if you ever read this book, know that my most common title given by customers was "the worst stripper ever," in reference to the fact that they all wanted to bring me home to meet their mothers—or better yet, their wives. My intention has *always been* to lift people up. Mom, Kathleen Kundert, you've always supported me in everything I do. You also showed me what it meant to be a goddess and to care for and love my temple. Thank you and Terry Vial for contributing to the book campaign. My baby sisters, Leah Wempner and Cali Freitag, you are pieces of my heart. You two are the most important women in my world and I am so grateful to have both of you in my life. My extended family, Rhea Consalvo, I'm so grateful to have a mother-in-love, because in-law was never my thing. Another strong mother in my world, Christine, and father Pierre-Jean Rollando, you will be forever missed. I appreciate your encouragement to strive for academic rigor. Mikey, Grandma K, Grandpa "Pres" Bob, a true revolutionary, your spirit lives on, and is a driving force in my life to change the world. Rest in peace.

Everyone who pre-ordered this book through the Publishizer.com campaign: Daniel Hoffer, Anita P Hoffer MS, PhD, EdD—clinical sexologist and educator, Eric Omuro, Leonora De Santis, Merrow Hart, Michele Victoria Aponte, Mira Cheval, Nadine Keller, The Cupcake Girls, Danielle Nonog, Dhara debbie, Laurie Mayer, Robert Tapella,

Kristian Poe, Andrew Rosas, Matthew Lessard, Chantell Tautua, Margaret Beim, and so many more. Thank you all for making it happen! Tara Thompson. You know why.

The stripper coach that I will leave unnamed, your coaching and your book changed the game for me. After your book, my dancer persona went from the quiet girl next door to elegant, respectable, and confident. I held my head higher and acknowledged my worth. I am worthy of everything I desire. Joe Mattia, you will forever be one of my greatest teachers. Thank you for being open and willing to take my midnight calls from the Rhino dressing room, to coach me on how to make the sale while maintaining poise and integrity. I will be forever grateful for each day you have cheered me on, made me dinner after work, rubbed my feet, picked out lingerie, and listened to endless hours of nightly recounts in the wee hours after dawn. We did a lot of growing up together, and you'll always hold a place in my heart.

A very, very, special thank you to William Leonard Pickard, who edited this entire manuscript by hand, released in 2021 from USP Tucson, a high-security U.S. penitentiary in Arizona. What a dream come true. I prayed that you'd be released when I sent you the manuscript. I am honored that you accepted this undertaking of editing my first book, (certainly not my last). I wish nothing more than to live in a world where someone with a brilliant mind such as yours is revered by all. Looks like we're moving in that direction. Being in your presence has been such a gift.

Saba Candari. My love. I couldn't have done this without you. That last push made it happen. Those twelve hours you spent editing will never be forgotten. Doing life with you is a dream. You are such a gift.

Pachamama, mother earth, for providing any and everything I need. May we all remember that we are not separate from her. In all of the roles we play in this one divine life, we have the opportunity to tread lightly and learn from the plant teachers who share the deepest wisdom; the wisdom of the earth.

Last but not least, thank *you*, the reader, for taking your precious time to come on this very raw, sacred healing journey.

BIBLIOGRAPHY

DeFour, Matthew. "Allied Dunn's Marsh in the Midst of a Rebirth after Years of Decline" (website). *Wisconsin State Journal.* Sept. 28, 2016, host.madison.com/wsj/news/local/neighborhoods/allied-dunn-s-marsh-in-the-midst-of-a-rebirth/article_140142c2-cbbe-54c8-9aa7-b54bc5eddba4.html.

Dodgson, Rick. *It's All a Kind of Magic: The Young Ken Kesey*. Madison: University of Wisconsin Press, 2013.

"Ken Kesey and the Merry Pranksters." Univie.ac.at. Accessed July, 28, 2017. https://newspaperarchive.com/madison-wisconsin-state-journal-dec-01-2004-p-39/.

ABOUT THE AUTHOR

LANA SHAY is a Midwestern-born, nomadic citizen of the world, based in Los Angeles. In 2008, she began her 10+ year career in the sex industry. During her informal education in gentleman's clubs across America, she discovered love, divorce, tantra, psychedelics, and a thirst for cognitive liberty.

In 2021, she exited the industry after a series of profound plant medicine journeys to co-create PsychedelicTimes.com, co-author a #1 International Amazon Bestselling book, become the Co-Founder of The Sensual Collective, and Entheo Ventures — a psychedelic consulting firm. Learn more about The Pure Way With Lana Shay at LanaShay.com.

Made in the USA
Middletown, DE
06 October 2022